History and Historians

History and Historians

Selected Papers of R. W. Southern

Edited by

R. J. Bartlett

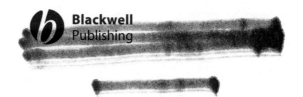
Blackwell
Publishing

BLACKWELL PUBLISHING
350 Main Street, Malden, MA 02148-5020, USA
108 Cowley Road, Oxford OX4 1JF, UK
550 Swanston Street, Carlton, Victoria 3053, Australia

First published 2004 by Blackwell Publishing Ltd

Library of Congress Cataloging-in-Publication Data

Southern, R. W. (Richard William), 1912–2001
  History and historians: selected papers of R. W. Southern / edited by R. J. Bartlett.
    p. cm.
  Includes bibliographical references and index.
  ISBN 1-4051-2387-7 (alk. paper)
  1. Middle Ages – Historiography. 2. Medievalists – Biography. I. Bartlett, Robert, 1950–
II. Title.

  D116.S67 2004
  909.07′07′2–dc22

                                                                    2004003050

A catalogue record for this title is available from the British Library.

Set in 10/12pt Sabon
by Kolam Information Services Pvt. Ltd, Pondicherry, India
Printed and bound in the United Kingdom
by MPG Books, Bodmin, Cornwall

The publisher's policy is to use permanent paper from mills that operate a sustainable forestry policy, and which has been manufactured from pulp processed using acid-free and elementary chlorine-free practices. Furthermore, the publisher ensures that the text paper and cover board used have met acceptable environmental accreditation standards.

For further information on
Blackwell Publishing, visit our website:

Contents

Part III Historians

Abbreviations

BL	British Library
CCCM	*Corpus Christianorum, continuatio mediaevalis*
EHR	*English Historical Review*
JEH	*Journal of Ecclesiastical History*
MARS	*Mediaeval and Renaissance Studies*
MGH	*Monumenta Germaniae historica*
OMT	Oxford Medieval Texts
PBA	*Proceedings of the British Academy*
PL	*Patrologiae cursus completus, series latina*, ed. J.-P. Migne (221 vols., Paris, 1844–64)
RS	*Rerum Britannicarum Medii Aevi Scriptores* ("Rolls Series") (251 vols., London, 1858–96)
SRG	*Scriptores rerum Germanicarum in usum scholarum (MGH)*
SS	*Scriptores (MGH)*
TRHS	*Transactions of the Royal Historical Society*

Place of First Publication

Part I Aspects of the European Tradition of Historical Writing

"Aspects of the European Tradition of Historical Writing 1: The Classical Tradition from Einhard to Geoffrey of Monmouth," *TRHS*, 5th ser., 20 (1970), pp. 173–96.

"Aspects of the European Tradition of Historical Writing 2: Hugh of St. Victor and the Idea of Historical Development," *TRHS*, 5th ser., 21 (1971), pp. 159–79.

"Aspects of the European Tradition of Historical Writing 3: History as Prophecy," *TRHS*, 5th ser., 22 (1972), pp. 159–80.

"Aspects of the European Tradition of Historical Writing 4: The Sense of the Past," *TRHS*, 5th ser., 23 (1973), pp. 246–63.

Part II History

The Shape and Substance of Academic History (Inaugural Lecture as Chichele Professor of Modern History, Oxford, 1961, repr. in *The Varieties of History from Voltaire to the Present*, ed. Fritz Stern, 2nd ed., London, 1970, pp. 403–22). Reprinted by permission of The University of Oxford.

"The Historical Experience," *Times Literary Supplement* (June 24, 1977), pp. 771–4 (the Rede Lecture, delivered in the University of Cambridge, May 3, 1977). Reprinted by permission of the *Times Literary Supplement*.

"The Truth about the Past" (unpublished paper delivered to the St. John's College Historical Society, Oxford, November 1988).

Part III Historians

Review of *The Letters of Frederic William Maitland*, ed. C. H. S. Fifoot, vol. 1 (Cambridge and Harvard University Press, 1965), *History and Theory* 6 (1967), pp. 105–11. Reprinted by permission of *History and Theory*.

"Sir Maurice Powicke (1879–1963)," *PBA* 50 (1964), pp. 275–304. Reprinted by permission of the British Academy.

"Vivian Hunter Galbraith (1889–1976)," *PBA* 64 (1978), pp. 397–425. Reprinted by permission of the British Academy.

"Richard William Hunt (1908–1979)," *PBA* 67 (1981), pp. 371–97. Reprinted by permission of the British Academy.

"Marjorie Reeves as a Historian," in *Prophecy and Millenarianism: Essays in Honour of Marjorie Reeves*, ed. Ann Williams (Harlow, 1980), pp. 1–9. Reprinted by permission of Pearson Education.

"Beryl Smalley (1905–1984)," *PBA* 72 (1986), pp. 455–71. Reprinted by permission of the British Academy.

Preface

A long-cherished project has been realized in the present volume. At once time-related and time-transcending, like all the finest historical writing, the papers of Sir Richard Southern here collected, and especially his four presidential addresses to the Royal Historical Society, offer profound insights into the aims and practices of historians, and the place of history in culture at large, in medieval and modern times. That the Society should enable these papers to reach a new generation and a wider readership is something we are confident Sir Richard himself would have approved.

The Society is extremely grateful to Peter Southern for his warm encouragement, to Alexander Murray for help of many kinds, to one of our Literary Directors, Andrew Pettegree, for piloting the volume toward its publisher, to Christopher Wheeler of Blackwell for taking it forward, and above all, to Robert Bartlett whose devoted and skillful efforts have seen the whole project through. At a time when history is attracting a larger audience than ever before, may this book signal both the mighty contribution of RWS, and the Society's ongoing commitment to history and historians.

Janet L. Nelson
President of the Royal Historical Society

Introduction

Sir Richard Southern (1912–2001) is widely regarded as one of the greatest medieval historians. His first book, *The Making of the Middle Ages*, published in 1953, translated into many languages, and never out of print, is a classic of its kind: a lucid exposition of an age that captures both the dynamism of the period and the inner workings of human thought and emotion. His studies of St. Anselm are standard works on that great monastic thinker; his superb synthesis, *Western Society and the Church in the Middle Ages*, vividly conveys "the history of the most elaborate and thoroughly integrated system of religious thought and practice the world has ever known"; his last but also one of his most ambitious projects was his multi-volume *Scholastic Humanism and the Unification of Europe*. Naturally, over the course of his life he also wrote numerous shorter pieces – essays, lectures, memoirs, and so on. Many of Southern's papers were collected in the volume *Medieval Humanism and Other Studies*, published by Blackwell in 1970. In that same year appeared the first of the series of reflections on medieval historical writing that Southern produced during his tenure as President of the Royal Historical Society. According to the custom of the Society, the four presidential addresses were published in successive volumes of the *Transactions* of the Society. Under the general title "Aspects of the European Tradition of Historical Writing," Southern dealt in turn with classicizing history, universal history, prophetic history, and, with the designation "The Sense of the Past," English antiquarian history, which he saw as aiming at "total recall of the past."

As in all his writings, the range is wide, the learning deep, and the insights penetrating. The essays belong together naturally and their republication here in book format is intended to make these writings by a master medievalist on such an important theme more accessible and convenient. They are supplemented by Southern's occasional pieces on two related subjects: the nature of academic history and appreciations of other medievalists, both his teachers and his contemporaries.

In the four addresses to the Royal Historical Society, Southern examined the historians of the past not as sources for events but as objects of study in their own right. He saw the limitations of "the tradition which regarded medieval chroniclers simply as repositories of facts and not as evidence of the minds and intentions of the authors." His avowed subject was exactly the "aims, methods, and limitations of the historians of the past." His first essay dealt with the classicizing, rhetorical tradition inspired by the writers of ancient Rome. Its most notable medieval example was Einhard, its most successful Geoffrey of Monmouth. Southern recognized that the invented speeches, the stock descriptions, and the stylistic elaboration of these writers were useless for "a modern historian in search of a fact," but that was not the point. They aimed to produce elegant works of art with an exemplary moral and must be understood in light of that aim. The universal historians who formed the subject of the second address were very different. Building especially on the foundations laid by St. Augustine, with his long view of history and his influential theory of the Six Ages, they developed a clear and coherent scheme in which all human affairs could be framed between Creation and the End, as depicted in Genesis and Revelation. The main example Southern chose here was the twelfth-century monastic theologian Hugh of St. Victor, whose historical conceptions he analyzed in detail. Although the foundations of Christian universal history were theological, Southern thought the enterprise deserved the label "scientific."

Prophetic history, Southern's third topic, was like universal history in that it built on the Bible. It was, however, interested in certain special parts of the Bible – those which could be used as keys to the future; and these biblical texts were supplemented by other prophetic materials, such as the mysterious predictions of the ancient sibyls and of the Celtic seer Merlin. From all this, learned and intelligent men and women sought to construct a picture of history that extended not only into the past but also into the future. Sometimes, as in the case of Joachim of Fiore, the most notable of medieval prophetic thinkers, their theories had tangible political consequences. The last of Southern's addresses began with the reflection that none of the three previous types of history he had considered – rhetorical, universal, prophetic – had the aim that he ascribed to modern historians, that of "reconstituting the thoughts and experiences of the past in their total environment." He also pondered what he called "the consoling sense of continuity and peace" which such a sense of the past could bring, before proceeding to address two moments in English history when historians of an antiquarian turn of mind had sought such consolation. One was in the aftermath of the Norman Conquest, when monks of the old English monasteries recalled the past "to give the community its identity in the present." William of Malmesbury was one of his main case studies here. The other moment was in the century after the Reformation. The main protagonists now were not English monks but English gentlemen, exemplified by the judge, antiquarian, and Kentish patriot William Lambarde.

Southern was very strongly aware that the intellectual traditions of the Middle Ages, which took shape in the twelfth century, did not expire at the touch of the Renaissance or Reformation, but continued with great vigor into the seventeenth century, and in part into the nineteenth. He wrote of "the relatively stable intellectual system which had been created in the Middle Ages and remained substantially operative till the mid-nineteenth century." This explains his willingness to take not only Joachim of Fiore but also Sir Isaac Newton as an example in his discussion of medieval prophetic history, or to conclude his analysis of universal history with a characteristic reference to the eighteenth-century *Universal History* on his shelves at St. John's College.

The wide chronological range of Southern's reflections on history is characteristic also of the three lectures printed in the second section of this volume. Indeed, they have much more to say about the nineteenth and twentieth centuries than about the Middle Ages. This is for two reasons. First, as Southern pointed out on more than one occasion, history only became an academic discipline in the nineteenth century. It was not studied in the medieval university, and was excluded from the general scholastic enterprise. Lacking authoritative texts and offering no body of systematic knowledge, "history remained a rag-bag among the sciences until the nineteenth century." For any academic historian, then, the nineteenth century is the age of genesis, where he or she must look for forebears. That is the general reason. A more particular one in Southern's case is that, as he was born in 1912, his teachers were themselves products of Victorian England and marked by its intellectual methods and priorities, its cultural flavors and its denominational divides. This was not an alien world for Southern. It came naturally to him to cite the great nineteenth-century novelists (*The Making of the Middle Ages* contains a famous use of Jane Austen to illustrate the dilemmas of secular patronage of the Church in the Middle Ages) and he was in constant intellectual debate with the controversial figure of John Henry Newman (1801–90).

The first piece in this second section is the Inaugural Lecture which Southern gave when he became Chichele Professor at the University of Oxford. It not only dealt with the creation of the academic discipline of history in Oxford in the mid-nineteenth century, but also advanced a program for practical educational change. Southern recognized that he himself was the product of the Victorian tradition of historical study and expressed his appreciation of many aspects of it, but he also saw its limitations, especially its disregard for "everything in history that could not be related to institutions and politics." The study of English constitutional history, with close analysis of original texts as its method and the continuous development of Liberty as its theme, had been revolutionary in its time, but its time was now over.

This lecture was given in Oxford, for an Oxford audience, and its concerns are (in a positive sense) local. The second piece in this section, "The Historical Experience," was given in another university, and it is on an altogether different scale. Here, after an illuminating account of what he considers his own first genuine historical insight, Southern looked at the revolutionary development of historical thinking in the nineteenth century, not this time in the sense of the birth of the academic discipline, but in the new awareness of change, of evolution, of development, to be found in many areas of intellectual and cultural life. His case studies are Darwin, Newman, Engels, and Renan, a curious quartet reflecting his wide reading, diverse interests, and sense of the centrality of the nineteenth century. He explored the social and intellectual background of these great figures, their wrestling with new ideas and situations, and, with particular emphasis, the moments when new formulations had crystallized within them. In the following piece, the last in this section, Southern's message to his undergraduate audience was that the purpose of historical scholarship should be "to recreate the minds of the past in all their aspects, and with close attention to times and places and personalities." This is exactly what he himself did in the case of Darwin, Newman, Engels, and Renan.

The third section of this volume contains appreciations of other medievalists, the first being a short piece on F. W. Maitland, who died before Southern was born, but who has a place in any consideration of the writing of medieval history. Maitland was a pioneer in method and approach and his contribution to medieval English history was not only enormous in its time but enduring. He is still the best place to start when studying medieval law and still a pleasure to read. As Southern put it, "all modern historical researchers are his successors." The other pieces printed here are appreciations either of Southern's teachers (Powicke, Galbraith) or of his Oxford contemporaries (Hunt, Reeves, Smalley).

Southern was very much an Oxford man. He came up to Balliol as an undergraduate in 1929 and he died in Oxford in 2001. All his permanent positions were at the University (Fellow of Balliol 1937–61, Chichele Professor 1961–9, President of St. John's 1969–81). These memoirs of teachers and contemporaries are thus a monument to, and a record of, the world of Oxford medieval scholarship over much of the twentieth century.

The year before Southern came to Oxford, Powicke had become Regius Professor there and Galbraith had been appointed to a Fellowship at Balliol, Southern's college. This fortunate eventuality shaped Southern's intellectual life deeply, and his memoirs of the two men exude gratitude and admiration, as well as a sharp appreciation of their qualities as historians and teachers. Galbraith was difficult to portray as a champion of the new history, breaking free of the old constitutional mold, because in fact the core of his work was in editions of texts and analysis of public records, but his sparkling personality and irreverent style come through clearly enough in Southern's memoir. Powicke is a different case and one senses that, as he wrote about him, Southern was seeking to capture something elusive, to record the "spell" that the older historian wove around him, a spell that others might well not have felt. He saw a visionary side to Powicke and his brilliant evocation of Powicke's *magnum opus, Henry III and the Lord Edward*, culminates with the arresting assessment – "history as perhaps Proust might have written it – episodic, fitful, haunting."

Both Powicke and Galbraith were products of the Manchester History School associated with the names of Tait and Tout, as well as of Oxford, and, in the case of Powicke in particular, could be seen as potential innovators in the Oxford scene. The study of history at Oxford, as it had developed in the mid- and late nineteenth century, was intended to give a general education to future administrators and politicians by grounding them in the constitutional history of England. In Southern's view, Powicke wished to alter the program in two ways, first by broadening the scope of study to encompass aspects of the religious and intellectual history of the Middle Ages, second by giving a new professional seriousness to post-graduate study (this was a time when post-graduate degrees were viewed skeptically by most Oxford and Cambridge dons). Southern himself did not seek a post-graduate degree, but clearly benefited from Powicke's interest and encouragement in the years after his graduation in 1932.

The theme of the widening of the range of Oxford medieval scholarship, beyond constitutional history and its handbook, Stubbs's *Select Charters*, to a more international and more cultural Middle Ages, runs through the last three pieces printed here, which are appreciations of three scholars of Southern's own generation (all a few years older). His picture of Marjorie Reeves, whose studies of medieval prophecy have done so much to turn a disregarded and quaint topic into a central concern of historical scholarship, starts with the attempts of "a young historian to break out of the narrow channels in which the academic history of the 1920s was confined." Similarly, Beryl Smalley was inspired by Powicke's own path-breaking work on the scholastic writing of Stephen Langton, archbishop of Canterbury, to undertake the studies of medieval biblical commentary that culminated in her *Study of the Bible in the Middle Ages*. Hunt was not a prolific publisher (his Oxford doctoral thesis of 1936 was finally published posthumously in 1984) but he was an influential scholar nonetheless and his contribution too was in the wide field of European intellectual history. All these scholars represent for Southern (and we can of course include him amongst them) a transformation of English medieval scholarship, away from the national and the constitutional to the international and cultural, creating a new picture of the Middle Ages which is symbolized in the title of Southern's last work, *Scholastic Humanism and the Unification of Europe*.

Southern won fame as a guide to the religious life of the medieval period and some of his best-known work concerns a saint (Anselm). His own strong religious principles are well known. Yet he was not blind to the material realities of the world – in *Western Society and the Church in the Middle Ages* he undertakes a calculation of the average cost of supporting a Benedictine monk compared to an Augustinian canon, concluding that the relative cheapness of the latter "was no doubt a powerful consideration for benefactors." A similar awareness of economic and practical realities can be seen in these appreciations of his teachers and contemporaries. He knows how difficult it was for a woman to obtain an academic position in the 1930s; he is alive to the worries and uncertainties of the years between graduation and a permanent job; he even tells us details of Galbraith's salary and the rent of his Hampstead flat (just over £2 per week in 1921). As in the case of his studies of medieval scholars and churchmen, intellectual and religious activity does not occur in a void but in a real, material, and sometimes difficult world.

The same concreteness applies to his evocation of the working methods and daily activity of these historians. Using their letters and notebooks with skill and sympathy, he is able to build up a detailed picture of scholarly donkey work – transcription, editing, the creation of committees to undertake long-term projects, as well as the task of lecturing, teaching, examining. In a curious sense, these minutiae bring the collection full circle, for the addresses to the Royal Historical Society are also concerned not merely with historical theorizing but with historical work – the business of a historian. The long story of historical scholarship, from its classical and Christian roots, through the antiquarians of the early modern period and the creation of academic history in the nineteenth century and on into its new variations in the twentieth, is a continuous one, in which, for all its transformations, practitioners can look with respect and interest at the efforts of other practitioners. That is what Southern was doing in these papers.

The core of this book is formed by the four addresses from the *Transactions of the Royal Historical Society* and it was one of Southern's successors as President of the Society, Professor Janet Nelson, who originated the idea of republishing them in book format. It was a suggestion willingly taken up by Blackwell. The advice of Alexander Murray was also very helpful in giving the volume its final shape. His biographical memoir provides the fullest and most recent account of Sir Richard Southern's life and work.[1]

Except in the case of "The Truth about the Past" (an unpublished talk), editorial revision has been slight. Systems of reference have been standardized and more modern editions of texts, and any English translations of them, have been indicated but no attempt has been made to give a full current bibliography on subjects discussed. English translations have been added to phrases cited in foreign languages and a few explanatory footnotes included.

Robert Bartlett
University of St. Andrews

Part I

Aspects of the European Tradition of Historical Writing

Aspects of the European Tradition of Historical Writing
1: The Classical Tradition from Einhard to Geoffrey of Monmouth

I hope the Society will not think that I am wasting its time in taking the European tradition of historical writing as the general theme of the addresses that I am required to deliver during my term of office. Although there have been many studies of the wide range of problems that fall under the general heading of historiography, the study of the aims, methods, and limitations of the historians of the past has been somewhat neglected, in this country at least.[1] There are of course some conspicuous exceptions. The historical attitudes and aptitudes of St. Augustine, Gibbon, and Macaulay have been examined again and again. But outside the great names comparatively little has been done to examine historical works for what they can tell us about the way in which historical writing is affected by the intellectual presuppositions and environment of the writer. As historians we are generally content to use the chronicles and histories of the past quite simply as quarries of facts that require to be sifted and purified to make them usable for our purposes, but do not require any profound investigation of the principles of selection, emphasis, or composition that determined their preservation. This is how Stubbs dealt with the many chronicles that he edited so admirably. They were the raw material for his own works and those of other historians. He examined them for reliability, and he asked whether they provided new facts that could not be found elsewhere. He had little concern with the minds of the men who all unknowingly determined what materials should be available for his workshop.

In many ways one must admire this insouciance. It arose from the confidence of the historians of a hundred years ago that they had discovered new methods, new questions, and new tools for the interpretation of the past. They had got so far beyond the old writers that the minds of these writers seemed scarcely worth the trouble of investigation. "What could not such a mind have done if it had not been fettered by such a method?" This was Stubbs's blunt reaction to Thomas Aquinas; but I fear he would not have thought that the minds or methods of the historians on whom he lavished so much care were sufficiently distinct to qualify for even this lofty enquiry.

The growing interest in the minds and methods of earlier historians is doubtless a sign of some lack of confidence in ourselves. But it is also a sign of a development in historical perspective that may in time produce important results. The founders of modern historical study were (as is the way with pioneers) highly selective in the type of evidence and the type of subject-matter which they thought suitable for the purposes of the historian, and they were inclined to think that there was only one way in which history could properly be written. They were much more interested in man as a social and political animal than as a thinking and feeling being. To me at least they seem to have put the accent in the wrong place, and my reflections on our historical tradition are to some extent a reaction against the limitations of the discipline in which I was brought up and to which I owe a debt that I can never adequately express.

I have perhaps already said too much by way of introduction, but since in three or four discourses the subject I have in mind can only be dealt with from a personal point of view, I may start by making an assertion that not everyone will agree with, and then proceed to examine the historical background of an attitude that has a long and controversial history. I shall begin then by declaring that the first duty of a historian is to produce works of art. By this I do not primarily mean works that are finely written, but works that are emotionally and intellectually satisfying, that combine a clear unity of conception with a vivacity of detail, and portray people whose actions are intelligible within the framework of their circumstances and character. It is thus that one might describe the aims of a Balzac or a Tolstoy: I say therefore that a historian should aim at satisfying the same emotional and intellectual needs as a novelist or poet. How he is to do this within the limits of the available data is the great question.

Now to start with, it must be recognized that this conception of the historian's task as primarily artistic runs directly against the main stream of European historical writing. Europe has produced a vast quantity of historical writing in the last fifteen hundred years, yet the amount of this huge bulk inspired by any artistic aim is very small indeed. The strength of the European historical tradition has lain in its annalists and

antiquarians. Historical scholarship has been more important than historical writing. The most influential historians have collected information for
many purposes – for legal and institutional purposes, to satisfy a thirst for
knowledge about a people or a province or a city, or simply for entertainment – but for the most part they have not troubled themselves with art.
In thus limiting themselves they were not simply taking an easy course.
They had intellectual credentials of the highest respectability for what
they did, and more especially for what they failed to do. Aristotle, to
come no lower, laid it down that between history and art there is a great
gulf fixed, and his view has too strong a foundation in common experience to be easily overthrown. We may therefore pause for a moment to
consider it.

In Aristotle's view history lacks the two main ingredients of serious art –
form and universality. It lacks form because the events of history have
no dramatic unity. And since it is the historian's task to record events
faithfully, as they happened, when they happened, and in the order in
which they happened, artistic form – the famous beginning, middle, and
end of Aristotle's definition – can have no part in the finished result.
Consequently the productions of the historian must be as chaotic as life
itself:

> The historian has to expound not one action, but one period of time and all
> that happens within this period to one or more persons, however discon-
> nected the several events may be.[2]

Artistic form is therefore excluded from written history. More important,
since the material of history lacks universality, the works of the historian
cannot have the universal truth which is the hallmark of great art:

> The historian describes the thing that has been; the poet the kind of thing
> that might be. Hence poetry is more important and philosophic than history,
> for its statements have universal validity, while those of the historian are
> valid only for one time and one place.[3]

These are familiar quotations but they are worth recalling for they sum up
a great deal that is implicit in the European sense of history as it has
developed through the centuries. The overwhelming mass of European
historical enquiry between the twelfth century and the nineteenth has been
inspired by an instinctive sense that Aristotle's view is right, and no historian who has wrestled long with the intractable material of his craft can
fail to have experienced the force of Aristotle's argument. We live daily
with the sense of the difficulty, sometimes it seems the impossibility, of
penetrating below the surface of events to those depths of human instinct

and volition, the proper sphere of the novelist and poet, where men of every age and place meet in their common humanity. We must often rage inwardly at our limitations; but there they are and they are basically the limitations that Aristotle pointed out.

Yet it is also true that the modern movement in historical writing began when the Aristotelian tradition, with its belittlement of history, wore thin. I am not today concerned with the long struggle in the late eighteenth and early nineteenth centuries to free history from the limitations imposed upon it by the Aristotelian tradition. It must suffice for the moment to say that history could only take its place among the academic disciplines when the criticism that it lacked form and universality of application had come to be widely disbelieved. We shall perhaps consider this struggle and its result on a later occasion. Today, however, I want to go back to the early days in the formation of a European historical tradition, before the Aristotelian freeze had set in, and when history was widely regarded as an art of a peculiarly elaborate, exacting, and artificial kind.

II

The writers of whom I shall speak belong to the three centuries from about 820 to 1140, from Einhard's *Life of Charlemagne* to Geoffrey of Monmouth's *History of the Kings of Britain*. I choose them because, although there is no scholar among them of the stature of Bede and no chronicler of contemporary events so copious or entertaining as Matthew Paris, the more ambitious historians of this period have an identity of aim and inspiration that we shall not find again on a European scale until the seventeenth century. The inspiration of these writers was predominantly classical, and they attempted to produce works of art based on the practice and precepts of antiquity. The extent to which they succeeded in this purpose will have to be considered somewhat carefully in assessing their achievement, and this in turn will help to explain why classical ideals of historical art were largely replaced by more pedestrian but more serviceable models in the course of the twelfth century.

The classical ideals which these writers inherited and attempted to revive had nothing in common with the views of Aristotle which I have already described. Aristotle's views on history had been pushed aside by ancient historians, and they were known in the early Middle Ages only in the form of an epigram about history being different from tragedy. But the source and meaning of this epigram were wholly unknown. The historical ideal of the West in the Carolingian and post-Carolingian period was derived from Sallust and Suetonius, from Virgil and Lucan, from Boethius and from the writers on rhetoric whose works were studied in the schools.[4] It was a miscellaneous bag, and to anyone who looks for a serious study of the practice of ancient historians it will seem woefully defective. Sallust is the sole representative of the great historians of Greece and Rome, and surely he is not the greatest. Yet it is doubtful whether more or better models would have made a greater or different impression. Men learn in the end only what they wish to learn, and the hints of authors far below the best will generally suffice to convey the acceptable lessons of the past. All the writers I have mentioned were very widely read and they transmitted to their readers some basic principles of ancient history.

In the first place they enforced the lesson that history is a branch of literature, and that he who aspires to write history must aim at producing works of art that are rich in color, distinctive in diction, and perfect in shape. Although the necessity for truth was a constantly reiterated require-ment, anyone familiar with Sallust and Suetonius would easily conclude that historical truth did not exclude a generous freedom to select, arrange, and fill out events to produce dramatic and intellectually satisfying con-frontations. If, in the exercise of this freedom, the disciples of these writers filled their works with appropriate speeches and documents of their own composition, they would certainly not have misinterpreted the spirit of their models. Early medieval scholars, who were educated in the rhetorical tradition of the ancient world, understood instinctively the liberties that ancient historians had taken, and they followed their example with enthu-siasm.

All these lessons, which chiefly concerned the literary presentation and ornamentation of historical themes, lay on the surface and could easily be learned. At a deeper level there were lessons about the structure of histor-ical events themselves. It was here that the poverty of the western inherit-ance of historical works from the past might have been a serious handicap. Polybius and Thucydides could certainly have imparted more serious views of historical causation than Sallust. Yet in Sallust, besides grand rhetoric, brilliant caricatures, weighty speeches, and generalizations about human affairs, the readers of the *Catiline Conspiracy* – which then as now was the most widely studied of his works – would find a large view of the stages by which society degenerates from its primitive vigor and moral purity as a result of the growth of wealth and luxury, until men of the highest talents seek to rehabilitate their dissipated fortunes at the cost of the general overthrow of the state.[5] Behind the rhetoric there is here the outline of a theory of social change and an account of the mech-anism of its progress that is quite enough to provoke thought about the general problems of historical causation.

In contrast to Sallust, Virgil was not interested in the causes and effects of social change, but he provided a view of the destiny of a nation sufficiently powerful to inspire the emulation of historians. Readers of the *Aeneid* found in it a secular parallel to the sacred history of man's Fall, Redemption, and Sanctification. Out of the flames and destruction of Troy there comes forth a remnant destined to restore the defeated people to a height beyond all previous imagining – to nothing less than world Empire. This remnant is battered and tossed hither and thither, the leader is exposed to overwhelming tests and temptations, the people suffer every kind of misfortune; but they persist, and in the end the new city is built which will bring peace and justice to all the world. All this is an example of a historical development which men may create if they collaborate with the will of God to fulfill their destiny. Nowhere, not even in the Old Testament, is it possible to find so powerful and poignant an account of the divinely assisted ascent of a people.

What effect did these various sides of the classical tradition have on the Carolingian scholars and their successors who aspired to write history?

III

We may begin with something which had no effect: there is no sign of any interest in Sallust's theory of historical causation. Nearly all our writers quote Sallust, some of them use him as their chief model, probably they had all studied him and would all have agreed that he was the most powerful historian in the ancient world.[6] But none of them so much as noticed that he had an overall theory of the development and decline of political societies. This total indifference is all the more striking in writers who were acutely aware of moral degeneration in societies as well as individuals. They frequently found an explanation of natural and political disasters in the obliquity of priests and people and in the sins of the ruler; but the explanation was not strictly historical – it was theological. It was God's anger that caused the disasters; and it was sin that made Him angry. There was no historical machinery that intervened. The signs and portents which accompanied or preceded disasters had a similarly supernatural role. Basically they were simply celestial signs of the divine wrath. Occasionally, if there was a sufficient delay between celestial sign and terrestrial disaster, the sign could be seen as a warning mercifully delivered to those who could understand. But historians knew almost nothing, and cared almost as little, about the secondary causes of events about which Sallust had so comprehensive a doctrine.

If we were to judge the influence of classical authors simply by the extent to which they stimulated thought about the problems of historical change our judgment would be brief and negative. But the lack of interest in this area was balanced by an intensity of interest in the problems of literary form. The doctrine that history is a branch of the art of rhetoric was accepted with eager acclaim. The presentation of great and noble events in language appropriate to the subject-matter, and the molding of this subject-matter into artistically contrived patterns, which emphasized grandeur and relegated pettiness to oblivion, became a major preoccupation of a long line of historians.

At first sight there seems a strange contradiction here. The period which produced the most highly polished works of carefully contrived history was also the greatest period for annals which were constructed without any attempt at cohesion or artistic elaboration. The modern reader will be apt to think that annals such as these, which sometimes extend over several centuries filling the empty spaces in liturgical calendars, are the most impressive historical products of the age. They are a resolute, undeviating record of human disorder in the midst of a cosmic order. This is how men seem instinctively to have looked on history; but it was not how they thought histories should be written.

The contrast between these annals and histories written in accordance with rhetorical rules is startling, but I think it is not quite beyond explanation. In the first place, although at one level of experience events seemed discontinuous and chaotic, there was another level at which they could be regarded as typical of an order that was beyond change. This ambiguity in history, which made it at once wholly irrational and wholly rational, at once wholly coherent and wholly incoherent, was one of the most carefully cultivated experiences of the early Middle Ages. The Old Testament with its various layers of historical truth was the basis of this experience of order in the midst of apparent chaos. And the point about this order was that it came from God not man; it was discoverable not by historical rules but by an inspiration beyond history. Men brought up in this tradition of interpretation had a strong sense of the confusion of events, and a weak sense of the distinction between (as we should say) facts and imagination. The facts of history, when heated in the fire of imagination, become malleable. If the chaos of Old Testament history could be resolved by a divine fire into a perfectly organized system of truth about man and God, it was not difficult to think that the chaos of contemporary history might respond to the fire of the liberal arts.

The fire came from rhetoric. This was an art that men thought important and studied with care, but could seldom use. The revival of classical learning in the ninth century had brought the art of rhetoric back to the supremacy which it had in the ancient world, and which it did not lose again until the twelfth century. But despite its importance in the educational program, most of its ancient uses had disappeared. Legal and political rhetoric, for which the ancient art chiefly existed, was dead; epistolary rhetoric, the chief subject of the medieval art, had not yet been born;

pulpit rhetoric still lay far in the future. History was the one branch of rhetoric that had lost none of its ancient opportunities.

The opportunities were especially great because there was never a time when display counted for more in public and private life than in the tenth and eleventh centuries. Great events were preeminently occasions of ceremony and pomp. Displays of pomp were a main prop of government; they were the highlights of the ecclesiastical year, and they marked the stages in the rise of churches and empires alike. It was easy to think that in writing worthily of such occasions, a writer was supremely fulfilling the duties of a historian. When the historians of the period apologized to their readers for not doing better, they never thought that their deficiencies arose from gaps in their information, which are manifest to us, nor from the problems they have left unsolved, nor from their failure to explain why things happened as they did. They deplored only their poverty of diction, their deficiency in rhetorical colors or *sententiae*, their failure to find words splendid enough for their theme.[7] It would be stupid to blame them for thinking of their task as historians in these terms, for history itself appeared as a kind of rhetoric in action.

This view of history does not now seem as silly as it once appeared. Recent studies of the place of ceremonies and symbolism in the organization of society have brought us nearer to the point of view of writers of the tenth and eleventh centuries than the great editors of their works in the last century. We see now that the display of outward splendor and the assertion of authority which it implied were central facts in social life. In depicting the glory of rulers, historians were not sycophants but interpreters of their time, and a grandiose style was the fittest garment to enclose what was thought to be the chief substance of history.

In order to obtain a harmony of style and matter it was necessary to find subjects that did not fall below the dignity of a grand effect. This necessity directed the historians of this period towards the lives of secular rulers, who were not only the most conspicuous objects on the landscape, but also attracted to themselves ceremonies of every kind – coronations, dedications of churches, feasts and funerals, councils and battles and acts of colorful treachery. These were the events that mattered; they were also the most suitable subjects for ornate prose. Besides, the prosperity of secular rulers – chosen by God, ordained by sacramental acts, resplendent in symbolic garments, the vicars of Christ, the fathers of their country, the heads of the world – provided mankind with their best hope of peace and plenty. People believed in the sacred mission of rulers as they have never believed in it before or since, and it is hard to think that the adulation which historians of these centuries heaped on their rulers came only from the thought that they had the means of paying for praise.

IV

It was Einhard who first opened this rich vein to historians and showed the way it could be worked. His *Life* of Charlemagne initiated a new phase in the development of historical studies in western Europe, characterized by a serious attempt to revive the literary and artistic standards of classical historians. No one ever again succeeded quite as well as Einhard in creating a contemporary character in a classical mold. However stilted and unconvincing some of the passages in his work may be, there emerges from the work a fresh and original portrait of a great barbarian with enormous appetites both physical and intellectual, with an instinct for government and a creative power in practical affairs which few men in European history have matched and which among Germans only Bismarck has equaled.

Einhard was fortunate in having a subject capable of filling a classical canvas. None of his successors was equally fortunate, and none of them knew their subject as well as Einhard did. Consequently they had to compensate for the flaws in their subject and the gaps in their knowledge by a growing extravagance of diction. The ornaments became more baroque as the subjects shrank in size. Sometimes the ornaments of later writers enlarged the range of historical feeling, but in the main their extravagance only confirms the impression of Einhard's superiority.

To say this is not discreditable to his successors. Einhard was a historian with an outstandingly alert and responsive mind. He not only appreciated the possibility of writing a secular biography quite unlike any that had been written for six hundred years; he also discovered the right model for such a biography. In the library at Fulda, where he was educated as a young man, there was a manuscript – so far as we know the only surviving manuscript at that time – of Suetonius's *Lives of the Caesars*. These tough and heartless biographies, with their interest in the private vices of the Emperors and their lucid arrangement of subject-matter, showed Einhard how to describe a man who was neither a saint, nor an institution, but a warrior and a creator of new forms of political life. The success of his work was immediate, and the testimony of over eighty manuscripts – a record number for any historical work between Bede and Geoffrey of Monmouth – confirms the praises of his contemporaries.

In order to achieve his effect Einhard took liberties with his material which have earned him the dispraise of modern scholars, and since this is a phenomenon we shall often encounter it may be well to examine the matter at this point. Briefly the difficulty is that the more successful Einhard is in handling his subject the less reliable he is as a source for modern historians. Louis Halphen, the first editor to examine his methods with care, was never tired either of pointing out his exaggerations and distortions, or of castigating his eagerness to apply to Charlemagne words and ideas that Suetonius used about Augustus.[8] To take only one example of habits that Halphen disliked, Einhard opens his description of the defeat of Charlemagne's army at Roncevaux with words appropriate to a victorious campaign:

> After crossing the Pyrenees and capturing all the towns and castles which he encountered, Charlemagne returned with his army safe and sound, except that on a ridge of the Pyrenees he happened to experience some small effects of Gascon perfidy on the way home.[9]

"Façon vraiment discrète d'avouer la défaite de Roncevaux [a truly discrete way to acknowledge the defeat at Roncevaux]," wrote Halphen. Einhard would not have considered this discretion a vice. On the contrary, it was a merit. He knew very well (if only because his contemporary source told him so) that the defeat was very much more serious than he admitted, and it is very likely that if he had been writing a series of annals instead of a work of art, he would have stuck as closely as possible to the facts. But here his purpose was to evoke an image of imperial greatness. It is a striking fact that men who wrote in the ancient rhetorical tradition seem to have been unable to admit any blemishes in the image they wished to convey. They were not romantics, and they knew nothing of the equally rhetorical but subtler use of the flaw which emphasizes a beauty; everything in their picture had to tell the same story. Acting on this principle, they thought it no more disgraceful in themselves to color and select the facts to convey the overriding image, than we should think it in a painter who rearranges the trees to bring out the character which he wishes to elicit from the landscape. In both cases the result must be judged, not by the photographic accuracy of the details, but by the impression of truth in the total effect.

Einhard had many admirers, but he had no successful imitators or successors for over a hundred years. Nithard, indeed, wrote an even better, because more pungent and disillusioned, history of the Empire in his day. Asser wrote a life of a ruler with a more attractive and more lovingly observed character than Einhard's Charlemagne; but as a work of literature it is very incompetent. The first entirely competent biography of a ruler after Charlemagne is Wipo's *Life* of Conrad II.[10] This is a well-organized and learned work, full of resonant phrases and with a fine smooth surface of splendor and success. It was written with the intention of provoking a comparison with Charlemagne and everything that words could do to build Conrad up to the stature of his predecessor was done.

Wipo had a wider range of authors at his command than Einhard, and equal skill in using them. But the work is pedestrian, partly because Conrad was after all much less interesting than Charlemagne, and partly because Wipo was a humble dependant. Einhard had written as a trusted friend and in some sense an equal of his hero; Wipo wrote as a schoolmaster and servant. This was the great weakness of the medieval rhetorical tradition: the writer was unequally yoked to his subject. In the ancient world rhetoric was used by statesmen and men of action speaking and writing for their equals; in the Middle Ages it fell into the hands of dependants who wished to please or instruct their superiors.

Even in these unfavorable conditions some impressive monuments of historical rhetoric were produced. The authors of these works had one great advantage over most historians; they knew exactly what they wanted to do, and their rules allowed them a wide liberty in doing it. It was in Germany that the best subjects suitable for treatment according to the rhetorical rules were to be found; and it was in Germany too that the chief schools existed where these rules were taught. But scholarship is an international asset, and the two works which most brilliantly imposed on recalcitrant material the dramatic unity and elevation of sentiment that the rhetorical ideal demanded were written by foreigners in England. The authors of these works wrote in praise of two English queens, Emma and Edith, the wives of Cnut and Edward the Confessor. They wrote as outsiders, and they wrote for benefits received or expected. Yet, even so, they managed to express a mysterious depth of national feeling quite unlike anything we find elsewhere. They were serious artists and in their own way serious historians.

The author of the earlier of these two works, which is known to modern scholars as the *Encomium Emmae*, made no secret of his primary duty of serving the honor and good name of the queen his patron. The story he had to tell was a simple one, but dramatic in its simplicity. He spoke first of the Danes – their military prowess, family disputes, and inner counsels; then of the ancient kingdom of England, torn apart by war and divided from its conquerors by bitterness and hatred; then of Cnut and his search for a wife; and finally of the divine providence which led him to choose a princess whom Englishmen could trust and who could interpret England to her alien husband. By her patience and skill in eliciting her husband's beneficence, the ruin and hatred that had ravaged the kingdom gave place to peace and splendor and religious harmony throughout his reign. Then on his death a renewal of family discord threatened further calamity and strife. But once more her prudence and foresight turned this dark and threatening scene into a new blossoming of peace and concord under the joint rule of her two surviving sons. So the story ends in a final chorus of praise and religious devotion as the sound of battle recedes into the distance. It is the story of a woman behind the scenes who saved a kingdom from ruin.

There is no need to examine the subterfuges which made it possible for the historian to reconcile this story with the facts of history.[11] Naturally these are very shocking to a modern scholarly conscience, though it is doubtful whether the author took any liberties with the facts of history that Suetonius and Sallust would not have felt free to take. If we grant these liberties, which are those of a historical method rather than an individual; and if we grant, as we must, that there is not a single speech, document, description, or insinuation of motive in any of the works written in this tradition that can be accepted unreservedly by a modern historian in search of a fact, then we may judge that the *Encomium Emmae* is not only a work of great literary skill, but even of some nobility and historical insight. Although the Danes are dressed up and speak like Romans, they act like barbarians in their love of splendor, their desire for cultural respectability, their awe in the face of the miraculous, their genius for discord, and their longing for domestic harmony. These are the genuine traits of the time which may be held to justify the author's high claim to be telling the truth despite all the equivocation which a modern editor can easily detect.

These reflections apply equally to the other great example of historical rhetoric produced by a foreigner in England in the eleventh century, the *Vita Edwardi Confessoris*.[12] The author of this work differs from his predecessor chiefly in having a more complicated task and a greater literary ambition. He wished to praise Queen Edith his patron; but, since she did no great works, he could only praise her by praising her husband, King Edward, and her father Earl Godwin, and all her brothers. This was not easy since the most conspicuous events of the reign arose from the enmity of the members of this domestic group. But the author managed to praise them all, nearly all the time, by using a simple and ingenious device. He elevated the king above the ordinary affairs of government and stressed the numinous quality of his rule. This allowed him the double liberty of blaming the king's errors on evil advisers, and of transferring to the queen's family all responsibility for running the kingdom, conducting military expeditions, and preserving the peace. In this way he managed to preserve and enhance the credit of all parties, and to keep a single theme running through the whole work: the theme of family unity. It was through unity in an amicable division of labor that the kingdom enjoyed a golden age that lasted throughout most of the reign.

Up to this point the author had a theme very similar to that of the *Encomium Emmae*, but in the end he had to face a final breakdown of the family unity on which everything depended. The two brothers, Harold and Tostig, quarreled, and this time there was no happy ending – only a succession of disasters to which the author could see no end. I know of no piece of medieval historical writing that ends with so little hope: history and tragedy are for once completely equated. Yet in facing the tragedy the author managed somehow to save everyone's credit and to raise his theme to a new height. For the nation the tragedy was complete, but in the king's sanctity there was a hope beyond temporal events. The intensity of the author's dramatic vision overcame every obstacle. He had set out to praise the family, and its greatest praise lay in the consequences of its disunity. It was a family on which everything depended, and the tragedy of its final break-up lay in a fatality beyond human control. The work is both a lament and a glorification of a family. The author had no eyes for other causes of ruin: to this one cause he attributed all the disasters of 1066 – he never mentioned the Norman Conquest.

A historian who could write about the disasters of 1066 without mentioning the Norman Conquest is evidently not a historian in any very pedestrian sense of the word. Like all the historians of this period he knew that the first duty of the historian was to tell the truth, and he was careful not to tell a lie; but within this limit he was a creator on a grand scale. The amount of poetry and Greek mythology in the work is a sufficient indication of the plane on which he moved as a historian. It is the plane of spiritual essences and eternal beings. At this level he would have claimed that his story is true, and we can only take his word for it. But if it is true, it is the truth that Aristotle allowed to the poet, not to the historian. But in Aristotle's sense all these writers were poets for they manipulated their materials to give form and universality to their productions.

V

The first great lesson that the historians of our period learnt from the classics was how to turn history into rhetoric. But there was another lesson which had a still greater future in its influence on western historical writing – the lesson that the destiny of nations is the noblest of all historical themes. Ancient historians had been deeply impressed – how could they fail to be? – by the spectacle of the rise of Rome to world-power. The appearance of inevitability in this movement, despite the follies and errors which hindered its progress, inspired the greatest writers of Rome with a sense of destiny that gave a purpose and direction to their history. This was the theme that the writers of our period found in Virgil. It was a theme that they were ready to absorb and turn to new uses.

In the tenth century several new peoples – Saxons and Normans in the first place, but also Poles and Hungarians – were beginning to achieve political importance and respectability. With this there came the conviction, or perhaps only the hope, that they were no longer barbarians but belonged to the civilized peoples of Europe. This in its turn bred a desire for a past, and a sense of awe at the providential steps which had brought them out of barbarism. In these circumstances the obvious source for a national history lies in the legends and myths of the people. But the new peoples of Europe were largely cut off from their mythological origins by their conversion to Christianity and by the Latin learning which stood between the literate part of society and its native past. Hence it was in Roman history that they found the broken pieces which they could build into a picture of their own origins and destiny.

There were two aspects of Roman history which they found especially useful for this purpose: it showed them how people in a distant and heroic past might be expected to speak and behave, and it provided a fixed point for the beginnings of the civilized peoples of Europe. The examples of speech and behavior were of course highly artificial, and when historians of the tenth and eleventh centuries made their national heroes speak and act like characters in Roman history they may have been fully aware of the artificiality, but the alternative was that they should not speak or act at all. As for the origins of the new races of Europe, everyone knew that they had come as conquerors to take over the Roman Empire and carry on the Roman tradition. But where had they come from and whence had they drawn strength for so great an enterprise? What was more likely than that they had come from the same root as the Romans themselves – from Troy? We smile; but very early – in the sixth or seventh century – a Frankish learned tradition had alleged that the Franks were the descendants of Trojans who fled from Troy to the Danube valley when Aeneas went in the opposite direction to the Tiber.[13] The Franks themselves do not seem to have attached much importance to this legend; but it became important for other races who had to struggle harder than the Franks for a place in the sun. In their claim to Trojan ancestry, first the Saxon and Norman, then the French and British peoples, began to build themselves up to a stature appropriate to their destiny.

The first writer to do this was Widukind the historian of the Saxons. Widukind was writing about 970, in the last years of the reign of Otto I, and the theme of his history was the rise of his people from obscure beginnings to universal power. As he surveyed the achievements of Otto I in extending Saxon rule to the furthest limits of Germany and Italy, in defeating the Greeks, subduing the heathen barbarians, assuming the crown of universal empire, he began to see the history of the Saxons as a reenactment of the history of Rome. How could this be explained?

I have said that the historians of this age had no interest in the mechanisms of historical change, and this is true if we think only of natural causation. But they saw that there were two requirements for political success: nobility of blood and heavenly aid. Noble blood meant primarily noble ancestry, and here Widukind took a hint from the Franks. According to the ancient Frankish legend, the Trojans had split into two groups of fugitives when their city fell: the followers of Aeneas who went west to Rome and the followers of Priam. This second group later split into two: one part went up the Danube to occupy the territory between the Rhine and the Danube. It was from this group that the Franks were descended. The second group went south into Macedonia and formed the conquering armies of Philip and Alexander the Great.[14] Widukind tells us that when he was a youth he had been told that the Saxons were descended from the remnants of the army of Alexander the Great, and he believed this to be probable.[15] The tone in which he speaks of this descent makes it fairly clear that it was a recent discovery, no doubt prompted by the rise of the Saxons to a world role and their desire to rival the Franks, whom they were supplanting, in nobility of blood. Widukind did not press the point very strongly, for he believed he could find in Josephus and Lucan ample evidence for the ancient nobility of the Saxon people. On any view the Saxons belonged to the noble races of the ancient world.

With regard to supernatural aid, he could be more precise. The commonest channels of divine favor were relics, and it was the transfer of the relics of St. Vitus from the Frankish Corbie to Saxon Korvei in 836 that signalized the transfer of Empire from the Franks to the Saxons. This transfer was confirmed by the translation of the hand of St. Denys from Paris to Korvei in 923.[16] This was the signal for Saxony to prepare itself for the great leap forward, which went on without a break till 973 when the Empire of the world seemed assured. It would of course be difficult to imagine a cruder mechanism of historical change than this physical transport of relics from place to place, but it sufficed. The relic was both an instrument of power and a symbol of power – the greatest force that was known.

Widukind thought he was writing of a new world-power. In fact it scarcely survived his own lifetime. The next hundred and fifty years brought forward new claimants to power and respectability, and the historians of these new peoples all told a similar story. The first in the field, some twenty-five years after Widukind, was Dudo the Norman historian.[17] He was an ambitious writer, and modern scholars have scarcely been able to contemplate his work without a shudder. To historians he has appeared as a historian who neglected a unique opportunity for recording the facts about tenth-century Norman society in order to indulge in the wildest fantasies about its origin and development. To students of literature he has appeared as a learned man who neglected no opportunity for loading his writing with false jewels of every possible kind. So, both for the opportunities he neglected and for those which he seized with avidity, he has won universal opprobrium. This is surely undeserved. What he set out to do, and – according to the standards and opinions of the best judges of his own and the following century – succeeded in doing, was to tell in the noblest style the story of a noble destiny. Without claiming that he produced a masterpiece of historical literature, he must certainly be given the credit of having successfully exploited the historical techniques that he shared with his contemporaries.

In the first place Dudo's elaborate prose, his reminiscences of classical and Christian literature, his frequent flights into poetry, were all designed to give his history the dignity of a theme which was basically the same as Widukind's: the rise of a people from the noble stock of Troy, through heroic wanderings strikingly similar to those of Aeneas and his companions, to their destined place among the Christian nations of Europe. These wanderings were punctuated, as were those of Aeneas, by divinely inspired visions and premonitions, and their end was baptism and holiness. To us every stage in this story is filled with historical absurdities: the myth of Trojan descent is based on false etymology and no doubt inspired by a desire to show that the Normans were equal to the Franks and Saxons in their nobility of blood; the visions, and the interpretations placed upon them, are no more than figments of the author's imagination; the concluding section of the work which portrays the dukes of Normandy as Christian heroes and martyrs, mainly concerned with the purity of their own lives and the endowment of the Church, contradicts almost every known fact in the lives of these men. And yet, behind all these absurdities, there lies the truth that by the early eleventh century the Normans were on the point of becoming the most influential Christian nation in Europe. Richer, the historian of the Franks, writing at almost the same moment as Dudo, still referred to Richard I of Normandy as "the leader of the pirates": Dudo wrote to show that this was out-of-date. In order to make his point he indulged in the wildest exaggerations, but his point was right, and even prophetic. No doubt his history was partly propaganda, partly admonition, but it was also an attempt to understand in the only terms available to a historian a mysterious phenomenon – the phenomenon of the conversion of a bloodthirsty crew into a Christian state, and a crowd of pirates into an ordered society.

After Widukind and Dudo, several nations produced writers who wrote similar histories for their own people and their rulers. Ekkehard [of Aura] wrote at the request of the Emperor Henry V a history which traced the descent of the German emperors from Troy to the Franconian dynasty.[18] In France, Suger and the monks of St. Denis began to collect materials to establish the claim of the Capetians to be the effective heirs of Charlemagne and, of course, Trojans also by origin.[19] Then in the fullness of time came Geoffrey of Monmouth to stake out the claims of the Celts to a historical destiny greater than any other.

Geoffrey of Monmouth's *Historia Regum Britanniae* is generally looked on as a new beginning in literature which helped to launch Europe in a wave of romanticism and fantasy. But as with all really influential works there is another side to the story.[20] If we look not at its influence but at its form and inspiration, we see that Geoffrey's *History* conforms to the same general pattern as those of Widukind and Dudo. Here, too, we have the history of an ancient and noble people, descended in blood from Troy the source of all worldly nobility, buffeted by fortune, guided by visions and heavenly visitations, and led to settle in a distant land. In the account of these wanderings the parallel between Aeneas and his descendant Brutus, the leader of the Britons, is never far from the surface. Then there follows a history of conversion, war, and a final period of peace and splendor under a great and religious king. In all this we see a pattern to which we have become accustomed. But at this point we begin to recognize two great differences between Geoffrey of Monmouth and all his medieval predecessors. In the first place his account of the distant past is far fuller than those of any previous author. Dudo is copious enough, but he has to inflate every incident with speeches and rhetoric to fill his pages. Geoffrey by contrast is overflowing with detail; he makes us conscious all the time of the confusion and unpredictability of real events. He gives his distant characters an independent, almost a plausible, life of their own. This was especially important for a writer to whom all history was ancient. Unlike Widukind and Dudo he had no story of success coming down to his own day. Instead, he told a tragic history of decline and destruction, the result of treachery within and barbarism without. Slowly the Britons withdrew before the onslaughts of the Saxons until they almost disappeared from the stage of history. But over this retreat there hovered the promise of renewal; Geoffrey's history here joined hands with prophecy and opened up the promise of a still greater future for this people predestined by God for universal rule.

It is these features of vivid detail and tragedy, together with the mysterious hope for the future, that put Geoffrey's history into a different class from those we have so far discussed. It must be left to the Celtic experts to discuss the sources of his strength. Personally I am convinced that the source which he claimed to have received from Walter, archdeacon of Oxford, really existed. But when we observe the freedom with which other historians in the same tradition treated their sources,[21] we shall not expect any exact correspondence between Geoffrey's source and the "translation" which he made of it. It is highly likely that in his treatment of his sources, whether literary or traditional, he used the freedom of invention that the literary tradition of historical writing allowed. But we may also think that like other writers in this tradition he used his freedom in the interests of some larger truth. He had seen in his own lifetime the

Bretons return to England as Conquerors. As he looked back he saw some divinely ordained design behind the chaos of events – a destiny once before fulfilled in Arthur and once again to be fulfilled in the future.

VI

We have traced two streams of classical influence in historical writing for about three hundred years from the rediscovery or rehabilitation of ancient models and ancient rhetorical teaching in the ninth century. During this period, alongside a great mass of annalistic compilation, there was a succession of writers who devoted their energies to the task of writing histories which were also works of art. The best results of their efforts can be seen in the biographies of rulers and the histories of the new peoples of Europe. These subjects were in various ways amenable to rhetorical treatment, and they could probably only have been given literary form under the influence of classical models. This combination of subject and method inspired a succession of writers who believed that the writing of history was an exacting literary art which demanded a wide range of secular learning and a full exercise of imaginative power. Consequently the histories which they produced were heavily loaded to produce an effect. They have very little assured fact that a modern historian can rely on; but they illuminate some of the main developments of their day – the sanctification of the secular ruler and the providential (as it seemed) emergence of new political powers in Europe. To these themes our writers have given a forceful and brilliant expression. Whether they went further than their ancient models in distorting the facts of history for their special ends is a difficult question and perhaps an irrelevant one. For the modern historian, who may be regarded as a share-holder in the facts of history, it makes a great difference whether the dividend of facts produced by these works is 2 percent or 20 percent; but if we look at the methods and aims of the writers the difference is accidental. Nevertheless we may all agree that in Geoffrey of Monmouth the dividend had shrunk to vanishing-point and it was time for history to come under a new management.

By this time too, the combination of learned interests and appropriate subjects which inspired these works was ceasing to exist. New forms of rhetoric were coming into fashion; new intellectual interests were replacing the literary and allegorical interests of the Carolingian period; secular rulers were losing their spiritual glamour; the peoples of Europe were nearly all provided with a historical background that sufficed till the nineteenth century. The *Life* of Henry IV of Germany was the last ruler-biography in the old rhetorical tradition; and, except for a few late-comers, of whom much the most important was Saxo Grammaticus, "research" into the distant past of European peoples came to an end. Historians began to take a more prosaic view of historical facts and to distinguish more rigorously between fact and fancy. When this happened the end was in sight for history as an art conceived in terms borrowed from the ancient world: Romance became separated from History. Art and science went their different ways to separate heavens, and history fell between the two with results that we shall perhaps be able to examine at a later date.

2

Aspects of the European Tradition of Historical Writing 2: Hugh of St. Victor and the Idea of Historical Development

A year ago I took the opportunity presented by this obligatory address to survey the working out of a classical formula for historical writing during the three hundred years which separate Einhard's *Life of Charlemagne* from Geoffrey of Monmouth's *Historia Regum Britanniae.* History written in accordance with these rules had many merits, and its emphasis is often right, or at least illuminating, but it never had a more than uncertain hold on the matter-of-fact world. Geoffrey of Monmouth was a historian who followed the old rules, but he did his job so well that he could have no successor except in the realm of romance. This is no place for us, and it is time for us to come down to earth again.

Chronologically, the phase of historical thought and writing to which I want to direct our attention today follows very closely on that which I have just outlined. But it comes from quite different origins and leads to totally different results. It is concerned not with grand subjects dealt with in a grand style, but with the greatest of all subjects studied in a scientific fashion. The subject is nothing less than universal history. The writers with whom we shall be chiefly concerned lie within the limits of the twelfth century, but in order to understand them correctly it will be necessary to look back to the system of thought which they inherited, and forward to the elaboration of this system until the moment of its final collapse.

The intellectual background of universal history is not provided by the rhetoric of the ancient schools, but by the framework of Creation, Fall, and Redemption, which Christianity gave to the western world. This cosmic plan gave birth to a new view of history which was the most important intellectual contribution that Christianity made to the stock of ancient learning. The ancient pagan world never had, any more than we now have, a clear and unambiguous picture of human history from its beginning to its end; but by the end of the fourth century Christian scholars had created a new view of a compact universe existing within clearly defined chronological limits and sharply distinguished from the eternal world of spiritual essences. The most striking feature of this view of history was its clarity. The details of the first moments of human life were known as unambiguously as those of yesterday, and thereafter there was scarcely a century without its quota of clearly ascertainable fact. It might be disputed whether the earliest events of history had taken place 5,000 or 6,000 years ago, and whether the final events were to be expected within 100 or 200 or perhaps another 1,000 years. But about the general time-scale there was no doubt. Few people in AD 1000 would have expected the world to last another 1,000 years, and probably no one another 2,000 years. The end was in sight almost as clearly as the beginning, and history was the story of a tight and compact world, of which the main outlines could be grasped without any disturbing uncertainty.

This certainty is an important fact in the intellectual development of Europe. The view of history which the Middle Ages inherited came to be supported by so much scientific evidence and critical scholarship that it proved to be the most difficult part of the medieval system of thought to shake. It took a revolution in thought to bring it to the ground, and it never looked so strong as in the last years of its life. During its fifteen hundred years of active life, it gave men confidence in dealing with the external world. Perhaps I suffer from a historian's delusion, but I cannot help thinking that the clarity of the historical picture was an important aid to the development of scientific thought. The complexities of endless time, of immense cyclical movements and unimaginable depths of change, could be excluded, and the mind could be fixed on clear facts capable of systematic arrangement. There was no need to strain the imagination by peering into the perplexed half-lights of past uncertainties. History was monolithic, and what men knew they knew without ambiguity.

Yet within this monolithic structure, the early Middle Ages inherited, chiefly from St. Augustine, a rudimentary view of historical development. The complexities of Augustine's historical vision lie outside the scope of this paper, but it is easy to identify his main contribution to medieval historical thought. In the last sentences of his City of God, and in several other places in his works, he sketches in the briefest outline the main phases of universal history:

Just as there are six days of Creation, so there are six ages of History: the first from Adam to the Flood, the second from the Flood to Abraham, the next three (as they are outlined in St. Matthew's Gospel) from Abraham to David, from David to the Babylonian Captivity, and from the Babylonian Captivity to the birth of Christ. Then comes the sixth age, in which the human mind was recreated in the image of God, just as on the sixth day of Creation man was created in the image of God. In this age we now live.[1]

The main outlines of this scheme have become so familiar through frequent repetition that it may seem superfluous to dissect it, but we shall not understand the later developments of the system without a brief analysis of its sources and main characteristics. First of all we must note that it is built on a bold interpretation of the first chapter of Genesis. The six days of Creation foreshadowed the six ages of history, and the seventh day of rest corresponded to the eternity beyond the end of history. Augustine's vision of history was an extraordinary flight of imagination springing from the mysterious depths of biblical truth. The first chapter of Genesis was the clue to the whole course of history; the genealogies of St. Matthew's Gospel were the clue to the precise boundaries of three of the six ages. So the main divisions of historical time were mapped out; and the faint outlines of a universal development came into view. Yet Augustine was not interested in development. For him, the only really significant division in history was at the intersection of the fifth and sixth ages, when the water of history was turned into the wine of Redemption. Apart from this division, history remained a chaos of human sin divided by acts of divine power.

It was left to Bede, a man with a more limited and more scientific mind, to establish the formal characteristics of the six ages of history and to introduce into their structure an element of autonomous development. Bede was not only the most expert chronologer and the most imaginative historian of the early Middle Ages; he was also the man who thought most seriously about the shape of universal history. He accepted Augustine's correlation between the six days of Creation and the six ages of history. Then he took a harder look at the six days of Creation and he related the course of each age of history to the movement within the corresponding day of Creation. For instance, just as the first Day began with the creation of light, continued with the separation of light from darkness, and ended with the fall of Night, so the first Age began with the creation of man, continued with the separation of the good from the bad, and ended with the destruction of the universal Flood. Bede applied this form of exegesis to each of the six ages. As a result, each age acquired a distinct momentum, similar in pattern but distinct in its results: at the beginning of each there was an act of restoration, succeeded by a period of divergent development leading to a general disaster which set the scene for a new act of restoration. I think that Bede is quite original in giving to each age this rhythm of dawn, growth, and destruction, containing the promise of a new dawn. It is a rhythm which has some faint similarity to the Hegelian dialectic of history, and this similarity is strengthened by the way in which Bede ties his ages of history together in a movement analogous to the seven ages in the life of man. The first age, Infancy, is the time beyond the reach of memory before the Flood; the second, Childhood, is the time before Abraham when human language was first formed; the third, Adolescence, is the time of potency, when the generation of the Patriarchs began; the fourth, Maturity, is the time when mankind became capable of kingly rule; the fifth, Old Age, is the time of growing afflictions; the sixth, Senility, is the time in which the human race moves into the decrepitude which precedes the age of eternal rest.[2]

Faithful to the teaching of Augustine, Bede did not attempt to give a precise shape to the sixth age, though he found a clue to its development in the seven seals of the Book of Revelation which later thinkers were to develop. The Book of Revelation is the most dangerous peak on which a historian can find himself, and I may find time at a later date to record some of the intellectual disasters that have overtaken climbers on this mountain. For the moment it is sufficient to record that in Bede's eyes it provided a shape, however obscure and incomplete, for the uncharted centuries of Christian history until his own day.

Bede brought history to the point at which it could be looked on not only as a succession of distinct ages with a development of their own, but also as a kind of biological process proceeding from age to age. Within this general framework he established a chronology which was better than that of any earlier scholar, and he opened up lines of future enquiry which (for better or worse) guided historical thought for the rest of the Middle Ages.

II

For nearly four centuries after Bede's death – during the period in which classical models dominated historical writing – there was no movement of thought which altered the pattern that Bede had established. There were intelligent and laborious calculators and compilers, but I cannot discover that any of them had new thoughts about the general movement of history. In history as in other fields of enquiry it was only in the early twelfth century that we find thoughts which go beyond those of Augustine and Bede. In saying this, however, I must beware of seeming to say too much. The intellectual climate of the twelfth century was not generally favorable to historical thought. It was favorable to systematization, and this was achieved by a method which was hostile to historical speculation, being based on the presumption that time and place and historical circumstances could be ignored in the search for the truth about the nature of man and the universe. This made everything easier for the systematizer. It meant that he could exclude from his already difficult task one vexatious complication. He could take texts gathered from all ages and from several different cultural environments, and use them as bricks in the edifice of truth: their historical context was irrelevant. Without this tacit agreement to ignore history, the theological, legal, and scientific summae of the twelfth and thirteenth centuries could never have been created. The centuries of systematic knowledge were, therefore, profoundly unhistorical in their approach to knowledge.[3]

Nevertheless, at the very beginning of the great period of systematization there was one man of high distinction, himself a systematizer on a grand scale, who had the instincts of a historian and had not yet learned that these instincts were incompatible with those of a scholastic theologian. This was Hugh of St. Victor, the dimmest of all the great figures of the twelfth century.

The details of his personal life are almost wholly obscure. Probably he came from the area of Ypres, but just possibly from Saxony.[4] All that we know for certain is that he was a canon of the Augustinian abbey of St. Victor in Paris and that he died in 1141. During the twenty years before his death he wrote a long series of works which exercised a mild influence on many branches of thought for several centuries. He was an almost exact contemporary of Abelard, Thierry of Chartres, and William of Conches, but in this sparkling company he is a faceless man. Like many of his great contemporaries he was a notable teacher;[5] but his name has not been associated with any single great original idea, nor with any major development of scholastic method, nor with the introduction of any new material into the curriculum of the schools. He wrote with distinction on almost every aspect of contemporary knowledge – on biblical exegesis, systematic theology, personal religion, the liberal arts – but it is hard to say that he had a distinctive place or a profound effect in any of them. A determined sobriety of thought does not easily warm the heart across a distance of eight centuries. Before my eyes were opened, I saw only a drab, respectable figure in a world of brilliant innovators and bold thinkers. Then, after much frustration and some boredom, the outlines of a distinct personality at last began to emerge. Will you be surprised to learn that what emerged from the undergrowth was the figure of a fellow-historian, a mild congenial spirit who pursued a certain vision of history through many works which superficially have little or no historical content?

In trying to convince you that Hugh of St. Victor would have been a suitable candidate for election to the fellowship of this Society, I must begin by acknowledging a difficulty. Although he wrote one historical work, it is not the work on which I should wish to base his claim to be an original historical thinker. His historical thoughts came to him not through writing history but through writing theology and biblical commentaries, and through teaching the liberal arts. It is to these areas that we must turn if we would understand his thoughts. But before we do so, we should notice that he had one natural asset. The fundamental requirement for a historian is the power of intense realization of remote situations. In the company of his great contemporaries, who either lacked this power or disesteemed it, Hugh of St. Victor stands out as one who possessed it in a notable degree. Very early in life, he tells us, when he was a schoolboy, he would lay out pebbles and mark the pavement and pace the areas of squares and parallelograms to convince himself of the truth of geometrical theorems; he would stretch strings on a wooden frame to test the doctrines of musical proportion; and he would spend long nights marking off the hours as he watched the stars.[6] These habits perhaps held no great promise of mathematical genius, but they showed an urge for the vivid realization of generalities in concrete terms which promised well for the growth of a historical imagination. It was this instinct at a later date which made him seek to give a historical setting to some of the texts used in theological debate, and to arrange his most important theological work on a historical plan. He is almost alone among medieval theologians in the importance he attached to historical situations.

A notable example of his historical bent is to be found in his discussion of the sacrament of Penance. Twelfth-century theologians found the obligation of annual confession to a priest peculiarly difficult to justify, first because the laity and some of the clergy were much opposed to it, and secondly because no precise text could be found to establish its origin. The biblical texts were inconclusive, as were the Fathers; and there was no legislative text to which the origins of the discipline could be traced. In the course of time the various strands were beaten into a coherent system to give a consistent result, but Hugh of St. Victor had an idea which seems to be quite his own.[7] It deserved more attention than it received. He arranged the inconclusive biblical texts in a plausible historical order, and he tried to show that the apparent gaps in the evidence could be filled by taking account of the historical circumstances. Thus, the simple statement "Thy sins are forgiven" belonged to the earliest period of Christ's personal ministry; then the phrases "Receive the Holy Spirit: whose soever sins ye remit, they are remitted, etc." belonged to the period when it became necessary to give an institutional basis to the personal activity of Christ; and finally St. James's admonition "Confess your sins one to another" belonged to the period when the slackness of believers in seeking the medicine for their souls made it necessary for the apostles to devise a code of discipline. The arrangement may be naive, but Hugh's way of dealing with the texts is intelligent and imaginative: it is a good illustration of his dictum that in meditating about history we search for perfect congruity of time and place and event.[8]

On a larger scale, Hugh organized his main work of systematic theology, *De Sacramentis*, on historical lines. Nearly the whole of his working life was a preparation for this work, and the arrangement can be traced back through successive drafts. The historical slant was not an accident: it was a long matured and deliberate decision. So far as I know there is no other important work of scholastic theology in which considerations of historical development have an important influence on the structure of the work. Hugh's work may be looked on as a first, and possibly last, medieval attempt to give Development a central place in theological discussion. He based his work on a division of human history into three stages in a continuous process of ascent towards God after man's Fall. The Fall left mankind wholly disorientated, feeble in body, weak in will, divorced from God. In this situation, the first thing that was needed was that men should discover the extent of their weakness through the experience of their moral, mental, and physical disintegration; and that from this experience they should come to desire and seek a Savior. Hence in this first period of human history, comprising some 2,000 years between the Fall and Abraham, God stood aside like a physician awaiting a call, while men learned how weak they were and began to desire a cure. This first age of history was the age of natural law when men groped around for remedies for their ills by the light of reason and experience. In the course of this search for a cure, there arose the varied sacraments of primitive man, the sacrifices and offerings by which they sought to give satisfaction to God for sin through external gifts. These sacrifices were a first step towards Redemption, acceptable to God as a token of faith in a Creator and Redeemer. Yet something stronger than this was needed to save mankind. The righteous were scattered across the face of the world like grains of wheat in a midden; they had no common rule of life, no community to which they could belong; they lived in isolation, knowing nothing of the future coming of Christ. They needed more knowledge and the strength which comes from being part of a dedicated community. These were to come in the second age.

The second age began embryonically with Abraham and fully with Moses. It was the age of written law when God intervened actively in human history to draw the righteous, or a main part of them, together in a recognizable community, and to establish an authoritative and complex system of sacramental union between himself and his chosen people. In this period, the further education of men took the form of teaching them by symbols the truths which they were not yet capable of receiving in undiluted strength. The sacraments of this period, though still external, were more personal and more closely associated with the life of each individual than those of the earlier age; and the faith which the sacraments expressed now explicitly pointed to a Messiah, though his person and mode of operation were still uncertain. What was now needed was not so much more knowledge as more humility and a more intense personal dedication. These were to come in the third age.

The third age began with the birth of Christ. It was an age in which Grace took the place of Law, in which the sacraments no longer expressed (as in the first age) shadows, or (as in the second age) images of the truth, but the substance of truth itself. An inner relationship with God took the place of the external relationship of earlier ages; a remedy for the sickness of the soul supplemented the remedy for ignorance which earlier ages had sought; the inspiration of the Spirit took the place of the commands which had bound men to God in the earlier age. These were the symptoms of the last age which would continue till all things came to an end.[9]

Even in this brief sketch it will be seen that we have here a dynamic view of history, in which men and God cooperate to produce a consistent forward movement from the first days after the Creation to the age in which we now live. Although most of the pieces from which Hugh constructed his historical model are as old as Christianity, the sense of movement from the primitive to the fully developed state of mankind is quite unlike anything in Augustine or Bede. We cannot read his account of the changing forms of faith without casting our minds forward to the publication of Newman's "Essay on the Development of Christian Doctrine" in 1845. It is a work which takes up many of the problems which had exercised the mind of Hugh of St. Victor, and brings a similar historical imagination to bear on them. Newman wrote on a rising tide of evolutionary thought, and his work has a place in the early history of a movement which has transformed western thought in many areas.[10] But Hugh's habits of thought were not those of his age, and they became less so as time went on.

Hugh's sympathy for the earliest and least articulate period of religious belief and practice aroused the strong hostility of Abelard. Abelard, despite (or because of) his own alleged aberrations, was always quick to jump on the deviations of others, and he denounced Hugh's views as those of a man alienated from the faith of the Church.[11] Hugh thought that the earliest sacrifices of men who knew nothing of Christ were acceptable to God: Abelard retorted that the formal consistency of the faith required from the beginning an explicit confession of Christ's birth, passion, and resurrection. Hugh laid his case before St. Bernard and won his approval, probably because his position was more Patristic, perhaps also because it was less Abelardian. Here we may simply notice Hugh's greater sense of historical plausibility. He pointed out that Abelard's view would mean either that very few men were saved before Christ, or that very many had received some special illumination. Both these suppositions seem to him contrary to common sense.[12] Besides, he said, it is clear from the Gospel narrative that not even the disciples, not even Peter himself, would have passed Abelard's test during the lifetime of Christ. Whatever its theological value this appeal to historical reality is something too seldom heard in the controversies of the twelfth and thirteenth centuries.

The idea of historical development is deeply impressed on Hugh's theology. It is also deeply impressed on his spiritual writings. Unlike the new scholastic theologians, Hugh was essentially a theologian of the practical religious life. Some of his best thoughts are those which describe the ascent of the mind from visible things to invisible causes, and from invisible causes to invisible essences, and so to the knowledge of God. Hugh described the early stages of this process in these words:

> The mind of man is plunged in the darkness of ignorance and cannot emerge into the light of truth unless material objects take him by the hand and lead him like a blind man to the contemplation and imitation of the things which he cannot see.[13]

A man's first perceptions of truth begin with material objects; then reason plays its part and extends a man's knowledge to invisible things. God for his part responds to this movement and supplements reason with illumination, extending himself to man in proportion as man comes to him, giving most to those who are nearest and least to those who are furthest off. The ascent of individual men to God is an exact replica of the ascent of the human race throughout history. Just as the individual starts his ascent with the material aids of sense, so mankind at the beginning of history took its first steps under the pressure of material needs and the promptings of nature. Just as God extends his illumination to the individual in proportion to his nearness, so the divine illumination in history grows clearer as mankind approaches the time of the full revelation of God. The individual is prepared for the full light of truth by figures and symbols proportioned to his understanding: so throughout history symbols and sacraments are adapted and refined to the growing disclosure of the truth. The educative process in history and in the life of the individual is everywhere the same.

Moreover, it is the same whether we look at religious growth or growth in secular understanding. Hugh wrote a handbook of the liberal arts. It is a thoroughly conservative work – except in one thing. No earlier work gives so coherent and philosophical an account of the rise of the arts within the framework of a broad historical process. The facts on which Hugh based his account were not new. A succession of authors from the fourth to the tenth century – mainly Eusebius, Isidore, and Remigius of Auxerre[14] – had collected myths, legends, and scholarly conjectures about the origin of the various branches of learning. Altogether it made up a great body of information – most of it wrong, some of it fantastic, all misconceived, but nevertheless the start of a great enquiry. The main misconception lay in the idea that a long series of heroes and super-men had "invented" the various branches of the arts and sciences. Classical mythology was ransacked to provide the facts to support this idea, and since these were the only facts available to scholars until the rise of archeology they formed part of the ordinary stock-in-trade of scholarship till the eighteenth century. Like everyone else Hugh of St. Victor accepted these "facts" and based his account of the origin of the sciences upon them. Yet even here, working with such unpromising material, he hammered out a philosophy of the development of secular knowledge which followed very similar lines to his philosophy of religious development.

There is evidence that Hugh gave much thought to this subject throughout his life and he sometimes changed his mind on the details – whether, for instance, Zoroaster, who invented astrology, was Shem the son of Noah under another name; and whether it was he who inscribed the outlines of the seven liberal arts on pillars of bronze and brick against the possibility of universal fire or another flood.[15] These are deep matters which I shall not attempt to unravel today. In any event, it is not to Hugh of St. Victor that we should go for light. We go to him for his general account of man's secular development, which is better than the stuff on which it was based.

He saw the growth of the human sciences as one side of the story of man's restoration after the disaster of the Fall.[16] Just as the faith and sacraments were the remedies for man's alienation from God, so the arts and sciences were the remedies for the disintegration of his natural powers and dignity. In both areas a long historical process was needed to find and perfect the remedies for successive stages of the disease. As we have seen, the supernatural evil caused by the Fall was man's alienation from God, and the remedy for this lay in the growth of faith and sacraments. The natural evils were ignorance, weakness of will, and frailty of body. For these evils, the instruments of restoration were philosophy, ethics, and technology. The first steps in the process of restoration are described by Hugh:

A great chaos of oblivion overwhelmed the human mind; men were sunk in profound ignorance and did not remember their origin. Yet a spark of the

eternal fire lived in them, and by its light, as of a spark in the darkness, they
could seek what they had lost...and they began to escape the evils from
which they suffered by the study of wisdom. Hence there arose the theoretical sciences to illuminate ignorance, ethics to strengthen virtue, and the
mechanical arts to temper man's infirmity.[17]

The chronological stages of the restoration cannot be so clearly distinguished as those of man's spiritual restoration, but there is a similar pattern. The first age was a period when mankind stumbled forward by
haphazard experiment:

Men wrote and talked before there was grammar; they distinguished truth
from falsehood before there was dialectic, they had laws before there was
rhetoric; they had numbers before there was arithmetic; they sang before
there was music; they measured fields before there was geometry; they observed the stars and seasons before there was astronomy.[18]

It was the role of reason to put in order this chaotic body of practical
experience, to shape it into ordered sciences, cutting out what was harm-
ful or superfluous, and giving a rational form to habits that men had
developed partly by chance and partly by natural impulse. In this way the
arts began to recreate the perfection that had once been man's by nature.

All the arts go through the same stages of growth, and their development has the same general chronological pattern as the restoration of
man's spiritual nature. The first age of man before Abraham was, generally speaking, the period of experiment. The age of rational system began
at about the time of Abraham's descent into Egypt. Thereafter the line of
development was fairly clear, beginning in Egypt the mother of the arts. It
was here that grammar was first invented in the time of Osiris, the husband of Isis; and it was here that – in the last and finest flight of mind –
Parmenides sat on his rock and discovered dialectic.[19] From Egypt the arts
were transmitted to Greece and thence to Rome. In all essentials they had
reached their final perfection when the third age of human history began
with the birth of Christ. They were ready to play their part in the full
unfolding of truth in the third and last stage of history.

In this story, one of Hugh's most original observations was the role of
physical necessity in prompting man's ascent. Necessity forced men to seek
a remedy for their weaknesses. The humblest needs were the earliest
training-ground for reason, and the sciences of the human mind (*logica*)
were the last to be discovered.[20] Since nature left men without a covering
to keep warm, reason had first to invent the art of clothing. Since man by
nature was without the means of defense, reason had to invent the arts of
fortification and arms to supply man's deficiencies. This is one more
example of the conformity of all historical development to a single

pattern: man starts with externals and works inwards; he starts with the most obvious material things and works towards the truths of the mind and spirit. This recognition of the importance of material things explains another significant feature in Hugh's system. Many men before him had discussed the divisions of philosophy, but he appears to have been the first to treat the mechanical arts on the same level as the theoretical ones, and to analyze their component parts with equal thoroughness.[21] This was a very important step. To place the mechanical arts on the same level as the liberal arts, to see them as equal partners in the restoration of human dignity, ran counter to the tradition of ancient learning. It implied a recognition, however dim or unformed, of a novel feature in western European civilization – some would think its most distinctive feature – its receptivity to technical change. In the place that he gave to the mechanical arts in his *Didascalicon* Hugh of St. Victor expressed the mental attitude which made this receptivity possible.

III

Hugh of St. Victor's view of history is remarkable for its general upward movement in every department of life. Although he says nothing to contradict Augustine, yet the uniformity of the movement of ascent, the co-operation of man and God in this movement, the single thread which binds the earliest efforts of man to the final result, and the close similarity between the general historical movement and the movement of the individual soul towards God – these features are certainly not Augustinian in inspiration. Their originality lies in giving a historical setting to a view of man which was the driving force behind the scientific movement of the twelfth and thirteenth centuries.

To this extent Hugh of St. Victor was a prophet of the new age. He had hoped to be more than this. He had wanted to make history a subject capable of systematic study among the other sciences of his day. If he had succeeded in this aim history might have had a beneficent effect in softening the outlines of scholastic theology. But in this he failed, and the failure was probably inevitable. We can see one reason for his failure in his Chronicle.[22] In this work Hugh attempted to produce a simple, memorable textbook of universal history. It was unlike other chronicles in making no attempt to be a record of events. It was, as we would say, a Handbook for the use of historians. Hugh thought about history, as he thought about everything else, systematically. In analyzing its composition he distinguished four elements: *time, place, people,* and *events.*[23] In this mixture, it is clear that events are the unpredictable, eccentric element. The other three are all capable of systematic treatment in the form of chronology, geography, and lists of rulers, and it was these alone that found a place in Hugh's Chronicle – hence its title: *Liber de tribus maximis circumstantiis gestorum, id est personis, locis, temporibus* [*Book of the three main circumstances of history, namely persons, places, times*]. It was, as he explained in his Preface, his intention that these elements, the main *circumstantiae* of history, should be memorized by beginners, as they memorize the outline of any science.[24]

Hugh's Chronicle, therefore, was a work of pedagogy, but it cannot be said to have had a great success.[25] A handful of manuscripts has survived from the schools of northern France, but they had little or no influence on education: history remained a rag-bag among the sciences until the nineteenth century. The reason for this is clear. However important the general problems of history might be, they offered no material for rigorous scholastic discussion. Hugh's historical speculations had no substantial body of historical fact to back them up. Without this, it was impossible to extend the area of systematic explanation much beyond the point which Hugh himself had reached. Consequently there is no "school" of Hugh of St. Victor among historians.

A single writer among Hugh's pupils, Richard of St. Victor, took over Hugh's historical ideas and attempted to fill out the substance of his Chronicle. He was a famous author in his own right and his *Liber Exceptionum*, which was based on Hugh's Chronicle, had an immense success.[26] But his success only underlines the cause of Hugh's failure to popularize the scholastic study of history. Richard made no attempt to write for the schools; he had his greatest success (so far as we can judge) among preachers and others who needed a compendium of allegorical interpretations of Old Testament history and a few facts about the main characters in ancient secular history. He pointed towards the two areas in which history had its greatest prospect of success in the later Middle Ages – in vast encyclopedias of learning and in collections of stories which could be used in sermons. Yet, in this general picture, there were a few writers in the twelfth century who filled some of the gaps which Hugh left; and over the centuries down to about 1750 there are learned historical compilations which drew together the social, political, religious, and intellectual history of the world into an intelligible framework of chronology and geography in a way that Hugh would have approved.

Among twelfth-century writers who may in some degree be looked on as Hugh's successors in historical vision I can mention only two: Anselm of Havelberg and Otto of Freising. They were both (perhaps like Hugh himself) Germans who studied in France in Hugh's lifetime, and they both found in history an answer to their pressing personal problems.

The problem of Anselm of Havelberg was a simple one. He was, like Hugh, an Augustinian canon, that is to say a member of one of the new religious Orders which proliferated in the early twelfth century. Naturally these new Orders came in for a good deal of criticism:

> Why (men said) – I quote the words of Anselm – are there so many novelties in the church? Why are there so many new Orders in it? ... Why does the Christian church make itself contemptible by displaying so many varieties, by being subject to so many innovations, agitated by so many new rules, heaving and swelling with so many customs almost annually under revision?[27]

Anselm found his answer to these questions in Hugh of St. Victor's view of history.[28] Hugh had shown how the faith and sacraments of the Church had developed from the earliest days of human history by a combination of experiment, reason, and divine providence. Anselm of Havelberg extended this process to the institutions of the Church, and he continued the story down to his own day. Everywhere he saw ecclesiastical history as the story of innovations. New ways of life, new commands, new directives, new prohibitions, new forms of worship, are the characteristics of every stage. Far from being signs of decadence and confusion, diversity and change were the necessary instruments of growth. Anselm could look on religious change in his own day, and particularly on the innovations of his own Order, with greater satisfaction when he saw a similar pattern working throughout history. He examined the twists and turns of historical change with a more lively interest because the variety of the past provided a way of understanding and defending the present. He is a notable example of the way in which a man's own needs and circumstances enlarge his historical understanding. He visited Constantinople, and he rejoiced to find that Greek, Armenian, and Syriac monks held the same Catholic faith, though they differed in customs, dress, food, offices, and psalmody from each other and from himself. He saw the untutored sacrifices of men outside the covenant with a more sympathetic eye because they strengthened the case for the experiments of his own Order. If Job, who was a Gentile in the time of the Law, could offer sacrifices outside the Law acceptable to God, surely there was room for the followers of St. Augustine beside those of St. Benedict in the Church. So he was brought to his great conclusion:

> It is necessary that the external forms of spiritual grace, which declare the same truth more and more fully, should grow from age to age ... This variety is caused by the variable infirmity of the human race and its temporal changes from generation to generation.[29]

This conclusion is basically the same as Hugh's, but it is fuller in scope and wider in its chronological sweep. Anselm enlarged more freely than Hugh on the benefits of variety within each period of history, and he was forced, as Hugh was not, by his own predicament to give the story of growth through variety a contemporary reference. As a result Anselm has a touch of passion, which Hugh lacked, as well as a visionary quality:

> The Church is by no means single or uniform throughout the course of its history, but it goes through many and various stages...and as it goes through these stages, each succeeding the other till the present day, it is renewed and will always be renewed like an eagle in its strength.[30]

The blessings of change and variety could scarcely be more warmly approved, or more happily vindicated by the whole course of universal history.

My other twelfth-century writer, Otto of Freising, has little in common with Anselm of Havelberg except that he too was a German student in Northern France when Hugh of St. Victor was at the height of his powers and fame, and he too had a personal problem on his hands. He was closely related to the imperial family, and he was clearly destined for high office in the Empire. But he was also deeply impressed by the pessimism of Augustine's view of history generally, and of the role of the Empire in particular. Where did it stand in the eternal enmity between the Two Cities – the one temporal, the other eternal; the one earthly, the other heavenly; the one of this world, the other made up of exiles from the heavenly city? At first Otto was in great perplexity. In his earliest work he sometimes spoke of the Empire as the modern Babylon, and he looked forward with complacency to its fall, along with the empires of the past.[31] But at other times he spoke in a different strain of the Empire as a divinely ordained power in the Church; and when he spoke like this he was inclined to say that history was no longer the story of the Two Cities, but of a mixed city, the single Church.[32] In course of time he inclined increasingly to the view that the Empire was an instrument of peace and that it belonged to the city of God – a view greatly strengthened by the accession in 1152 of his nephew Frederick I, who promised to bring an end to the confusion of the past and the beginning of an age of peace. He began to see history no longer as a tragedy, but as a story of joy.[33] It was in this spirit that he began in 1157 to write the life of Frederick.

This was the background of Otto's historical thinking, which produced two large histories – the one about the whole of history, the other about Frederick – but both about the place of Empire in the world. We are concerned with only one small part of this theme. Like Hugh of St. Victor, Otto was interested in the growth of learning from the earliest days of man, and he observed that it had a curious connection with the growth of

Empire. He found the bare bones of this idea in Eusebius, but he enlarged it and brought it down to his own day. Eusebius had observed that the succession of ancient empires began in the East and moved westwards. By Otto's time the succession had moved one step further West: Babylon, Greece, Rome, and now Germany. As for learning, it was common ground to all students that it had taken a similar, though not identical route: beginning in Babylon it had passed to Egypt, from Egypt to Greece, from Greece to Rome, and in the last days from Rome to France and Spain:

> Note well (he wrote) that all human power and knowledge began in the East and end in the West, so that in this way the variability and weaknesses of all things may be made clear.[34]

Otto gives us the names of a strangely incongruous trio of scholars who had in the previous generation taken over the crown of learning from the philosophers and poets of antiquity. They were Berengar of Tours, Manegold of Lautenbach, and Anselm of Laon.[35] It is an odd list, but since it appears in Otto's earlier and more pessimistic work, it may be intended to illustrate the decline of Empire and learning as they move westward towards their final senility.

In making the connection between the movement of Empire and the arts Otto was not yet speaking as an optimist. But those who came after him and made the same connection generally did so with a high degree of cheerfulness. At the end of the century the admirers of the kings of France were glad to trace the rise of the French kingdom to their love of learning. From the observation of this historical connection Alexander Nequam drew an axiom of government:

> The glory of a kingdom grows so long as the study of the liberal arts flourishes in it. For how shall enemies prevail over a kingdom which has mastered the sciences? The cunning skill of men, who have followed the secret flight of subtle essences into the bosom of nature, will not be overcome by the stratagems of their enemies.[36]

This is a doctrine which has acquired some ominous overtones in recent years, but in its original course it was very comforting to learned men; and, like many of the great ideas which took root in the twelfth century, it had its most confident expression in the eighteenth century:

> In happy climes the seat of innocence...
> There shall be sung another golden age.
> The rise of empire and of arts,
> The good and great inspiring epic rage,
> The wisest heads and noblest hearts...

By future poets shall be sung.
Westward the course of empire takes its way;
The first four acts already past,
A fifth shall close the drama with the day;
Time's noblest offspring is the last.[37]

So the great Berkeley in about 1730. Another act has been added to the drama, but there is still the same imperial pattern: Babylon, Greece, Rome, Germany – now the fifth act, America; and then the end.

The grand historical visions of the twelfth century continued for centuries to float about the world. But it was only late in their career, chiefly in the period from 1550 to 1750, that a great effort of scholarly accumulation and criticism made possible a full and apparently unshakeable account of the progress of government, learning, and religion from the days of the Creation. To unfold the intricacies of this scholarship, which Newton thought not unworthy of his attention, would need another address and another President. I shall mention only one fragment of the story.

I often have before my eyes a large work of scholarship in which the historical developments outlined by Hugh of St. Victor and enlarged by his followers received a final and (it might have seemed) permanent expression. It is a *Universal History* of mankind published in eight folio volumes in London between 1736 and 1750, the cooperative work of scholars of Oxford and Cambridge working for a consortium of London publishers.[38] It was a very expensive work, complete with plans and maps and tables; but it seems to have had a large circulation – and rightly, for it summed up the scholarship of centuries. The authors avoided every form of extravagant speculation: they castigated "the figments and deceits of the Jewish Rabbins," and looked coldly on the specious conjectures of Christian chronologers. They still told the old story that the study of astronomy had been founded by the sons of Seth, who wrote their inventions on pillars of brick and stone against a future fire or flood; yet they analyzed their sources with care and confessed that there was not much to be collected from Scripture about this period of history.[39] Their materials were the same as those of our twelfth-century scholars, but their scholarship and critical acumen vastly greater. Everywhere in this work calm reason and assured scholarship speak with quiet authority. One is almost convinced by the tone of voice. Hugh of St. Victor's dream of an assured and systematic history of mankind seemed to have been finally realized in this last great expression of the view of history which had dominated Europe since the fourth century.

Within a few years of the publication of this *Universal History* the whole system lay in total ruin. In its main outline it has gone for ever, but among the ruins there are some ideas which deserve to be rescued. Among these I would number Hugh of St. Victor's account of man's historical development; and I think we should miss something if we neglected the echoes of this idea in a few writers who lie on the other side of the evolutionary flood which has overwhelmed the world in our own Age.

3

Aspects of the European Tradition of Historical Writing 3: History as Prophecy

A year ago I took as my theme the origin of that comprehensive but limited view of human progress which dominated European historical thought from the twelfth century to the eighteenth. This idea of historical development had the great merit of embracing every aspect of human life from the first moments of history to the last days. It brought together in a single pattern of development the improvement in man's material condition, the discovery and perfecting of the sciences, the movement of empires, and the enlargement of man's spiritual life. Taken as a whole it was one of the grandest expressions of the beneficent unity of nature, reason, and revelation, which has stamped the chief products of European culture during the greater part of its history. From the time of Hugh of St. Victor to Voltaire, it continued despite many setbacks and aberrations to be refined and enlarged by scholarship – and never more confidently than in the last moments before its collapse. In the end the system collapsed as a result of a totally unexpected failure in the foundations on which it was based.

A main part of the collapse in the eighteenth century was due to the failure of prophetic utterances to support the weight which had been placed upon them. It is not too much to say that the whole structure rested on the conviction that prophecy was the most certain of all sources of historical information, and that it could provide an assured framework for the whole course of history. A consideration of the role of prophecy in history, therefore, arises naturally from the survey which I attempted last year, and I shall take it as the theme of today's discourse. Prophecy impinged on history at very many points. It provided some of the most important facts of history, disclosed the meaning of many more, and set them all within a systematic shape. Finally, it was the only source of information about the future – information which was in itself absolutely certain, though obscure in its manner of presentation and needing careful investigation if its meaning was to be established. Prophecy was at once a source of information and interpretation, of hope and fear, and of assured truths which needed to be distinguished from the grossest errors and frauds. The source of prophecy was inspiration, but its interpretation was a science, and more than any other science it called for the coolest discrimination and for profound scholarship. Prophecy filled the world-picture, past, present, and future; and it was the chief inspiration of all historical thinking. In order to understand how this could be, it will first be necessary to enter into some slight theological explanation.

We are not now concerned with prophecy in the vulgar sense of prediction, though the power of prediction has always been the final test of prophetic inspiration. One commentator expressed the popular view when he said "Prophecy is the history of the future." But this, though true, is only one part of the truth. According to Thomas Aquinas prophecy is divinely revealed knowledge of matters, past, present, or future, lying beyond the scope of human observation: "the further removed the facts are from human cognition, the more they belong to prophecy."[1] Thus the prophet brings news of otherwise inaccessible events in history: in the past, of the Creation of the World, of the days before the Flood, of the Flood itself; in the present, of events beyond the physical horizons of human perception; and in the future of any events whatsoever. Since the indeterminate future, shaped by the free will of many men, is further beyond ordinary human cognition than anything else in the world, it is here that prophecy is most fully itself and most widely distinct from every other mode of knowledge.[2]

Thomas Aquinas, in common with most medieval writers, imposed no limits to the range of prophetic knowledge. It came to many men who were neither good nor pious, and to unbelievers who did not understand the prophetic message which they conveyed by word or deed.[3] Whoever the agent might be, prophecy had always the stamp of the divine truth upon it, compelling men to see, say, or do, things which disclosed the hidden structure of historical events. The ubiquity of prophecy both as to the area of knowing which it illuminated and the persons to whom it might be disclosed, can scarcely be overstated.

It is important to emphasize these elements of prophecy – its certainty, its divine origin, its wide range of agents, and its universal subject-matter – if we are to understand the place which it had in shaping the outline of historical thought for several centuries. Of course, even during these centuries, it was recognized that there were snags to be encountered in any deep study of the subject. The first of these snags was that, though all genuine prophecy was unalterably true, not all genuinely prophetic predictions were fulfilled. There were various reasons for this. One was that prophecy sometimes related only to events which would happen if men continued on a certain course of behavior. These were prophecies with an often unexpressed condition: "If things go on as they are, this and this will happen." Although they were capable of being frustrated they were still prophetic, for only the prophetic spirit could foresee and help to change events. The failure of a prophecy was not therefore a proof of its falsity.[4] Jonah's prophecy of the overthrow of Nineveh was an example. He prophesied that Nineveh would be overthrown in forty days. It didn't happen, and yet it was a true prophecy. The people of Nineveh unexpectedly forestalled the disaster by repentance. This was the kind of disappointment that prophets had to learn to live with. But it did not threaten their prophetic stature.

Another snag was that the vocabulary of prophecy was often amazingly obscure. Indeed, ambiguity of imagery or statement was so common in prophetic utterances, that obscurity was sometimes adduced as a proof of genuineness.[5] Many reasons could be given for this characteristic obscurity, but whatever the reason the fact was undeniable. Even when prophets spoke most plainly, they spoke a language in which animals stood sometimes for kingdoms, sometimes for persons, sometimes for classes of people; and the contortions of elemental forces in nature sometimes stood for political disasters, sometimes for moral disorders, sometimes for eschatological events. This of course was very bewildering, but no more bewildering than the facts which have to be taken into account in many sciences. A meticulous examination of the language and imagery of the prophets, and a careful correlation of their statements with known historical events, could (it was thought) produce a body of information of the greatest value for mankind. It could bring understanding of the course of past history, of the present state of affairs, and provide a means of predicting the future. But to do all this, or even any part of it, required a science of interpretation at least as complicated as the study of the combined philosophies of Aristotle and Plato. In some ways the study of prophecy was rather like the study of ancient philosophies: it led at once to a number of satisfying results; but it soon led the enquirer into an area of doubt, and before long into a wilderness in which investigators were supported only by the conviction that perseverance would at last bring success.

II

Throughout all these investigations it was recognized that the main body of material for the science of prophecy was to be found in the Bible. It was here that the plainest, most weighty, and most clearly inspired prophecies were to be found. The prophetic account of the Creation in the first chapter of Genesis was the source of the whole general chronology of history, with its division into six Ages, and its providential plan of Redemption. This one chapter provided at a single blow a clue to the whole structure of history, and it was of course prophetic, since it provided historical information beyond the scope of any possible human experience. The details of the general plan were to be found prophetically foreshadowed in the remainder of the Old Testament, and it was in the study of this evidence that the western world first learnt to think about history in an orderly and comprehensive fashion.

By the beginning of the twelfth century the main lines of historical events, so far as they could be made out from the prophecies and symbols of the Old Testament, had already been discovered. But there were still some prophetic passages in the Bible, and many more outside it, which had not yet been explained. So far as biblical prophecy was concerned, there were two relatively unexploited areas. The first was in the seventh chapter of the Book of Daniel, the second in the sixth chapter of the Revelation of St. John. Both these passages would seem, even to the most superficial enquirer, to contain some message about the course of history.

With regard to the Book of Daniel, some important progress in detailed historical interpretation had already been made before the twelfth century and then largely forgotten or rejected. Let me remind you of the text. Daniel had a dream in which he saw four beasts coming up from the sea: the first like a lion; the second like a bear; the third like a leopard; and the fourth with great iron teeth, more terrible and dreadful than the rest. Already by the first century A D these beasts had been interpreted as the successive empires of the Assyrians, the Persians, the Greeks, and the Romans.[6] This interpretation was given general currency by Jerome's *Commentary on Daniel*, and with minor deviations it was universally accepted. So far, so good. Daniel's dream, however, continued further. The fourth beast, i.e., the Roman Empire, had ten horns, and in the midst of them another little horn came up and plucked three of the original horns up by the roots. This little horn was the most terrible of all: "He shall speak great words against the most High and shall wear out the saints, and change times and laws, and reign for a time, and times, and half a time."[7] These strange words have probably had a more disturbing effect on European minds than any others in the Bible. If prophecy meant anything at all, the interpretation of these words was a matter of great moment. Yet what they meant no one knew. Jerome left the question undecided. Perhaps, he said, the ten horns were the ten most fierce rulers between Alexander the Great and Antiochus the Great; or perhaps they were the ten kings who would destroy the Roman Empire at the end of the world and be overcome by the eleventh, who would be Antichrist.[8]

Here the matter rested until, in the ninth century, a group of persecuted Christians in Moslem Spain found consolation in their sufferings by finding, as historians often do, that the present threw light upon the past and enabled them to give a new and important meaning to Jerome's suggestion about the ten horns.[9] As they gathered together the threadbare remnants of their Christian tradition and brooded over their wrongs, they found an explanation for Daniel's dream which strangely anticipated the explanations of many bitter and disappointed men in Europe in the later Middle Ages. They saw that the first ten horns of the fourth beast must be the ten barbarian peoples who had destroyed the Roman Empire – the Goths, Franks, Burgundians, Huns, etc. But, further – and here was their real discovery – they saw that the eleventh horn rising in the midst of the first ten, that terrible little horn which would change times and laws and speak against the Most High, could be none other than Mahomet, with his new system of dates, his new Law, and his many blasphemies. As with the mysterious "time, and times, and half a time" during which he would reign, it was generally agreed that this meant $3\frac{1}{2}$ times or epochs. If now we ask the length of an epoch, no suggestion could be more obvious than a period of 70 years, which (besides being an important symbolic number) was the period given by the Psalmist to the life of man. With this key to history, the rest is mere arithmetic: $3\frac{1}{2}$ epochs of 70 years gives us 245 years as the total period of Moslem rule before the end. Since the Moslem era began in AD 622, it was clear that its end must come in about 867; and since these calculations were made in 854, it was equally clear that only some 13 years of persecution remained before the beginning of the great and final Peace of the saints.

I have shortened and simplified the calculations in the interests of brevity, but even if I were to explain them in much greater detail you might still think that their author had taken a number of short cuts which were scientifically somewhat unsound. Yet even the most prosaic scientist will be tempted to take a few leaps in the dark when the pieces of evidence begin to fall into place; and our scholar had the additional excuse that he was working under great pressure in the midst of great suffering. His thoughts have some of the marks of a great historical idea: simplicity of conception, broadness of treatment, a strong sense of actuality, and a convincing congruity between fact and theory. These qualities must give a historian a warm sympathy for the author of these interpretations of the dark sayings of Daniel. Compared with many writers on this subject who came after him he may even be called a rigorous thinker. But whether rigorous or not, his account was soon proved wrong by events. Islam did not end, and the Christian minority for whom the writer spoke soon disappeared into the compliant multitude who were either converted to Islam or shaped their lives in such a way as to give no offense to their conquerors. The interpretation of Daniel's dream, which had pointed to the year 867 as the likely end of Moslem rule, was soon forgotten. I mention it here only because it foreshadows with remarkable accuracy and unusual clarity the kind of argument that was to become very common in the later Middle Ages.

To turn now to the Book of Revelation. The most important passage for historical thought was the description of the opening of the Book of the Seven Seals.[10] Here we have a passage which easily lends itself to historical interpretation. The horses of various colors, the voices, symbols, strange sayings, and upheavals of nature, which accompany the opening of each of the seals in turn, all seem to speak mysteriously of historical events which are not easy to identify. It may have been this difficulty of identification which made early commentators slow to give a historical interpretation of the passage. Even Bede, the most historically minded of early biblical scholars, gave an account of the opening of the seals which was only mildly historical.[11] For him the first seal referred to the splendor of the primitive Church; the second, third, and fourth to the successive attacks of tyrants, false brethren, and heretics; the fifth revealed the glory of the blessed after their sufferings; the sixth, the final persecution by Antichrist; the seventh, the beginning of eternal rest. In all this there is clearly an element of historical progression, but the chronological development is confused by quite general symbols of different aspects of the Church's life, throughout history.

In most of Bede's successors the historical view is even less sharply defined. Most commentators were interested only in unfolding the wealth of symbolic meanings without regard to historical, or any other kind of order. For them richness was all. So the seven seals became indiscriminately the sevenfold mysteries of the Old Testament, the seven gifts of the Holy Spirit, the seven mysteries of Christ, the seven tenses of the verb, and so on. This tradition of miscellaneous symbolism was continued by twelfth-century commentators and became canonized in the great biblical compilations of the later Middle Ages.

The only commentator in the middle years of the twelfth century who took the historical thought of Bede a stage further was Anselm of Havelberg, about whom I spoke last year. I then spoke of him as a writer who extended Hugh of St. Victor's large view of historical development. I must now mention that he also gave a strong impulse to the historical interpretation of the Book of Revelation. He made the stages in the Church's history, which Bede had dimly outlined, much clearer and more coherent.[12] These stages were symbolized by the opening of the seals, and in each of them a new persecution called forth a new response of vigor and understanding. In the first stage, the Apostles brought the illumination of miracles; in the second, the martyrs brought a growth in patience; in the third, the great heresies promoted the growth of understanding; in the fourth, the proliferation of false brethren brought, by reaction, the foundation of new religious orders which enlarged the Church's life. This process was still going on: the Benedictines had recently been afforced by Cistercians, Augustinians, and most recently by Templars. The Church was still in the fourth of seven stages of development. Consequently there were still three more stages to come before the end. The end seemed sufficiently remote to excite no speculation. Anselm was the prophet of progress not of doom; and in this he spoke for his whole generation.[13]

Until the very end of the century most scholars showed little interest in the end of the world. They were interested in other problems: in extending the area of intelligibility and order in the existing world; in clarifying the relations between past and present; in bringing order out of confusion. They had no strong impulse to take a leap into the unknown future. Anselm of Havelberg was of the same mind as his contemporaries, and it is a tribute to the confident rationality of the middle years of the twelfth century that he should have been able to extract from the blood-stained imagery of the Book of Revelation the calm and comfortable doctrine of the steady enlargement of man's powers throughout history. It was a *tour de force* which most of Anselm's contemporaries did not attempt. They too were interested in the application of prophecy to history, but they did not go to Daniel or the Book of Revelation to satisfy their historical curiosity. They did not even in general go to the Bible, but to more secular sources. They sought to draw into the circle of Christian thinking sources which had previously lain outside or on the edge of it. This too was symptomatic of the enlarging intellectual ambitions of the period.

III

There were three non-biblical sources of prophetic insight which were growing in importance about the middle of the twelfth century. They may briefly be labeled as pagan, Christian, and cosmic. The pagan contribution embraced in the first place the large assortment of prophecies believed to be of ancient sibylline origin.[14] This untidy rag-bag of pretentious nonsense (as it must appear to us) owed its credibility in the first place to the predictions of the birth of Christ which were to be found embedded in it, and to the example of Aeneas's consultation with the sibyl in the sixth book of the *Aeneid*. But at a deeper level the sibyls met a widely felt need for a bridge between Christian and pagan revelation, similar to the bridge which had slowly been built up over the centuries between pagan and Christian learning. To us the sibylline documents are absurdly implausible documents, and it is hard to believe that they were ever taken seriously.

Yet men did take them seriously, partly because they lacked the techniques for historical criticism, but partly too because they had a strong psychological need for the existence of such documents. They filled a gap in the chain of revelation. The existence of blindly inspired women in a distant past, drawing from the well of eternal truth and communicating to the pagan world the truths which were fully disclosed in Christ, enlarged, however uncertainly, the otherwise intolerable narrowness of the stream of salvation which flowed through the Jews to the Christian Church.[15] The sibyls were a bond between the chosen people and the outside world. They were a guarantee of the unity and beneficence of creation. These qualities, which were believed to exist in principle, were verified by the existence of the sibyls.

The more refined men's sensibilities became, the more they needed the sibyls. Hence the sibylline literature, infinitely tedious though it is, crops up almost everywhere from the mid-twelfth century onwards. Though it always promised more than it ever delivered, it continued to strengthen its imaginative grip on western Europe till the end of the Middle Ages and beyond. The men whom we know to have taken an interest in sibylline literature were generally men of high culture and intelligence. For instance, when Joachim of Fiore (of whom more later) first came to the Pope in 1184 to win acceptance for his prophetic studies, the Pope gave him an immediate test.[16] He asked him to explain some sibylline fragments, which had been found among the literary remains of a recently deceased cardinal, Matthew of Angers.[17] The fragments, as we know, were highly bogus, but Joachim did his best with them and evidently impressed the papal curia. The cardinal to whom they had belonged had been a man of high intellectual pretensions, a pupil of Abelard, a university lawyer, and a scholar called to the curia by Pope Alexander III to assist in the dissemination of canon law throughout the Church. When we approach the sibyls, therefore, we are not dealing with any popular mumbo-jumbo but with matter of grave intellectual concern to serious and practical men.

The same must be said of the still more widely disseminated prophecies of Merlin.[18] Here again we have the strange phenomenon of apparently unrelieved gibberish claiming the anxious attention of men of high intelligence and sophistication, and here again we can only explain the phenomenon by the need which men felt to believe in a wide dissemination of divinely inspired truth about historical events throughout all ages and peoples. Like the sibyls, Merlin, half-man, half-demon, half-Christian, half-pagan, was a link between the ancient pagan and the modern Christian world, between the worlds of reason and inspiration, between the subnatural and the supernatural. It was not naivety which made men search the cloudy imagery of Merlin for some hint with a contemporary relevance. It was, rather, a too ambitious view of the knowledge which is accessible to man. The keenest students of Merlin, as of the sibyls, were university men with intellectual aspirations. We find, for instance, John of Salisbury in the midst of the Becket controversy attempting to interpret events in Brittany in the light of a sentence of Merlin about the eagle of the broken covenant.[19] He spoke as a man does who has a tool of unknown power which he doesn't quite understand, and he referred his correspondent for a second opinion to Master Alexander of Wales who was more skilled in this special subject. Another contemporary of these men, and another intellectual in government, was Master John of Cornwall, who translated and commented on some newly discovered prophecies of Merlin at the request of the bishop of Exeter, himself a distinguished canonist and administrator.[20] At about the same time, Gerald of Wales, who was one of the most ambitious and experimental historical writers of the late twelfth century, went further than anyone else in seeking unknown prophecies and trying to fit them into his contemporary histories. He seems to have had the idea of making a complete fusion between contemporary history and ancient Celtic prophecy, writing what he called a *Historia Vaticinalis*.[21] It was all very solemn. He found nothing funny in the idea that Prince John, blundering around Ireland, was fulfilling the obscure predictions of Celtic bards.

English historians in the twelfth century were more exposed than any others to this type of prophecy. In some of them the search for prophecies to illuminate events became an obsession. Even William of Newburgh, who alone refused to give any credence to Merlin, was deterred not by any lack of interest in prophecy but by an austere theological objection to prophecies of demoniac origin. He gave a ready welcome to prophetic utterances of less exceptionable origin.[22]

IV

The interpreters of Merlin and of the sibyls were the more intellectual part of a much larger army of interpreters of contemporary Christian dreams, visions, and voices, seen and heard by countless people, especially in religious communities. The monasteries were full of stories of visionary experiences of a prophetic kind, generally relating to strictly local affairs and to monastic interests. Most of these revelations aimed no higher than the discovery of relics or the vindication of local saints, but they were evidence on a local scale that historical events could be known by prophetic revelation.

Out of the great company of local visionaries, there arose here and there authoritative figures whose existence gave a stronger impulse to the conviction that the power of prophetic vision had not failed. Of these by far the most attractive and persuasive was the German nun, Hildegard of Bingen.[23] Her visionary experiences began in youth in the early years of the twelfth century and continued until her death in 1179. During the last thirty years of her life, she was sought out by great men from all parts of Europe, anxious to gain from her some inkling of the shape of contemporary events. Here too the ever-active John of Salisbury is a witness to a general interest. In the midst of all his other concerns, he wrote to a colleague in Cologne asking him to find out if there was anything in Hildegard's revelations to indicate when the schism would end.[24] Like the majority of his contemporaries, he sought enlightenment from prophecy about the practical outcome of present events, not about the end of the world; but fifty years later, when the climate of thought had changed, Hildegard's works were systematically searched for news of the final catastrophe.[25] Thereafter her prophecies became part of the stock-in-trade of later medieval apocalyptic.

V

Before we come to this great change in historical thinking there is one more weapon in the prophetic armory which must be briefly examined: the growing power of astrological prediction. At first sight the stars may seem to have nothing to do with prophecy, but in fact the two subjects were closely related. The movement of the stars contained within themselves the movements of history, in much the same way as the prophetic voices of Daniel and the Book of Revelation showed the shape of things past, present, and to come. It was as if God spoke to men about history in two different languages, through the prophets on earth and the planets in heaven. In order to get the message the appropriate language had to be learnt. The message of the stars like that of the prophets could only be extracted by a careful study of their language, and in both cases careful study might be expected to produce results of great importance. It is not therefore surprising that both branches of study rose and fell in the same movement of thought. Before the twelfth century, although men did not doubt the influence of the stars, they had neither the technical equipment nor the detailed knowledge to make an effective study of their influence. It was the introduction of Islamic science in the early twelfth century, first with the astrolabe and then with the tables and exact observations that became current in the middle years of the century, which made possible the science of prediction and opened the way to the full development of astrological prophecy.[26]

By the middle of the century the study was going briskly forward and it had its first great chance to prove its value as a practical historical tool in

1186.[27] It was known well in advance that in this year there would be a series of remarkable celestial events and there was a widespread European interest in producing the right prognosis of the terrestrial consequences. The predictions which survive seem neither much better nor much worse than most forecasts. One foresaw thunder and lightning, with much evil to be feared from the Saracens, and an urgent need for a conference of prelates. Another anticipated an earthquake and a great wind, with dust storms in the East which would destroy Babylon and Mecca, and discords and dissensions in the West. Another pooh-poohed the predictions of high winds, and foresaw nothing more alarming than poor wine and a mediocre harvest, accompanied by many deaths by the sword and many shipwrecks. In fact nothing happened, or nothing much. It was all rather absurd. If the disasters which happened in 1187 and put an end to the Latin kingdom of Jerusalem had come a year earlier science might have gained a resounding, though undeserved, success. As it was, there was a general feeling that the stars had failed. Yet science is never to be deterred by a failure, however resounding, especially when a great deal of intellectual capital has been committed to the hypothesis of success. Hence the year 1186, instead of being the end, is only the first European milestone on the long road of anticipation and disillusionment which had to be traveled before the astrological aid to the study of history was finally buried.[28]

VI

This then completes the armory which prophecy offered for the study of history: biblical prophecy, pagan prophecy, Christian prophecy, astrological prophecy. Together they made a formidable array of interlocking sciences claiming to tell men something about the shape of historical events. They owed their strength to their cohesion. By their mere existence they expressed a view of the relationship between time and eternity, between the mind of God and the minds of men, between the pattern of past events and the future, which most people found compellingly persuasive. The conjunction of these sciences meant that there was no area of the divine plan for mankind totally unilluminated even for those who were outside the Church. Besides they offered unimaginable practical benefits. Roger Bacon summed the matter up in a letter which he wrote to the Pope about 1267:

> If only the Church would examine the prophecies of the Bible, the sayings of the saints, the sentences of sibyl and Merlin and other pagan prophets, and would add thereto astrological considerations and experimental knowledge,

it would without doubt be able to provide usefully against the coming of Antichrist. For it is a great question whence he will arise and who he will be, and if the Church would do all it can, I believe that God would give a fuller revelation, especially if a special prayer for this were ordained throughout the whole Church. For not all prophecies are irrevocable and many things are said in the prophets about the coming of Antichrist which will come to pass only through the negligence of Christians. They would be changed if Christians would strenuously enquire when he will come, and seek all the knowledge which he will use when he comes.[29]

The plan of study which Bacon sketches might have been put forward at any time in the previous hundred years. It is implicit in much late twelfth-century historical writing. But in one respect Roger Bacon's plan marks a significant shift of interest between the twelfth and thirteenth centuries. In the middle of the twelfth century, the end of the world was a remote expectation in most people's minds. A century later many knew, and most feared, that the end was close at hand. This apprehension had come to fill a great part of the historical scene.

VII

The chief agent in bringing about this change was the Calabrian monk Joachim of Fiore who died in 1202. Dr. Reeves has recently written an important book on his influence in the later Middle Ages, and there is no need to attempt to summarize the many new facts and materials which she has brought together for the first time.[30] I am concerned only to show how Joachim emerges from what I may call the scientific and intellectual enquiries of the twelfth century, and how in the very last stages of his influence a final attempt was made to restore the subject to the cooler and more rational atmosphere of pre-Joachimite enquiry.

I have already mentioned Joachim's first appearance in 1184 as an interpreter of sibylline sayings. For nearly twenty years after this date he continued to grow in power and influence, and he gained the reputation of being a prophet with an emotionally highly charged and original vision. He himself claimed not to be a prophet but a scholar with a special insight into the meaning of texts which his predecessors had been able only partially to explain. He thought that by diligent application he had reached a fuller understanding of biblical prophecies than any earlier expositor. He had worked harder, and thought more, and submitted to a more rigorous discipline than others. He could reasonably claim that his fuller understanding came not from any new method of interpretation, but simply from taking a stage further the well-established methods of interpretation developed by his predecessors. As Joachim brooded in the isolation of his south Italian monastery he came to believe that he had found the clues which they had missed. He had the most powerfully imaginative and comprehensive historical mind of the Middle Ages, and he was never at a loss for historical parallels and explanations. They sprang up in his mind in fertile abundance. As new information and new events poured in on him, old events began to take on a new significance, and he began to see the whole shape of history with a clarity and pictorial detail which no one before him had attained. It is very seldom in the Middle Ages that we can see a mind at work applying a well-tried method to a mass of material, pushing this method a little further than earlier scholars, evolving a leading idea, elaborating it, filling in the details, sometimes changing an opinion, always plagued by uncertainty, but in the end producing a substantially new and complete reconstruction of a very large subject – nothing less than the systematic ordering of the whole course of human history. This is the process we can observe in Joachim over a period of twenty years.[31]

He clearly did not know at first where his studies were going to lead him, but he had from the beginning a sense of practical urgency which distinguished him sharply from his immediate predecessors in biblical interpretation. In his interpretation of the Seven Seals of the Book of Revelation he was similar to Anselm of Havelberg in seeking an orderly chronological sequence of events to fit the symbolism of the opening of the seals. But here the similarity ends. For Anselm the process was full of hope: persecution and suffering were simply a mechanism for the enlargement of life. Joachim, by contrast, saw menacing dangers closing in on the Church from outside, and springing up from within, in a way that would have been scarcely imaginable thirty years earlier. When he first spoke to the Pope in 1184 he had not yet clearly seen that Islam was the central threat. Three years later he had the evidence he needed. Jerusalem had fallen, and a new Moslem hero had burst upon the world as Islam's answer to Christian expansion. From this moment the scene grew darker, and as it grew darker Joachim's vision grew brighter. He began at last to see clearly the pattern of the Church's persecutors from the beginning to the end. The succession of persecutors ran from Herod, the massacrer of the infant Church, to Nero, the persecutor of the early martyrs, to Constantius, the Arian emperor and symbol of the heretics, to Mahomet, the great schismatic, then to the recent Berber invaders of Spain, and finally to Saladin, the penultimate enemy of the Church. This was the view of history which Joachim expounded in 1190 to King Richard and the Crusaders at Messina. The world was moving into its last age. It only remained for "the king who is properly called Antichrist to appear." Joachim in 1190 was still groping for light on this question. He thought that Antichrist had already been born in Rome, but that he had not yet come to power. These were startling words for his listeners from England

and for the many visitors who now came to hear what Joachim had to say. Many disagreed with him. But they all had to take him seriously.

There were several reasons for the seriousness with which he was heard. In the first place he was a man of great religious power and simplicity, deeply impressive to all who met him. Then too he could claim to be a conservative scholar pursuing old methods of biblical scholarship: he was no revolutionary in intention. It would be difficult to point to anything in his methods of interpretation which is not to be found in earlier interpreters of biblical prophecy. His power of bringing order into the tumultuous imagery of the Book of Revelation made a strong appeal to a generation which had become accustomed to regard order as the main aim of intellectual enquiry. Joachim was doing for prophetic history what scholastic theologians were doing for the general structure of theology: bringing order into thought by a stricter application of the methods and interpretations of the past and by giving a clear and logical arrangement to the results. Above all he claimed attention because his science simply anticipated other men's apprehensions. What he said about the present was slowly becoming apparent to everyone. New dangers had arisen for the Church of a quite unprecedented size.

In giving Islam a central place in the later stages of the Church's history, Joachim was reverting to an old idea which had been discovered in Spain in the ninth century and then forgotten. But the old idea had now acquired a new plausibility. The ninth-century scholars had been obsessed by their own local difficulties. They had worked, out of touch with the main stream of thought, with few books and little material. Joachim, by contrast, was able to take a European-wide view. The signs which the Bible had taught men to look for as symptoms of the approaching end were accumulating rapidly on all sides. The abomination of Islam was in Jerusalem. The false doctors were in Languedoc. The end of the Roman Empire, whether in its Greek or Hohenstaufen form, seemed to be at hand. In the Bible this was one of the clearest signs of the end of the world.[32] All the other signs were present also. The Gospel had, to all appearances, been preached to the ends of the world, the wars of nation against nation were visible to everyone. Joachim had met most of the greatest men of his time and the views which he expressed expressed what everyone who could survey the scene thought likely to be true. Even Innocent III, of all the popes of Joachim's lifetime the least inclined to encourage him, believed that the Number of the Beast denoted the 666 years that Islam was destined to last. Since nearly six hundred years of this allotted period had now passed, the end of the world was near.[33] The universal stage seemed to be set for Antichrist, and this was not simply the view of fanatics or men maddened by persecution, it was the view of sober men taking a full view of the whole course of history.

In his aims, and with one half of his mind, Joachim belonged to the scientific scholarly world of the twelfth century. But, despite his disclaimers, he was also an original prophet who opened up new opportunities for revolutionary speculation. His idea that Antichrist would arise from within Christendom, that he would be born in Rome and hold high office – it could scarcely be less than the highest – in the Church, added a new dimension to the growing distrust of ecclesiastical institutions. And his further idea that after the opening of the seventh seal, the last age of universal peace when institutions would wither away, would be enacted *within* (and not beyond) history, added a new and practical zest to the religious fervor of the later Middle Ages.[34] Both these ideas were well grounded in biblical exegesis, but they cut loose from all earlier interpretation. In a very precise way they make Joachim the Karl Marx of medieval prophecy.

The only weakness of this new apocalyptic was that it laid itself open to the final disproof by events; but, as with the disappointments of astrology or Marxism, this was not such a serious drawback as might at first sight appear. The desire for a view of history which will embrace a sizable portion of the future is too strong to be quenched even by repeated and shattering disappointments. Predictions are capable of much manipulation. The expected catastrophe could be, and was, postponed from 1260 to 1290, to 1305, to 1335, to 1350, to 1360, to 1400, to 1415, to 1500, to 1535.[35] Not only did the dates move relentlessly forward without losing their power to persuade, but the chosen actors of destruction and redemption were assigned their allotted places with undiminished assurance. Indeed each failed Antichrist gave an additional plausibility to the claims of his successor, just as in tossing a coin a long succession of "heads" arouses a strong expectation that the next toss will turn up "tails." It takes a very long time for the suspicion to gain ground that we are dealing with a two-headed coin.

It took nearly 500 years from the death of Joachim for this suspicion to become irresistible. Meanwhile Joachim remained a dominating figure in the whole vast area of prophetic history. The list of poets, theologians, philosophers, and statesmen in the later Middle Ages, who fell at one time or another under the sway of his prophetic vision, seems endless, and the number of fragments of prophetic prediction is beyond computation. The elements are always the same. Whenever five or six prophecies were gathered together, Joachim was always there in the midst of them with the sibyls, Merlin, Hildegard, and the astrologers.

This mixture of sources, which had appeared in the twelfth century to offer a hope for the scientific interpretation of history, showed in the later Middle Ages its incapacity to promise anything more than a variegated sequence of real disasters and illusory expectations. With Joachim the prophetic technique for investigating the shape of history, and consequently for predicting the future, had reached the end of the road. This was not apparent so long as the system of thought, on which these hopes and fears were based, remained intact. So long as the system held, everyone was kept busy by arguments about times and places and people and their respective roles. But no system can for ever survive if it can only promise what is never fulfilled. By the end of the seventeenth century the whole complicated pattern of prophetic history was tottering to its fall.

VIII

Before it fell however a last effort was made to save the most substantial and intellectually most firmly based part of the structure by removing the clutter of flimsy additions with which twelfth-century scholars had tried to complete the system. Merlin and the sibyls, the visions and dreams of pagan and Christian seers, had to go. Divinely inspired prophecy was restricted to the Bible, and within the Bible to two short periods of human history. The picture of a broad though erratic stream of divinely inspired prophetic utterance throughout history, which had consoled the minds of medieval enquirers, was cut down to the bare minimum required by the biblical texts. The claims of astrology put up a stubborn resistance, and it was hard to deny the possibility that this science might survive as a subsidiary aid to biblical interpretation. With this one doubtful astrological outpost, the ground was cleared for the defense of the central prophecies of the Bible.

The most illustrious advocate of this reorganization of prophetic science was Sir Isaac Newton. Newton's prophetic works have often been dismissed as the expressions of the lunatic fringe of a great scientific mind. But, if we come to him with medieval rather than with modern preconceptions, he never appears more soberly scientific than in his *Observations upon the prophecies of Holy Writ particularly the prophecies of Daniel and the Apocalypse of St. John.*[36] His aim in this work was to cut away the accretions which had encumbered prophecy, especially since the twelfth century, and to recall biblical interpretation to the modest dimensions of earlier days. He wanted, though he probably did not know this, to restore the subject to the state in which Hugh of St. Victor and Anselm of Havelberg had left it, while making use of some of the historical insights to which Joachim of Fiore had given currency. Newton wanted to use biblical prophecy as a means of understanding the past and not as a way of foretelling the future:

> The folly of interpreters hath been to foretell times and things by this prophecy (of St. John), as if God designed to make them prophets. By this rashness they have not only exposed themselves, but brought the prophecy also into

contempt. The design of God was much otherwise. He gave this and the prophecies of the Old Testament, not to gratify men's curiosities by enabling them to foreknow things; but that, after they were fulfilled, they might be interpreted by the event, and his own providence, not the interpreters', be then manifested thereby to the world.[37]

No one would have approved this declaration more strongly than the pre-Joachimite scholars of the early twelfth century. Equally they would have approved Newton's firm conviction that of all historical sources the prophetic statements of the Bible were the most certain:

The authority of emperors, kings and princes is human. The authority of councils, synods, bishops and presbyters is human. The authority of the prophets is divine and comprehends the sum of religion ... Their predictions of things to come relate to the state of the church in all ages; and amongst the old prophets, Daniel is the most distinct in order of time and easiest to be understood; and therefore in those things which relate to the last times he must be made the key to the rest.[38]

Newton was the last great scientific mind in European history to accept biblical prophecies as a source for the detailed study of historical facts. He accepted the imagery of biblical prophecy with the calm competence of a scientist dealing with puzzling but well-authenticated material, for which reliable techniques of interpretation existed. The dream of Daniel was for him still the chief clue to the shape of world history – a clue of such difficulty that it demanded the severest concentration of scientific attention. Much of the work of the past could be allowed to stand. The ten horns of the fourth beast of Daniel were still the ten kingdoms into which the Roman Empire had been divided. But much required a new effort of interpretation. The eleventh horn was no longer Islam but, with greater plausibility, the temporal power of the popes. Newton traced with great clarity and scientific objectivity the rise of this kingdom and the fulfillment in it of all the details noted by Daniel in his dream. The "time, and times, and half a time" were still taken to be $3\frac{1}{2}$ periods, but not the periods of seventy years which had satisfied an unsophisticated age; they were "1260 solar years, reckoning a time for a calendar year of 360 days, and a day for a solar year." In plain English, they were 1260 years from the rise of papal temporal power in the eighth century, after which the kingdom would be given to "the people of the saints of the Most High, whose kingdom is an everlasting kingdom."[39] In this reconstruction with its climax pushed forward into a relatively distant future, we are back in the calm and rational atmosphere of the early twelfth century.

In Newton's lucid and masterly survey of universal history carried out with the aid of the books of Daniel and Revelation, reason everywhere presides. Yet no one can see clearly the pattern of history without having some anticipations of the future. Even Newton's pulse quickened as he came nearer to his own day. Although he protested that for the present "we must content ourselves with interpreting what hath already been fulfilled," he could not help seeing that, when so much of the pattern was already laid out, the day would come, and perhaps quite soon, when the study of the future would become a safe and secure area of scientific investigation:

> Among the interpreters of the last age there is scarce one of note who hath not made some discovery worth knowing; and thence, it seems, one may gather that God is about opening these mysteries. The success of others put me upon considering it; and if I have done anything which may be useful to following writers I have my design.[40]

These words suggest that if Newton had started his prophetic studies earlier, or if he had devoted more time to prophecy and less to the *Principia*, he might have become another Joachim of Fiore. But fortunately he was content to leave this role for an actor temperamentally better suited to it – Karl Marx.

4

Aspects of the European Tradition of Historical Writing
4: The Sense of the Past

In the first three of these papers I have examined three aspects of the European historical tradition – aspects which I may briefly characterize as classical, early scientific, and prophetic. The models for all these modes were derived from the ancient world, and all three have played an important part in the development of western attitudes to history. Yet no one who looks dispassionately at the works produced by these three modes of studying history will think that they are the main sources of our modern ways of thinking about and writing history. So we must now ask whether it is possible to identify any central tradition in historical study leading to the practice and assumptions of most historians today.

It may help to clear the ground for our enquiry if we begin by asking what were the aims of the historians of the three types which we have so far examined. The brief answer to this question is that the aim of the classical imitators was to exemplify virtues and vices for moral instruction, and to extract from the confusion of the past a clear picture of the destinies of peoples. The aim of the scientific students of universal history was to exhibit the divine plan for mankind throughout history, and to demonstrate the congruity between the facts of history revealed in the Bible and the facts provided by secular sources. As for the prophetic historians, their aim was first to identify the historical landmarks referred to in prophetic utterances, then to discover the point at which history had arrived, and finally to predict the future from the still unfulfilled portions of prophecy.

These purposes cover all the main aims traditionally put forward to justify the study of history. But one has only to mention them to know that they are not those of modern historians. If we ask what these are, no doubt widely different answers can be given. But there is one aim which, whether as an end in itself, or as a means to other ends, nearly all historians will either acknowledge or in practice pursue. This is the aim of reconstituting the thoughts and experiences of the past in their total environment of social relationships and material and mental resources. The hope of success in this task is something new in modern historical writing, and it has created a new relationship between past and present. Even though the historian may reject the thoughts and experiences he describes, and would find them very repellent in practice, yet the act of understanding them creates a bond between past and present, which is all the stronger if these thoughts and experiences are in some sense his own. Whether or not this is the fundamental aim of modern historical study, it is a condition of success in any further aim which the historian may have, and it requires a careful and deliberate cultivation of what we may call a sense of the past.

As an avowed aim of historical study this cultivation of a sense of the past is a fairly recent development. In its most articulate form it is a product of the breakdown of the relatively stable intellectual system which had been created in the Middle Ages and remained substantially operative till the mid-nineteenth century. When the breakdown of this inherited system became widely apparent, and when as a consequence the past ceased to be a repository of true doctrines and became an incoherent heap of errors and inhumanities, sensitive people were threatened with the most serious alienation from their past in the whole course of European history. One remedy for this threatened alienation was an increasingly vigorous and sensitive cultivation of historical understanding. The result of this was to replace intellectual certainty by an emotional cohesion within which all the experiences of the past could coexist. The doctrines of the past might be false, but the experiences which had given rise to the doctrines were indubitably true. By the imaginative appropriation of these experiences, people could still possess the past, while rejecting the intellectual structure which it had once been the role of the historical process to hand down intact from age to age.

This struggle between alienation and desire for union with the past provided the impetus – so it seems to me – for the great outburst of historical activity of which we are the heirs. An appreciation of the therapeutic value of this historical activity was not confined to historians. Indeed it was non-historians who rejoiced most abundantly in the cure which it worked; and, since history was a cure for alienation, it is not surprising that it was aliens and exiles who experienced most vividly its healing power. Among these none were more eloquent than Kipling and Henry James. It was the returned exile Kipling – in my view the most gifted historical genius this country has ever produced – who created the most vivid imaginative pictures of the successive phases of life in England going back to a remote antiquity. But it was Henry James I think – and the wide sweep of the historical impulse can be seen in its powerful effect on a man so different in taste and character from Kipling – who first used the phrase "the sense of the past" to denote the impact of an immensely complicated and varied scene on a historically sensitive mind. He certainly expressed with greater sensitivity than any other writer the mixture of alienation and desire for union which underlies a great mass of late nineteenth-century historical work. This mixture is to be found in innumerable passages, but a single example will suffice. When Nick Dormer in *The Tragic Muse* looked over the estate which he would never inherit, what came over him was

> simply the sense of England – a sort of apprehended revelation of his country. The dim annals of the place appeared to be in the air (foundations bafflingly early, a great monastic life, wars of the Roses, with battles and blood in the streets, and then the long quietude of the respectable centuries, all cornfields and magistrates and vicars) and these things were connected with an emotion that arose from the green country, the rich land so infinitely lived in, and laid on him a hand that was too ghostly to press and yet somehow too urgent to be light. It produced a throb that he could not have spoken of, it was so deep, and that was half imagination and half responsibility.

One could go on for ever in this vein, and of course Henry James virtually did. But, however embarrassing these effusions may seem out of their context, they are valuable witnesses to the consoling sense of continuity and peace which historical studies everywhere in Europe brought to minds bruised by the perplexities of Darwinism, Socialism, and industrial society. This consolation may now seem a feeble thing to minds toughened by long familiarity with these perplexities. The cultivation of a sense of the past now appears rather as a private luxury than as the medicine for the universal ill. But a hundred years ago, the study of history offered a sense of stability, permanence, and the gentleness of change, in place of a long vista of meaningless and inhuman errors. Hence it became the most cultivated area of intellectual activity for the better part of a century.

Historical study has now lost this position, though I am not persuaded that the task which it took up in the mid-nineteenth century is either completed or unnecessary today. On the contrary, it has only started. It is not, however, my intention tonight to provide an exhibition of the historian as propagandist or prophet. I have mentioned the immediate past not as a basis for prophecy, but as a starting point for looking further back. I want to ask whether situations of alienation in the past have produced outbursts of historical activity similar to that which we find in the nineteenth century, to examine the nature of these outbursts and the effect they have had in forming our habits of historical work.

If we look back with these questions in mind, it is at once clear that there are two periods which require attention. The first is from about 1090 to 1130 and the second from about 1560 to 1620. These are both periods of a conspicuous renewal in historical studies, when there was an abundance of activity among a relatively large number of workers, and when their methods of work were substantially new. Both periods, moreover, came after a crisis in national affairs which seemed to alienate men from their past. To these periods I now turn.

II

The first historical revival began about twenty-five years after the Norman Conquest of England. The features in the situation which provoked it were these. The old English aristocracy had disappeared; the English language, which had recently been the medium of all social life and a surprisingly large area of religious life, was no longer in use in the upper strata of society. The literature, educational manuals, prayers, rituals, laws, and legal procedures, which had employed this language, were rapidly becoming unintelligible curiosities. At the level of literate and aristocratic society, no country in Europe, between the rise of the barbarian kingdoms and the twentieth century, has undergone so radical a change in so short a time as England experienced after 1066. The distant eye of the historian can detect many signs of continuity, but to cultivated contemporaries these signs must have been very inconspicuous. The main reaction of men who had known pre-Conquest England was one of outrage, resentment, and nostalgia. As late as 1120 William of Malmesbury, who was only half English and no enemy to the Normans, could write of the state of England:

> It is the habitation of strangers and the domination of foreigners. There is today no Englishman who is either earl, bishop or abbot. The newcomers devour the riches and entrails of England and there is no hope of the misery coming to an end.[1]

And this was not an isolated voice. It was the voice of a whole generation of literate men who had English ancestors.

The only people who were in a position to observe, feel, and express their reaction to these changes were Benedictine monks in monasteries sufficiently old and wealthy to evoke an acute sense of the difference between the present and the past. The members of these communities lived among the evidences of ancient greatness, and they were exposed more continuously than any others to the dangers of the present in the multiple forms of the loss of lands, the destruction of rituals, the plundering of ancient treasures, and the overturning of old habits of life. Many, probably most, members of ancient monasteries in 1100 were men of English descent. They were the lucky Englishmen of their generation, for compared with their relatives who belonged to the dispossessed or depressed aristocracy, they had survived with their way of life relatively intact. They were not unaware or ungrateful for their good fortune, but it made them all the more sensitive to the places where the shoe pinched most. Most irksome of all, they felt their exclusion from all promotion. This was one cause of internal tension within monastic communities, and it drew English monks together in defense of their past.

The men of English speech in the monasteries felt themselves the special custodians of the monastic past, and this gave them some compensation for their exclusion from high office. Besides being bound to the past by blood, they were the only members of the community who could understand the documents in which much of the evidence of the past was preserved. Yet it must not be thought that they were the only members of monastic communities who valued the past greatness of their monasteries. Everyone who lives in an ancient community is sooner or later drawn into the task of defending it against all comers. In the last resort commitment to the community knows no limits. But in the post-Conquest monasteries the threat of the outside world evoked responses of varying degrees of intensity. The crudest threat was to the monastic lands, and all members could combine wholeheartedly to resist this. The many intruders into monastic estates could be repelled only by constant vigilance and frequent reference to early documents. In making these documents available for instant use, the English monks were doing a service which all their brethren would applaud. They could be less sure of applause in their efforts to repel the threats to local rituals, to domestic legends, to traditional claims to respect and authority. On these points the newcomers in the community required instruction, and we can sometimes see with extraordinary clarity how the English monks set about this task – surreptitiously at first, and then with growing confidence and success. Superficially, the written evidence at their disposal was not impressive. There were many silent shrines:

> This is a state of affairs which you will find in many places in England: the evidence has been destroyed by the violence of enemies, so that only the names of saints remain and their modern miracles, if any.[2]

In the days of their prosperity the old monasteries had relied on established usage, on the support of kings and nobles, and on popular veneration, to preserve all that they valued in their way of life. Consequently the evidence was scattered, fragmentary, and difficult to interpret. Yet there was an abundance of ancient charters; the bodies of the saints lay thick on the ground; although many manuscripts had been destroyed or stolen, there were still ancient volumes which preserved the outlines of the old monastic culture. All these documents told something about the ancient saints and patrons of the community, and there were many legends which enforced the intimate connection between the prosperity of the kingdom and the greatness of the monasteries. The task of bringing this fragmentary and widely dispersed material together, and extracting from it a story which would impress hostile or indifferent contemporaries, was very urgent, but it was also very difficult.

It was not only in England that Benedictine monks felt their position threatened in the early twelfth century. In Germany, especially, there were monks, like Rupert of Deutz, who bitterly resented their depreciation by the world and expressed this bitterness very copiously. Rupert of Deutz tried to restore the scholarly reputation of the monasteries by undertaking vast works of biblical and liturgical interpretation, and by engaging in ill-advised controversy with scholastic theologians.[3] There is nothing like this in England. The English reaction was peculiar in its strong historical bias, and there was an obvious reason for this. The Norman Conquest provided an event in the past to which every evil could be traced: "the fatal day for England, the mournful end of the sweet country, the coming of the new lord."[4] All hope of revival, all hope of resistance to further depreciation, depended on reanimating the pre-Conquest past and showing that the Conquest was no more than a tremor in a long development.

It was from this situation that the English historical movement developed. It developed spontaneously in monasteries which were widely separated geographically, but they all had the same problem and all possessed similar material for dealing with it. Canterbury, Malmesbury, Worcester, Evesham, and Durham were the outstanding places in the movement; but Abingdon, Rochester, Glastonbury, Thorney, Peterborough, and Ramsey all made a contribution. The movement had its great names – Eadmer, William of Malmesbury, Symeon of Durham, Wulfstan, Florence and John of Worcester, chief among them – but it was not inspired by the personal tastes of a few antiquaries. It drew its inspiration and gained its momentum from the necessities of corporate survival – at the lowest level mere physical survival; at the highest, the survival of an ancient monastic culture, a religious and intellectual tradition, and a position in the world. What was important for success in this task was the cumulative weight of many men working on similar material for similar purposes in many different places. It was this that gave consistency to the historical work of the period. Circumstances forced scholarly monks all over England to become historians, to examine the historical content of material which had never been used in this way before, and to extract from unpromising documents a new picture of antiquity.

The mistake is often made of looking for evidence of a historical revival only in the histories which it produces; and this mistake has obscured the character of the work done by these monastic scholars. Just as the finest work of the modern historical movement is to be found in editions of texts, catalogues of materials, and critical notes on sources, symbols, and social habits, so in the twelfth century the historical revival is to be seen as a continuous process of collecting and arranging charters, transcribing documents, and carrying out minute investigations into chronology and topography, studying monastic buildings and inscriptions, assembling the texts of ancient learning, writing estate-histories, chronicles, and biographies – and only at the end of the day the histories which we all know.

The initial impulse was sternly practical, but the work diverged in different directions according to the needs and resources of the community, and the scholarly talent which each community contained. At Worcester the practical impulse is very clearly expressed in the preface to the collection of charters made by the monk Hemming in about 1095:

> Wulfstan, bishop of this see, caused this book to be written to teach his successors about the things which have been committed to their care, and to show them which lands justly belong (or ought to belong) to the church, and which have been unjustly seized by evil men – first, during the Danish invasions; later, by unjust royal officials and tax collectors; and most recently, by the violence of Normans in our own time, who by force, guile and rapine have unjustly deprived this holy church of its lands, villages and possessions, until hardly anything is safe from their depredations.[5]

It would be hard to think of anything more practical than this. Yet bare practicality can scarcely have inspired research into the depredations of Danish invaders two centuries earlier, or of royal officials in the tenth and eleventh centuries. By no conceivable process of law could these losses be made good, and very few of the documents in Hemming's cartulary can ever have been produced in a court of law. In its totality the collection provides, not a practical handbook, but a complete picture of past glories, most of them beyond human powers to restore, but all of them laid up in heaven and apprehensible on earth only by the historical imagination. This imaginative reconstruction of the monastic past inevitably grew out of the initial impulse to regain lost lands and to save those which remained. It was part of a large effort to make the past alive in the present. Even in the act of stating his practical aim Hemming at Worcester illustrates the extension of purpose which was common to all ancient monastic communities.

Worcester, however, also illustrates a quite different historical extension taking place at the same time. Bishop Wulfstan, who promoted the collection of charters, also promoted the enlargement of monastic history from a local to a universal setting. The process of enlargement can be observed in the manuscript of the Worcester chronicle preserved at Corpus Christi College, Oxford (MS. 157). The volume starts with a historical account of the origin of the see of Worcester and of the possessions given to it between 679 and 1093. Then after various other preliminary matters – lists of consuls, popes, and bishops, genealogies of kings, Easter Tables, sacred sites (the basic materials of universal history) – the manuscript contains the most learned of all contemporary attempts to fit the facts of English history into a universal chronology. It is worth noting that this scholarly purpose, and consequently the whole movement of thought which the Worcester volume represents, is wholly obscured in the only generally available edition. The editor – true to the tradition which regarded medieval chronicles simply as repositories of facts and not as evidence of the minds and intentions of their authors – printed only the insertions relating to English history and entirely ignored the body on to which they were grafted. To get a truer picture we have to go back to the edition of 1592, and only a photographic edition could adequately represent the various streams of thought which converged to make up this volume.[6] It was not a mechanical task which the compiler undertook; it required an elaborate series of chronological decisions, a wide learning, and a continuous search for new sources. The Corpus manuscript with its many corrections and changes of hand brings us into immediate contact with the long continued effort which these processes entailed, and it makes intelligible the fame of the monk (in the phrase of his contemporary admirer) "whose subtle learning and laborious scholarship made this composite chronicle pre-eminent over all others."

If Worcester illustrates the historical movement at its two extremes of territorial intensity and universal extension, Durham illustrates a different kind of movement. Here too the practical impulse of self-protection is very conspicuous, but the historical manifestations of a single character, St. Cuthbert, stand out more clearly than anything else in the past. No community had more physical objects which recalled its past than Durham, and the most important of these were associated with the many journeys of the saint's body in the centuries from 875 to 1070. In the cemetery there was the stone cross made by Bishop Aethelwold in about 730, broken by the Vikings in 793, repaired, and carried with the body of St. Cuthbert till it finally came to rest at Durham. On the altar there was the Gospel Book written by Bishop Eadfrith about 700, bound by his successor Bishop Aethelwold, and ornamented by Billfrith the anchorite.

This too had accompanied the saint from Lindisfarne, and it bore the traces of its miraculous survival after immersion in the sea in the course of these travels. Beside it on the altar there lay the Book of Life, with the names of monks, friends, and benefactors of St. Cuthbert begun in the eighth century and continued to the present day. Outside, on the monastic estates, there still lived descendants of the men who had carried the body from 875 to 883 and could trace their genealogies back to the years of travel. And most impressive of all, there were the many gifts of lands, books, and ornaments given by King Athelstan in recognition of St. Cuthbert's help in uniting the kingdom under his rule.[7]

These may seem small matters, scarcely worth detaining the Society for the length of time it takes to tell them, but taken together they built up a complicated sense of the past, which must always be made up of small things vividly perceived.

The post-Conquest historical revival was very rich in historical perceptions. Each community added some feature of its own. At Christ Church, Canterbury, the main corporate interest was at first concentrated on the great collection of saints' bodies which lay around in disarray. The writing of their biographies, the authentication of their miracles, the preservation of their Feasts, were the primary tasks of historical effort. Here too, as elsewhere, the charters were collected, annotated, and transcribed, to resist attack. Too often, more often and more radically than elsewhere, they were brought up to date, for at Canterbury new problems had arisen for which the past could provide an answer only by being taken firmly in hand. The fatal dispute about the primacy and the great political issues of St. Anselm's time gave a new direction to the historical interests of the community, and especially of Eadmer its best historian. He had as great a love of the English past as anyone, but he was spoilt as a researcher by his opportunities for observing the present. As the companion of Archbishop Anselm he had moved more freely among the great men and issues of his day than any of his contemporary monks. These experiences altered his view of the past. He looked for contemporary issues in past events, and his *Historia Novorum* was an explicit attempt to provide the kind of evidence he would have liked to find:

> When (he wrote) I see men of the present time, hard-pressed by misfortunes, anxiously scanning the deeds of their predecessors for consolation and strength, and unable to get as much as they wish, I conceive it will be a great service to posterity to commit to writing the deeds of the present for the use of the future.[8]

The objects of research were everywhere influenced by locality. At Glastonbury, the oldest of the English monasteries, the main interest of the monks lay in extending their history backwards as far as it would go – to St. Patrick, and ultimately to King Arthur.[9] At Abingdon the main interest was in the history of the estates;[10] at Evesham in the miracles of the saints.[11] Thorney and Peterborough did most for the revival of Anglo-Saxon scientific learning.[12] At Rochester the monk who put together and transcribed the monastery's charters also made the fullest collection of Old English laws and legal texts, stretching from the laws of Aethelberht in about 600 to Henry I's Coronation Charter in 1100. The arrangement and correct transcription of these texts in Old English was a notable scholarly achievement, and the impulse behind it can only have been the desire, which the compiler shared with his English monastic contemporaries, to demonstrate that the Norman Conquest had only shaken, but not interrupted, a long development.[13]

Finally there is the community which produced the most talented of all the researchers of this period: William of Malmesbury.[14] Unlike Eadmer, his only rival as a historian, William never deviated from the corporate monastic purpose of recreating the Old English past, and of all the monastic scholars of his day he knew best how to use ancient materials.

His virtuosity can best be studied in his small work on the antiquity of Glastonbury, which was once the most despised of all the historical productions of this time. Armitage Robinson, nearly fifty years ago, restored it to respectability, though not to the fame which it deserves, by freeing it from later imaginative accretions.[15] It was in its origin a polemical work, designed to show that the earliest of the post-Conquest Canterbury historians had been wrong in saying that Dunstan in 942 was the first abbot of Glastonbury. The monks of Glastonbury gave William access to all their materials and he had no difficulty in proving his main point. But the peculiar excellence of his work lies in the way in which he used his materials. Eight hundred and fifty years before J. H. Round he discovered how to use charters as a historian.

Several monastic scholars of the day discovered that a history of the monastic estates could be extracted from charters, but William alone saw how many-sided this history could be. He read charters with an eye open for every hint they could give him. He saw that they told a story, not only of losses and gains throughout the centuries, but also of kings and bishops with intelligible wills and purposes. He used witness lists to establish the succession of bishops and abbots. He drew on them for archeological details. He noticed the nationality of early donors, whether they were British or Saxon, and he remarked that Cadwalla, while he was still a pagan, already used the sign of the cross to authenticate his charters. And to the evidence of the charters, he added the evidence of tombs and inscriptions, crosses, reliquaries, books, and ornaments. From the whole mass of fragments he constructed a history in which local men known only by their names mingled with some of the greatest names in English history. By the standards of modern scholarship William was a primitive operator, but he had grasped the essential principle that in studying a period for which there is little evidence no detail and no kind of evidence are unimportant.

The methods which he employed in his history of Glastonbury are to be found in all his works. He himself thought that his ecclesiastical survey of England, his *Gesta pontificum*, was his most original work, and in this he was right, though not altogether for the reasons he gives. He thought that his originality consisted in doing something which no one had previously attempted:

> Here I am destitute of all help; I feel the palpable darkness of ignorance, and I have no lantern of an earlier history to guide my footsteps.[16]

All this is fine and true. But his more important originality lay in extending to the whole kingdom the corporate aims of each monastic researcher of his day. He used the materials of every monastery he could visit, or from which he could get information – their chronicles, charters, legends, ornaments, inscriptions, and buildings – to make a survey of the whole kingdom. He traveled widely to gather material for his book, and he is the first of a long line of historians whose sense of the English past has been developed in the course of extensive journeys, notebook in hand, recording inscriptions, examining charters, and writing descriptions of the places he visited.[17] His brief descriptions of Canterbury, Rochester, Glastonbury, London, Hereford, York, Durham, Crowland, Thorney, the vale of Gloucester, and the fens are the first accounts of ancient places in this country seen through the eyes of a man with a critical and developed sense of the past.

If his *Gesta pontificum* is the most original of his works, the account it contains of Aldhelm, the founder of his own monastery, is his masterpiece of historical method, doing for a single man of the late seventh century what he had earlier done for the monastery at Glastonbury through several centuries. The attempt to evoke a figure of so distant a past from such fragmentary materials – for he had no contemporary biography to guide him – was a daunting task. He had to rely on a mixture of charters, inscriptions, archeological remains, pictures, legends, and chronicles; and to these he added Aldhelm's own theological writings and letters. In its complicated texture, its critical assessment of the evidence, and its total use of the evidence, it is – in the whole body of medieval historical writing – the piece which leaves the strongest impression of modernity.

William was well aware that he was writing history in a manner widely different from that of historians writing in the rhetorical tradition. He inveighed against the use of rhetoric to add bulk to an exiguous work: he had made it a rule, he said, to add nothing except to put the meaning of an old author in a clearer light. He denounced the commonest of all rhetorical devices, the introduction of imaginary speeches: "the memory of the *deeds* of the past has scarcely come down to us," he wrote; "how much less the *volatile* words?"[18] He had a strict idea of what he meant by *integritas* in historical writing: it meant the frequent quotation of texts and a close reliance on his sources. If his ideas of relevance and of the relative importance of events sometimes seem very bizarre to us, we must remember that the whole school of scholars to which he belonged would have rejected our notion of importance. What mattered to them was the web of associations which made objects or events, however trivial, part of the life of the community. Every object in the church and every portion of land, and all their associations with past events and people, had a place in the composite picture. The prime object was to connect the community with its past by making its physical being a vehicle for the remembrance of a great army of benefactors, craftsmen, saints, and enemies. The aim was a total recall of the past in order to give the community its identity in the present.

The historical scholars who worked for this end were inspired by ideals quite different from those of classical, universal, or prophetic historians. They rejected both the form and the rhetoric of classical models. They accepted unpredictable confusion as the ordinary state of men in history, and they found a uniting thread, not in the working out of a grand design, but in the memories of small communities accumulating over several centuries. Their only contribution to universal history was to fit these microscopically small events into the system of earlier scholars. They took no account of the end of the world, which (in their sense) ended where the monastic property began. By way of compensation for their limitations, they had a vivid interest in the texts of old documents and an eagerness in collecting and scrutinizing them. Their whole effort was anchored in the countryside and in the defense of a long established way of life. Out of their local knowledge and their local materials they created the image of a phase of English history which would scarcely have existed without their efforts: substantially they were responsible for bringing Anglo-Saxon history into existence.

III

If time and ability allowed I should have liked to show how the methods and aims of the early twelfth-century monks, and the necessities which moved them to undertake their work, were revived in the antiquaries of the sixteenth and seventeenth centuries. From this point one could trace

the stages by which their work became the foundation of modern historical studies. But the time for such a survey has not yet come. Despite all
the work that has been done in recent years, the bulk of unexplored
material is still very large. Instead of losing myself and my audience in
this jungle, let me simply offer a slight sketch of a Tudor researcher at
work, with a few remarks on the type he represents.

For my sketch I choose neither the most original nor the most influential
– neither, on the one hand, Laurence Nowell, who revived the study of
Anglo-Saxon at the point where it had been abandoned in the early twelfth
century, nor, on the other, a great entrepreneur like Camden – but a man
between Nowell and Camden in time and influence: William Lambarde.[19]
Nowell was his master in Anglo-Saxon; Camden his supplanter in fame. He
came from the level of society which produced most of the hard-working
antiquaries of the next hundred years, and he displays most of the features
of the type. He was a small Kentish landowner, the newest of the newcomers in his class, for his father – a London draper and alderman – had
bought the small manor at Greenwich, which his son inherited, only ten
years before he died. William was eighteen when he succeeded his father in
1554. Before he was thirty he was a member of the House of Commons,
where he narrowly escaped being associated with Peter Wentworth.[20]
When he was forty-one he became a bencher of Lincoln's Inn and two years
later a Justice of the Peace. At fifty-five he was appointed a Master in
Chancery, at sixty-one Deputy Keeper of the Rolls, and at sixty-five Keeper
of the Records in the Tower.[21] His last appointment was in 1601, and he
died in the same year. For a brief period in Parliament, and for a long time
in local affairs, at Quarter Sessions, and in the Court of Chancery, he was a
very busy man, but it is as a historian that I commemorate him now.

He was not an antiquary of the type which became common in the
eighteenth century, when men of abundant leisure took an interest – more
or less profound according to their abilities – in every kind of curious or
ancient object. With Lambarde it was his business, not his leisure, that
made him a historian. In all phases of his life he felt an intense urge to
give his position a historical dimension. In the 1560s, before he had settled
down and when he was briefly active in Parliament, he took all England
as his theme, and he then planned an ambitious "description and History
of our whole Realm." Then,

> after such time as it had pleased my good God, by marriage of a wife, to
> bestow me in Kent, I resolved for sundry just respects to draw out of that
> my Topographical storehouse a particular discourse of Kent.

This resolve produced, in 1571, his *Perambulation of Kent*, the first of our
county histories.[22] Nine years later, on August 6, 1579, he was put on the

Commission of the Peace in Kent, and at once began "in greedy haste" to study the history of his new Office. The first draft of his work on this subject bears the date of the very month of his appointment. It was published two years later, in 1581, as *Eirenarcha, or of the Office of Justices of Peace*, and for the next twenty years he continuously revised it, thickening his illustrations from the past and enlarging his views of the future.[23] His work as a Justice led him to probe more deeply into the lower offices of the shire, and to produce in 1583 a volume on the duties of "Constables, borsholders, tithingmen, and such other lowe Ministers of the Peace."[24] Having, in the course of these studies, become convinced that "the base courts of the Shires, Hundreds, Boroughs and Manors do yet remain in a manner the same in substance that they then (in Anglo-Saxon times) were," he turned his attention to the Courts of King's Bench, Star-Chamber, Constable's Court, Admiralty, etc., and showed (as he thought) that they had all sprung from the same root in the King's court.[25] By this time he was becoming closely associated with the central legal administration, and a few months before his appointment as a Master in Chancery he produced his *Archeion, or a Commentary upon the High Courts of Justice in England*, in which he traced the history of the various branches of the royal courts of justice.[26] Meanwhile his experiences in the House of Commons led him to make a collection of ancient treaties and notes on the proceedings of Parliament.[27] And, in his last years, his work as a lawyer in the Court of Chancery caused him to collect precedents, which were later published as a volume "out of the labours of Master William Lambert."[28] Everywhere he discovered that the roots of his daily work were hidden in deep layers of the past. *Periit et inventa est*: this motto on his volume of 1583 might apply to his whole search for the past – "It was lost, and is found."

His life provides as perfect a conjunction of history and practice as we can find. Yet a man's thoughts always range more widely than his business. In the sixteenth, as in the twelfth century, practical and psychological needs might provide the initial impetus, but the result was a new vision of the past beyond all the claims of necessity. We can follow the growth of Lambarde's vision most clearly in his notebooks and annotations. They are the raw material for his printed works, and they show how widely he ranged and how varied were his sources and his friends. His earliest extracts seem to have been chiefly from chronicles, often transcribed in collaboration with his "dearest friend" Laurence Nowell. The earliest date in these notebooks is 1560, when Lambarde made extracts from Gerald of Wales's *Itinerary* and *Topography of Wales*.[29] Later, his interests expanded to include records of many kinds – Perambulations of the Forest, fiscal returns, surveys of the courts of Chancery and Exchequer, lists of castles, and landowners in Kent who had obtained an alteration in the terms of their tenure. One of his manuscripts contains taxation records for Knights' Fees and ecclesiastical benefices from 1483 to 1581. In another he constructed an imitation of an Anglo-Saxon Easter Table from 1571 to 1600 with all the appropriate apparatus of Indictions, Epacts, Golden Numbers, Sunday Letters, and Feast Days. The latest dated transcript of his I have seen is a copy of a fourteenth-century treatise on the coinage made in 1588.[30]

Anything that was old and English, especially if it was also Kentish, was noted, extracted, and indexed. But it was long a puzzle to him to know how to use all his material. At first he thought of bringing everything together in a Topographical Dictionary of England.[31] The book on Kent was an experimental volume extracted from his material. He sent this at the beginning of 1571 to his fellow Kentish landowner Thomas Wotton with a letter explaining his method and his hope of expanding the work into "a description and story of the most famous places throughout the Realm." For several years he continued to collect material for the large work, but his hopes of completing it (if indeed they were still alive) were dashed in 1585 when he received a pre-publication copy of Camden's *Britannia*, which anticipated his own plan. In its first edition, Camden's *Britannia* was a jejune and inferior performance but it had the merit of having actually appeared, which Lambarde's would probably never have done. Lambarde's letter of thanks is a model for anyone who finds himself in a similar position:

> In reading these your painful topographies I have been contrarily affected; one way taking singular delight and pleasure in the perusing of them; another way by sorrowing that I may not now, as I wonted, dwell in the meditation of the same things that you are occupied withal. And yet I must confess that the delectation which I reaped by your labours recompensed the grief that I conceived of mine own bereaving from the like: notwithstanding that in time past I have preferred the reading of antiquities before any sort of study that ever I frequented...To be plain, I seem to myself not to have known Kent till I knew Camden.[32]

After this act of renunciation, he went on in the second edition of his *Perambulation* to express an opinion which is a charter for all later work undertaken by county historians:

> Nevertheless, being assured that the inwards of each place may best be known by such as reside therein, I cannot but still encourage some one able man in each shire to undertake his own.[33]

Lambarde's discovery that history is best written from inside, and that it was his own task to write it in this way, came at the end of a long search.

In 1577 he was still engaged on his Topography "digging and raking together the antiquities of this realm which (as metall conteyned within the bowells of the earth) lie hidden in old books hoarded up in corners." But he may in the end not have been sorry to find that Camden had forestalled him, and that his own task was to be confined to the country-side he knew best and to the history of the offices and courts with which he was familiar through personal experience.

IV

This is the picture of a Tudor researcher at work. There had been a few – a very few – like him in the hundred years before 1550, but he and his friends, and the similar groups who were beginning to appear in other parts of the country, were the first body of workers since the historical revival of the early twelfth century to devote themselves to a systematic examination of records and chronicles over a wide area of country. They turned over great masses of unexplored documents searching for material of historical interest. They analyzed and transcribed indefatigably; and they exchanged their results. As in the earlier period, so in the sixteenth century, the writing of great histories was not the primary aim. These workers felt (as Lambarde described himself) like miners digging great masses of ore out of the earth, casting it into rude lumps, and then looking round to see what they could make of it. Slowly the books began to emerge, but the first aim was simply (in Lambarde's words) "to attayne to some knowledge and understanding of the antiquities of this realme."

If we ask why they wanted to do this, the reason seems to be that – like the English monks nearly five hundred years earlier – they were the fortunate but uneasy survivors of a great upheaval, and they wanted to overcome the sense of alienation from the past, which was threatened by the destruction of old institutions and the growing unintelligibility of old books and records. This desire to make the present intelligible by linking it with the past affected all men of a certain position in society. The dedications and acknowledgments in Lambarde's books tell us who they were. Above all they were the "Gentlemen of England." Most of them had landed property; many were beneficiaries of monastic estates; some had ancient documents on their hands; and all were surrounded by many evidences of past life and institutions. These evidences were at first sight obscure and repulsive, but if attacked with sufficient determination, they proved that local and national affairs had for centuries followed a pattern which was still familiar and could be stabilized if it was understood. It is unlikely that antiquarian research was motivated, as it had been in the twelfth century, by the need to defend titles to land, but in a more general way it satisfied a need to understand the offices and title-deeds of a large class of men: the nature of their tenures, their position in society, and the claims of their families, however recently established, to a respectable antiquity. Men newly established in county society and in ancient titles and functions wanted to feel at home in their properties, to understand their dignity and offices, and to be identified with the landscape. These were needs which historical research alone could satisfy.

The researchers of the period after 1560 were the secular successors of the post-Conquest monks. They were engaged in the same task of bridging a gap between past and present which made them uneasy and diminished their stature in society. But at this point an important difference has to be noticed. The post-Conquest monks were sure that they had a great past, but they were uncertain of their present and future. Their post-Reformation secular successors were relatively sure of the present but uncertain of their past. The monks felt the danger of losing their lands; the new landowners felt the danger of holding their lands without having the ancient respectability which would give dignity and stability to their position. The monastic antiquaries searched the records to give detail and lucidity to their inherited conviction of greatness; the secular antiquaries searched to discover what it was they had inherited. Hence their interest in family history, and the consequent importance of the College of Heralds in the historical researches of the Tudor and Stuart periods. Hence also their interest in institutions and in the descent of landed property, and the consequent importance of lawyers in the historical movement. Heralds and lawyers were the men who handled ancient documents as part of their daily work, and they became the interpreters of these documents to their generation, just as the English monks in the post-Conquest monasteries had been the interpreters in their time.

Despite the difference of emphasis, the researchers into the past in the two periods had a similar function; but their work had a different fate. The researchers of the earlier period had fulfilled their purpose and exhausted their material within a period of about thirty years. By 1130 their work was done. In historical research they had no successors. The monastic historians of the later Middle Ages abandoned historical research for contemporary journalism, and relied on their predecessors for their record of the past. Even a laborious scholar like Ranulf Higden regarded the past as an accumulation of compilations from which he made his own mountainous abridgment. The Tudor researchers had a better fortune. The methods they revived and the materials they unearthed have continued to attract workers from that time to this. The various stages in the evolution of this work, from being the absorbing passion of a whole generation to becoming the pleasing habit of a leisured clergy and gentry, cannot concern us now; but even in the mid-nineteenth century, when a new and much more powerful impulse than ever before stirred men to historical study, the tradition of research, which had been started in the twelfth century and renewed in the sixteenth, was still strong enough to give a distinctive character to English historical writing. Stubbs learnt to be a historian by studying family history at Knaresborough and by compiling lists of bishops at Navestock. Maitland learnt by copying legal documents in a conveyancer's office in London. They were starting where Hemming had started at Worcester and Lambarde in Kent. This starting point has the great merit of beginning with the ordinary needs of life, and not with any intellectual program whatsoever. Therefore, in the end, it proved stronger than any of the other traditions of historical scholarship which we have examined. So far as there is a central tradition in our historical writing, it arises from this recurrent need to understand and stabilize the present by reviving the experience of the past.

Part II

History

5

The Shape and Substance of Academic History

There is no statutory obligation to give an Inaugural Lecture. It may therefore seem strange that professors, who sometimes complain of the lectures required of them by the statutes, should undertake this voluntary task, especially when their admonitions are generally so quickly and so completely forgotten. In their defense it may be said that these occasions serve three purposes not otherwise provided for. They give an opportunity to take an academic farewell of our predecessors, to survey the past, and to glance at what we presume may be the future.

On the first point, I can happily be brief. Ernest Jacob is still with us; no farewell is called for. He is in the full tide of his activity as a historian, as his latest volume, published at the moment of his official retirement, testifies. We look forward to many years of his friendship and counsel, and to the fruits of his labor in the years to come. No man is more securely established in the affections of the members of his Faculty, and no man has done more to earn this affection. May we all long enjoy his peaceable and benign influence.

With regard to the future I can also be brief. I have never been convinced that historians have any greater claim to the gift of foresight than any other body of men. I certainly can make no such claim. Besides, apart from lacking the gift of prophecy, I have been too long a college tutor to believe otherwise than that the future of the History School in this University lies in the hands of the college tutors. It is they who must be chiefly responsible for shaping the subject to the needs of a new generation. But it may not be inappropriate today to turn our attention to the development of historical studies in the past, and to examine some general principles which may guide their development in the future. I do not wish to exaggerate the importance of this theme. We all know that intellectual friendship and discussion are the most important things a university has to offer. The precise syllabus of studies is of comparatively little importance. This is true, but it makes it easy to acquiesce in many anomalies and outworn practices. In the active life of a tutor almost no academic change seems worth the sweat of bringing it about; it will in any case be mutilated in the process and it will probably not serve the ends for which it was first devised. Yet it is a mistake to give up the laborious task of criticism and improvement. If we do so, we may find ourselves back in the position of this University just over a hundred years ago. The situation then was that a large part of public opinion outside the University, and some few persons inside it, considered that the studies of the University no longer met the needs of the time. It was from this crisis in our affairs that the History School had its rise. Our affairs are not in so critical a condition as they were in the 1850s; but the experience of that time, and the experiments which developed from it, have some interest and some lessons for us.

In the century that has passed between then and now the academic study of history has grown from nothing to the status of a considerable national industry occupying the full-time energies of several thousand persons of considerable skill and ability. It was in Oxford that this movement had its origin, and Oxford has probably done more than any other university to mold it by its inspiration and example. A hundred years ago, modern history formed part of a great and beneficent revolution in academic studies. But like all revolutions, an unfriendly observer might be tempted to say, its best days and brightest thoughts came early. Nearly everything that we now do in the History School goes back to the 1870s. The definition of the subject, as we now know it, was a rapid process; and the growth in the numbers studying it did not lag far behind. During the first quarter of this century nearly one undergraduate in three was reading history. It was an astonishing victory for the new subject, and it showed the extent to which the reformers of the period from 1850 to 1870 had fashioned an instrument which met a large variety of intellectual and practical needs during the last days of British supremacy in the world.

That the situation today is less promising I think no one will deny. During the period of growth, historical studies filled a gap which nothing else could fill. In the first place, history was the most exciting area of speculation in the last half of the nineteenth century. And secondly, in those unscientific days, history provided the ideal bridge between speculation and government, fitting its students for the direction of affairs in a leisurely world. In both of these directions historical studies have lost ground in the course of the last thirty years. The loss of ground shows itself in various ways. We may reconcile ourselves without regret to a decreasing proportion of university students reading history. It is inevitable and right that this should happen; but still the fall is significant. Whereas in the 1920s, over 30 percent of our undergraduates were reading history, by 1938 the proportion had fallen to just under 25 percent.

The latest figures show that it is now just over 15 percent. The same trend is to be observed in other universities, and it will certainly continue.[1]

More important, however, than this numerical decline, are the symptoms that some of the props of academic history, which were built up in the last century, are beginning to wear away without being replaced by any others of equal strength. At the risk of anticipating some of the things which I shall later talk about in greater detail, it may be said that, arising from the early controversies about history as an academic discipline, three main ways were discovered of giving cohesion to the subject. These were: an emphasis on institutions, an insistence on continuity, and a predilection for geography as a determinant of historical events. Some of us remember how these principles were made evident in the final examinations of thirty years ago in the "Outlines of Constitutional History," in the papers on continuous political history, and in the obligatory geographical questions. It may seem a small thing that these have all gone, but behind these pedantic details lies a larger change which raises some important problems. It is these that I wish to bring before you this evening.

In order to get our problems in perspective we must begin at the beginning, that is to say in the year 1850.

In this year the studies of the University were still governed, in principle at least, by the Laudian Statutes of 1636, which were themselves an attempt to preserve and modernize the medieval system of studies. This system was one of the most complete and coherent syllabuses of study ever devised, and the Hebdomadal Board in 1850 went so far as to declare that the Laudian Statutes presented a course of study "admirably arranged, at a time when not only the nature and faculties of the human mind were exactly what they are still, and must of course remain, but the principles also of sound and enlarged culture were far from being imperfectly understood."[2]

This handsome commendation did not of course prevent the disregard of almost every detail of the system in practice. But whether in theory or in practice, modern history had no place in the studies of the University. Yet at the very moment when the principles of the Laudian Statutes were being endorsed by the Hebdomadal Board, they were on the point of being buried for ever. A first step in this act of burial was the statute, passed by Convocation on April 23, 1850, setting up a combined School of Law and Modern History. This was part of an attempt to bring about a modernization of the University from within, and to allay by timely and moderate concessions the widespread public dissatisfaction with the narrowness and archaism of the education provided by the University. Like most other internal reforms, however, it was not sufficient to ward off the threat of reformation from without. On the same day that Convocation passed the new statute, Mr. Heywood, the Radical member for North

Lancashire, moved in the House of Commons a resolution to the effect that "all systems of academical education require from time to time some modification"; that "in the ancient English and Irish universities the interests of religious and useful learning have not been advanced to an extent commensurate with the great resources and high position of these bodies," and requesting the issue of a Royal Commission of Inquiry into the state of the Universities "with a view to assist in the adaptation of these important institutions to the requirements of modern times." Despite Gladstone's opposition to this "resort to an intermeddling and inquisitorial power which is neither supported by history or law," Lord Derby's government accepted the resolution and appointed the Commission, which issued its report two years later. One of the Commission's recommendations was that five Fellowships at All Souls should be suppressed in order to provide emoluments for a single Professor of International Law and Diplomacy, and another five to provide for a Professor of Modern History. It was as a result of this recommendation that the first Chichele Professor – frail instrument of reform – was appointed in 1862, and that I stand here today.

It would take too long to give more than a cursory glance at the motives which made the study of history the spearhead of an academic revolution a hundred years ago. But, briefly, the study of history seemed to provide an escape from the endless dogmatic wrangles which were both the glory and the disgrace of the University of the 1840s. By 1850 the University was tired of the charges and counter-charges, the deprivations, degradations, and condemnations which theological dispute brought in its train. Looking back in old age at this crisis, Jowett put the matter in a nutshell. He described how the forties had been dominated by Newman. After doing justice to the extraordinary power of Newman's appeal to the young, and to the revolutionary effect of his teaching on "active minds cut loose from their traditional moorings and launched on a sea of speculation over which they at last floated to a great diversity of havens," he added: "In some of us Liberalism soon took the practical shape of an effort to reform and emancipate the University, to strike off the fetters of medieval statutes, to set it free from the predominance of ecclesiasticism, recall it to its proper work, and restore it to the nation."[3]

In this task of restoring the University to the nation, the study of history presented itself as one of the most powerful tools. It was professedly undogmatic. At a time when the academic study of natural science was barely in its infancy, history had already on the Continent, and especially in Germany, made gigantic strides towards academic maturity. Besides, it had long been in the air that history was the subject of the future. It had established the same kind of mysterious power over men's minds that science has gained in our own day. In history, many believed they had found an education for gentlemen, for men of affairs, for open-minded men, free from the cobwebs of useless learning and ancient error.

There remained, however, one great difficulty. It was all very well to establish modern history as an academic discipline; the question still remained, how was it to be studied? There was only one kind of serious discipline known to the old academic world: the study and commentary of ancient and authoritative texts. For this type of activity there was an established routine. But how could it be applied to history? This was a question which, in various forms, greatly exercised the controversialists of the 1850s. I quote from one of the pamphlets of the day in which these questions were asked:

> Is the subject suitable for Education? Is it an exercise of the mind? Is it not better left till Education is completed? Is it not sufficiently attractive to ensure a voluntary attention to it? Is it a convenient subject for Examination? Where is the standard author like Thucydides, etc.? If there is no standard author, how are the comparative merits of the candidates to be judged? Will it not supersede those subjects where a severer discipline is required?[4]

We cannot fail to catch the hostile ring of these questions. But even those who were in favor of the new discipline found the questions difficult to answer. J. A. Froude, writing in 1855, struggled to find some more or less inerrant text on which the study of modern history could be based. There were lacking, he complained, those writers, who abounded in the ancient world, who were not only distinct, detailed, and lucid, but, "best of all, may be followed with all but implicit credence."[5] This is an amazing statement from a historian. It shows how deeply rooted was the idea that ancient texts were somehow more truthful than modern ones, and therefore more suitable as a basis for an academic commentary.

This search for an all but infallible authority worthy of an academic commentary is exemplified in the little book which did more than anything else to secure the election of Montagu Burrows as the first Chichele Professor of Modern History in 1862. He was a man of the reformed Oxford. A naval man by profession, he retired, read the School of Law and Modern History, set himself up as a coach in the new school, and wrote a book to teach others what books they should read. Gunnery officer of HMS *Excellent* in 1852; Professor in 1862. He was immensely surprised: "not even my First Class astonished me more" – especially, he added, "as some of the five electors were Liberals." However, his little guide to academic strategy, *Pass and Class* as he called it, met an undoubted need at a time when colleges had no tutors in the new subjects. For English history he recommended Lingard as the chief authority, though with the warning that "even for more hasty readers some other view of English History besides Lingard's will be desirable. That author, though quite the best, on the whole, that can be followed, exhibits the tendencies which may be expected from a Romanist by birth and conviction." In addition to Lingard, and as a counter-weight to him, there was Hume; and there was a new book in three volumes which had recently appeared – the *Annals of England*, a work which avoided all dangerous tendencies by having no thread of discourse whatsoever. But above them all towered one final authority: "The Professor of Modern History, whose lectures it will always be found worthwhile, whatever the pressure of work may be, to attend, will be the living reference on all obscure and controverted points."

This search for an authority solid enough to bear the weight of an academic discipline now raises a smile. But the universities of Europe had been built up since the twelfth century on the discipline of commentary and disputation on an authoritative text, and even the revolutionaries of the 1850s knew no other way of going about the business of academic study. I find, for instance, the following notice dated April 21, 1863: "The Regius Professor of Modern History will read with his Catechetical class this term the History of England, commencing with the Roman Conquest of Britain, and using as his Textbook the *Annals of England*."

"To read" meant, in the jargon of the medieval schools, "to go through and comment on a basic text," and this is precisely what the Regius Professor was doing. And if we ask how he did this, we have the answer in Sidney Lee's biography of Edward VII. The Prince of Wales came to Oxford in 1859 and had special lectures from the Regius Professor. Four other carefully chosen members of Christ Church were, in the rich words of the royal biographer, "suffered to join the Prince at his special courses": "The Professor's lectures took the form of epigrammatic comments on the *Annals of England* as he hurriedly turned over the pages."[6]

The Prince seems to have been singularly unimpressed by the annual record of Parliaments, statutes, murrains, deaths, pestilences, famines, and the foundation of colleges thus cursorily wafted before his eyes. What was wrong with it all? Some of the professor's lack of success might be put down to the Prince's stupidity, but there were other explanations less flattering to academic pride. Could it be that there was a certain lack of method in the whole procedure, and that the idea of a "living reference on all obscure and controverted points" was defective; even perhaps that the whole notion of "reading" the *Annals of England* was absurd?

The truth was that history had attained academic status in 1850 on a wave of opposition to theological dogmatism and impatience with ancient restrictions, without anyone being clear whether the subject had a method, or a public, or indeed whether it was a recognizable subject at all. These were questions which had yet to be answered. For the first seventeen years of its academical existence "history was struggling out of that condition in which it was looked on as no special or definite study, but as part of that general mass of things, which every gentleman should know." These words were written in 1867 by J. R. Green, one of the most sensitive and eager observers of the historical scene, and all the evidence we have confirms the truth of his observation. Freeman pronounced that the History School in these years was "an easy School for rich men," and the Regius Professor said that its purpose was "the better education of the gentry." The surviving examination papers tell the same story. They are printed on blue notepaper, with a space (a small space) left for the answers, and the questions have a lofty indifference to the finer points of historical science. All the history papers were papers on set books, but the books set, besides being secondary authorities, were mostly those of a previous age – Smollett, Hume, Robertson, Lingard, Gibbon, and the by now venerable Hallam, with Guizot and Ranke just beginning to make an appearance. The difficulty of finding a list of writers whose works could be read with "all but implicit credence" could scarcely be better illustrated than by this ragged, and by 1850 largely antiquated, army.

II

By 1867, however, the picture had substantially changed. History was on the point of being separated from law; the attempt to link the study of history with the study of set textbooks had been abandoned, and in their place special subjects to be studied from the original sources had been introduced. Most important of all, Stubbs had just arrived in Oxford from his country parish as professor.

Stubbs is a name always to be mentioned with veneration in the Oxford History School. He is without doubt the greatest of Oxford historians, as Maitland is equally preeminent among Cambridge men. They have no peers. During the seventeen years in which he was Regius Professor, from 1867 to 1884, the History School changed from being "an easy School for rich men" into an academic discipline of a serious kind.

It gradually became clear that if academic history was ever to have any cohesion or intellectual form it would have to find it in some other procedure than the commenting on the work of earlier historians. The cohesion would have to come, somehow, from within the subject itself. The discovery of lines of organization within the historical process was one of the great problems of the day. Even men who had not heard of Marx and who looked with horror on Darwin – the two most powerful organizers of history in the decade after 1850 – could not altogether escape the influence of Newman's *Essay on the Development of Christian Doctrine*,[7] or Buckle's *History of Civilization*. At the most lowly level of all, everyone recognized that the mere fact of continuity in history provided some thin line of causal connection and raised history ever so slightly above the level of discrete happenings. The insistence on continuity was the earliest, because the least controversial, of all methods of organizing history from within. It was a shallow stream of thought that bound together history so conceived, but it had a long ancestry, and it only received its death blow the other day when the "continuous history of England" from the beginning ceased to be required from all honors students in modern history in this University.

Another method of organizing history from within was discovered in relating events to their physical background. In 1857 Buckle started to publish his *History of Civilization in England* with Parker's of Oxford. His main contribution to general historical ideas lay in his insistence on the interaction between physical environment and the development of human faculties. I do not suppose his views ever had wide acceptance in Oxford; but they helped to draw attention to geography. In the search for systematic elements in history, geography recommended itself as more substantial than bare continuity, and less monotonous than the class-war. It had a long popularity, and it held its own, in the mundane form of "starred" questions, from 1886 till 1932.

But neither continuity nor geography provided the Oxford historians with the principle of order which the survival of the subject as an academic discipline required. This was provided by the study of constitutional history, and it was here that Stubbs made his massive contribution to academic history. Constitutional history was a wonderful instrument for the purposes with which the History School was coming to be identified. Intellectually it was highly respectable. It was systematic; it gave an organic unity to a large assortment of otherwise disconnected events. It was difficult. In Stubbs's famous phrase, it could "scarcely be approached without an effort"; and this was important in proving that history was no longer an easy school for rich men.

Constitutional history helped to make the subject both severe and secular. Besides all this, it had still higher claims to regard. The central theme of constitutional history was Parliament, the long-matured and best gift of England to the world. Its origins could be traced back to the dim recesses of the German forests, and its development could be brought forward through the most famous events in English history to the moment at which it seemed destined to enlarge the area of freedom and responsibility in this country and throughout the world. Here was the noblest and most generous theme for secular history ever propounded.

With constitutional history firmly established as the central theme of the Oxford History School, we might imagine that Stubbs would have left

Oxford in 1884 a happy man. Surely he had had a success beyond anything that most professors can hope for. Yet he was not happy. So far as his sober and level-headed attitude to life and his satisfaction in original work allowed, he left Oxford a disappointed man, passing severe strictures on the School of History which had grown up round him. Since the school is essentially the same now as it was in 1884, these strictures, so far as they were justified, are as cogent now as they were then. It is therefore worth asking the cause of Stubbs's disillusionment.

In his Inaugural Lecture of 1867 Stubbs had spoken with confidence of the "good time coming" in historical studies with a historical school built "not upon Hallam and Palgrave and Kemble and Froude and Macaulay, but on the abundant collected and arranged materials now in course of publication."[8] He foresaw a time not far ahead when history could cease to be a mere task for children, or an instrument "to qualify men to make effective speeches to ignorant hearers, and to indite brilliant articles for people who only read periodicals," and become a thing "loved and cultivated for its own sake," entailing a "widespread historical training which will make imposture futile and adulteration unprofitable."

What had gone wrong with this vision? To put it bluntly, England had not kept pace with Germany and was falling every year further behind. In 1867 Stubbs had been aware, but not I think very keenly aware, of the great work of the editors of the *Monumenta Germaniae Historica*, and, after all, he could reflect, England had its own Record Publications, and its own Rolls Series, in which more than seventy volumes had been published in the ten years between 1857 and 1867. In view of this record, Stubbs may be excused for not having understood in 1867 that the situation in England was quite different from that in Germany. By 1877, still more by 1884, he could not fail to mark the difference. In England the flow of printed sources had fallen off; many deficiencies in the scholarship of those already published had been disclosed. In Germany not only had the work of publication gone on apace, and at a conspicuously higher level of scholarship than in England – a painful difference which would be even more marked if Stubbs's own publications were removed – but the work of the German editors was being supplemented every year by a more and more formidable array of monographs. It is fashionable now to sneer at these monuments of Teutonic diligence, but no serious scholar will feel inclined to sneer; and to anyone who saw it happen, it must have appeared the most prodigious event in the history of scholarship. There had never been anything like it before.

The Germans were conquering every area of history, ancient and modern, papal and European as well as German. In English history alone, Stubbs could enumerate the important contributions of Schmid, Lappenberg, Mauer, Pauli, Ranke, Jaffé, Dümmler, Wattenbach, and Sickel;

and he might have added the most devoted of all, Felix Liebermann, whose earliest work must already have reached him. By contrast the English historians were not only increasingly sunk in English history – "Carlyle's Frederick II," said Stubbs, "is really the only great work on German or European history which has appeared in England for nearly half a century" – but the steady jog-trot of tutorials and examinations was killing the historical aspirations of tutors and undergraduates alike.

The testimonies to the contrast between academic history in England and on the Continent in the period after 1870 are quite unanimous, and almost everyone who knew the two systems spoke with disparagement of the English one. Briefly the contrast lay in the much greater scientific seriousness of the Continental system. A Belgian visitor to Oxford in 1884 found the main work of the school in the hands of thirteen tutors teaching a rather elementary kind of history with no profound study (not even in the special subjects) of original sources, to three or four hundred students, most of whom aimed at getting a BA "without nourishing for History any scientific passion."[9] I am quite sure we must acquiesce in this description and regard it as not very different from the description that the same observer might have given today.

Whether we acquiesce in the disparaging tone of the comparison with France and Germany is another matter. Personally I am quite sure that the Oxford tutors of the 1870s and 1880s chose, or were impelled along, the path which was best for our particular needs. The simple discipline which these tutors devised has served us well. They not only made history an academic discipline suitable for the needs of their time, but they perfected a method of general education that has never been bettered. They made the very deficiencies which had hindered the early growth of history as an academic subject – its lack of certainty, of system, and of generality – into a virtue, using these defects as a vehicle for enlarging the minds of men who would meet just these conditions in the world they were to rule. As the stream of dissertations from Germany poured in on Stubbs, the Oxford tutors concentrated not on training historians, or even on communicating any very subtle understanding of history, but on encouraging their pupils to express their thoughts with ease and clarity, to argue with sense and vigor, and to enlarge their practical sympathies and experience by contact with the statesmen and institutions of the past. Long walks, muddy boots, an abundance of discursive talk were the features of their method that most impressed an observer of the system fifty years ago, and Sir Lewis Namier, a greater historian than his tutor, has acknowledged the debt which his writing owed to the sudden illuminating criticism of A. L. Smith: "You have built a long drive to a very small house." Thirty years ago, when I was an undergraduate, all these features were still present, and retained their power, as I can testify with gratitude, to set the minds of the young on fire. Today, the boots and the mud, and some of the discursiveness which they encouraged, have gone. Perhaps the talk and the criticism have lost something thereby.

Meanwhile Oxford threw out most of the historians whose works are still read, and naturally many of them spoke ill of Oxford in return, and taught others to envy the universities of Waitz, Wattenbach, Bresslau, Dümmler, and Sybel. The writings of these scholars, in contrast to those of their Oxford contemporaries, are still indispensable to other scholars today. We, who have seen the fate of their universities, will not be disposed to envy them. Nevertheless, the German system, with all its faults, had one great virtue. It introduced into the universities the atmosphere of the workshop in which everyone was collaborating in original creation. Whatever our virtues, I do not think that this has commonly been one of them. Intellectually it has been our greatest failure.

The creator of the German system was preeminently a single man – Ranke, the greatest academic historian the world has ever known. The seminar which he started in Berlin in 1825 deserves the same place in modern history that the foundation of a new religious order has in the Middle Ages. One cannot mention academic history without mentioning this extraordinary man who united the whole force of German romanticism and German scientific genius in a single machine of awe-inspiring power for the production of historical scholarship. It was the contemplation of this creation which made Stubbs feel humbled and frustrated. Nor do I think that all the efforts made since Stubbs's day to graft on to our History School a school of advanced learning which would emulate the virtues and achievements of the school of Ranke have come within a thousand miles of succeeding in this purpose. There were too many forces working in the opposite direction, and Vinogradoff who came nearest to establishing in Oxford a seminar on the Continental model was driven to his often repeated conclusion that "the young men in Oxford do not love the higher education."[10]

So be it. We need have no regrets. But we should know what we have missed. I was privileged to have the friendship of the last of the great scholars who came to maturity in Ranke's lifetime, and whose methods were those of the great master. He was a Frenchman who combined the scientific fervor of the German schools with the marvelous rapidity and intelligence of France. I refer to Ferdinand Lot, and I cannot forbear, as an epitaph on the greatest age of European historical scholarship, to describe my last meeting with him. It was in the spring of 1945. Twelve years earlier in Paris I had attended his seminars on Carolingian history. Even then they had seemed to belong to the passionate intellectual life of an earlier age, for Lot's first book had been published in 1891. In 1945 I found him in his paintless flat in the suburbs of Paris at Fontenay-aux-Roses.

He received me with kindly emotion, and seized with birdlike avidity and pleasure on the few cigarettes and chocolates I had brought. His table was heaped with the familiar piles of fiches from which he produced with an air of innocent triumph his reports on his pupils of twelve years earlier. The best of them, his son-in-law Jean-Berthold Mahn, had been killed in the war. Most of his comforts and friends had gone, leaving him a lonely figure in a shabby world. Yet he spoke of the war with remarkable resilience and insisted – rightly as it turned out – that it would be over sooner than I would allow. I left him, thinking that the next news I should have would be of his death, for he was then nearly eighty. But for the next seven years scarcely a year passed without bringing some new work from his pen, on the population of medieval towns, on the Barbarian invasions, on the art of war in the Middle Ages, on the letters of Gerbert; works not of his finest quality, but showing all his old intelligence and originality, the fruits of a lifetime's reading. He died in 1952, and with him the epoch in historical writing and teaching inaugurated by Ranke in Berlin in 1825 may be said to have ended. Neither the excitements nor the achievements of that epoch can now be recalled, much less restored, here or anywhere else; but we should remember them when we compare what we are with what we might have been.

III

We need, I say, have no regrets that we did not take the road recommended by our critics from the time of Vinogradoff onwards. But only on condition that we can maintain the peculiar mixture of intellectual excitement and practical usefulness which characterized the Oxford school in its most prosperous days. At the beginning of this lecture I gave some reasons for thinking that this mixture has lost some of its first beauty. Let me now examine one or two aspects of this decline.

In the first place: English constitutional history. It is hard to think that it can ever regain the position which it held eighty years ago. Historical facts, for many of us at least, simply do not arrange themselves in the way which Stubbs and his contemporaries found so illuminating. It has lost its emotional appeal and most of its intellectual coherence. If we compare the work of Stubbs with the work on the history of Parliament now in progress we cannot fail to seize the difference. Stubbs's work, difficult though it is, communicates a vision; what we are now engaged on is a series of post-mortems, and the result will be a book of reference for scholars, fascinating, indispensable for many subjects, but not visionary.

Constitutional history, as Stubbs and his contemporaries conceived it, has been pushed further and further into the background in the History

School, and the same thing has happened to all the simple lines of development and rules of coherence which they devised. Rightly so, in my view. But what has taken the place of this familiar framework? On the whole it has been replaced by a greater elaboration, a greater efficiency, a more professional air, and a more exacting standard of information.

One of our difficulties is that the founders of our school were only too successful in proving to themselves and to the world that history was not an easy study for rich men and that it had a discipline of its own. They perfected a syllabus and a system of examination which was coherent and rigorous. Their success made radical change difficult and for a long time impossible. But their virtues naturally were achieved only at a cost. The main part of this cost was the omission of those parts of human experience which are not related to public affairs. At the time this was a wise omission. But it cut short many of the most promising developments in the historical interests of the earlier years of the nineteenth century – the interest, for example, in art and architecture, liturgy and worship, and in most aspects of European history which have never found a secure academic home with us. Nothing is more striking about the Oxford historians of the late nineteenth century than their disregard of everything in history that could not be related to institutions and politics. They left out that which is most interesting in the past in order to concentrate on that which was practically and academically most serviceable. In a rough and ready way these exclusions, which were in any case determined by instinctive sympathies rather than any consideration of policy, were sensible enough. In the shaping of a subject suitable for men of the world weary of dogmatic wrangles they were necessary for the survival of history as an academic discipline. By some instinctive process of natural selection, the study of history was sternly canalized to ensure its survival.

But of course the mood and circumstances which guided this process of canalization are now as remote as anything in our history. The weariness with dogma and the preference for large indefinite truths finds little sympathy today. Do we not almost all prefer clarity and definition, in however small a field, to a large-hearted imprecision? I do not say we are right or wrong, but the fact is obvious wherever we look. Or again, the circumstances. The founders of our school were conservatives acutely aware of the need to withdraw at some points in order to preserve their central position: they were defenders of the Church who recognized that unless they secularized the universities, enlarged their studies and adapted them to the world, they would all be swept away in a rising tide which looked very menacing in 1850. I applaud their purpose and admire their success. More has been preserved than the most far-sighted could have expected. But the same prescription will not ensure the survival for another hundred years of the things they cared about, or of anything else. Nor will the history which they formed into an academic discipline minister now, as it then undoubtedly did, to the stability of society and the greatness of England. As I look down the list of publications of my academic ancestor Montagu Burrows, I feel myself drawn into a world which disappeared for ever in 1914: *Constitutional Progress, Imperial England, Parliament and the Church of England, Wiclif's Place in History, Alfred the Great, Worthies of All Souls*. These are the titles of some of his publications, and in them we see the outlines of the system he helped to create. And if the titles suggest a world essentially secure, I assure you that the contents do so far more. They were wise and right to do so, and it would be folly to forget all the lessons of a century of effort. But even more foolish to learn no others.

The question, how far the undergraduate study of history can be enlarged without destroying the subject as an academic discipline, is one of immense difficulty. The answer of the great generation of Oxford tutors was in favor of limitation. They broke with law, which had at first provided a systematic background to historical change; they ignored the study of literature, which at one time stood in the syllabus. We can see why they did this. It made the subject suitable for practical men, and kept it manageable. But there are many reasons why this is no longer sufficient. In the first place, the study of history has lost much of the practical drive which made this limitation sensible. History will always provide sensible men with a discipline that can be turned to account in practical affairs, but this purpose can no longer provide – as it did in Oxford sixty or seventy years ago – a main incentive to its academic study. The world does not now want the institutions of our past. But there are other fields of experience, some of them very distant in time, that have never been more alive, never more necessary to us. It is these that now make history worthy of academic study. The study of environment can never lose its interest; but all this is preparatory to the study of the thoughts and visions, moods and emotions and devotions of articulate people. These are the valuable deposit of the past.

Whether or not you agree with this, at least we have receded too far from the simple certainties of our founding fathers to retain their self-imposed limitations. We have abandoned continuous political history and compulsory geographical questions; even constitutional history is now optional. We have established new posts in the history of art, science, medieval philosophy, and in other branches of history unknown to the old Oxford curriculum; in St. Anthony's, in the new Oriental Institute, in the Institute of Social Anthropology, there are historical developments of the greatest interest; the Ashmolean is equipped to make a contribution to our studies quite undreamt of a hundred years ago. In all this, have we simply made broad our phylacteries; or have we been responding to the changing interests of the world and the excitement of discovery? I should hope the latter; yet our best friends might think we historians have not quite known what to do with our new adornments. The greatest developments in historical thought have been on the periphery of the old syllabus, the centre has remained comparatively unchanged. It is quietly ceasing to be the centre. Yet our best history graduates, if they consider their future, will be cautious of venturing far from the well-trodden paths of English politics and institutions; how much more, therefore, our undergraduates?

There is no easy solution to these problems. We cannot maintain the old limitations because we have already abandoned the framework which made them intelligible. We cannot enlarge the syllabus without abandoning something already there. Yet unless we enlarge it we commit ourselves to a view of historical study which will become every day more archaic. In this predicament I make only one suggestion: that we should boldly allow an individual choice in the omission of some large part of the traditional syllabus; and that we should allow this remission to anyone who submits, instead of some of the examination papers now required, a piece of work, or perhaps several pieces of work, written at leisure during the three years of undergraduate life. I am not thinking here only of dissertations, or pieces of original research, but also of surveys of problems or of tracts of history which have at present no place in our syllabus. The business would need a good deal of regulation; but it would provide a way of escape from the dilemma I have outlined. It would enlarge the area of freedom and bring new possibilities of growth; it would open the whole school more fully to the influence of our newly established professors, readers, and lecturers. It might, even at this late hour, without submitting us to the evils of the German professorial system, give us some of the advantages of their intellectual variety.

It would be rash to claim too many advantages for one small change, which may in any case find no acceptance. But I may add one further advantage which I foresee from such a change: it would provide some relief from the dull despotism of examination papers. I speak with feeling on this subject, for one of the saddest experiences of a tutor's life is reading these papers, and to examine them is slavery. They have some usefulness as a method of displaying intellectual powers, but none at all in helping to develop these powers in mature people. Too often a comparison between the entrance papers of schoolboys and the final papers of honors candidates suggests that the result of three years' study has been to add weight without muscle, and to crush precision of thought and lucidity of style under a barbarous weight of information, or – failing this – to envelop thought and style alike in a cloud of ambiguity. I do not wish to put the matter too strongly. But let us remember that our modern examination papers replaced an earlier well-tried system of examination, which had in practice become absurd. As an exercise of the mind they belong to a period, not very long ago, when it was necessary to prove against a host of enemies that history was a suitable subject for examination. The danger now is that, far from seeming unsuitable for examination, it will seem suitable for nothing else.

On this subject I may quote one last witness writing when the academic study of history was in its infancy. The writer had been the greatest Oxford man of his day, but he had had no part in the reforms of 1850. Quite the contrary. A large part of the reforms were a reaction against his views. He was in exile, but he remained the most eloquent exponent of the principles for which Oxford stood. He was engaged in laying the foundation of a new University, founded, as he believed, on truths that Oxford had rejected. Nevertheless the old University had had virtues that he feared might be lost in the new zeal for righteousness. Oxford had at least not been a "foundry or a treadmill":

> Even if it merely brought a number of young men together for three or four years, and then sent them away again, as the University of Oxford is said to have done some sixty years since ... (this system produced men) with more thought, more mind, more philosophy, more true enlargement, than those earnest but ill-used persons who are forced to load their minds with a score of subjects against an examination, who have too much on their hands to indulge themselves in thinking or investigation, who devour premiss and conclusion together with indiscriminate greediness... and who too often, as might be expected, when their period of education is passed, throw up all they have learned in disgust, having gained nothing really by their anxious labours, except perhaps the habit of application.[11]

These words of J. H. Newman were written in 1852, when the Oxford School of Law and Modern History had just come into existence. The threat which he foresaw is one which hangs heavily over academic history today. Such persons as he describes are to be found in distressing numbers up and down the country. I speak of the country as a whole and not specially of Oxford; but we have a special responsibility, for it was here that many of the decisions were taken which are still the effective guides to academic historical studies in this country. If there are such persons among us as Newman described, I plead for their freedom. They have a whole world of historical enjoyment and enlightenment before them, and almost nothing to lose but their chains. Enlightened enjoyment cannot be ordained by legislation, but something can be done to encourage it. We have, on an average, undergraduates who are cleverer, better trained, more hard-working than those for whom the English system of academic history was first developed. Our situation has changed; our interests have changed. To meet these changes we must be prepared to sacrifice something of academic convenience, and even of theoretical perfection. This was the problem that faced the University in 1850. We know the answer of that time. In the face of bitter criticism, the distinguished clergymen of the Royal Commission and their clerical friends in Oxford chose to abandon an ancient academic system, alleged by the Hebdomadal Board to be almost perfect, in order to "restore the University to the nation." They destroyed some of the virtues of the old University for uncertain advantages. And, despite their mistakes, they were right to do so, for they judged that it was pointless to perfect a system of academic studies if this entailed a devotion to subjects of ever narrower and narrower interest. Their decision is one that deserves to be reaffirmed now, and especially by us, the historians of Oxford, the true and undoubted heirs of the revolution of 1850.

6

The Historical Experience

In 1524 the executors of the late Chief Justice of Common Pleas, Sir Robert Rede, endowed three courses of lectures on ancient literature, logic, and philosophy. In doing this they could not have imagined that they were opening the way for a sizable number of lectures on history. The only place in their scheme where history could have found a place would have been as a relatively minor branch of ancient literature. Yet, when in 1858 the Rede Lectures were reorganized, it was inevitable – even in Cambridge which took less readily than Oxford to history as an academic subject – that history would take a large share of whatever remained of Sir Robert Rede's benefaction. How has it come about that historians have been able to put their scythes so freely into other men's harvests? It is really a most unlikely development with many sides to it, and I can do no more than provide an outline answer, concentrating on the fundamental question of the change in the nature and importance of our experience of the past, which has been reflected in the titles of many Rede Lectures since 1858, and not least in the title of this. Since experience is something that can best be described from within, I will venture to begin with the most primitive elements in my own historical experience; and then enquire why experiences of this kind have seemed more important during the last one hundred and fifty years than ever before. Finally I shall ask what kind of importance, if any, such experiences are likely to have in future.

I

In the complete historical experience there are three stages: first the individual perceptions which are the bricks out of which our historical edifices are built; then the ramifications of these perceptions to every area of social or private life to form large areas of intelligibility; and finally the arranging of this material to form works of art of a special and distinctive kind. These are, as I conceive, the activities proper to a historian, and all three stages deserve a careful study. But this afternoon there is time to examine only the first and most primitive stage of all – the sources and characteristics of the initial perceptions.

Nothing in the past is usable until it has been the subject of a vivid perception, and it is important to know what it is we are expecting to perceive. The situation of the historian is like this. He has in front of him some object: it may be a charter, or a prayer, or a legal document, or a work of art, or a symbolic object like a crown, a throne, a scepter; or something of common use like a word or a pot, or the foundations of an ancient hall, or the arrangement of chapels in a great church. He who views these things as a historian is not concerned with their esthetic qualities, but only with the ways in which they express the minds, intentions, problems, and limitations of those who created them or for whom they were created.

If it is a charter he will want to know not simply what it was designed to do, but (even more) what social conventions, intellectual equipment, legal and linguistic resources and technical skills, went into its making. He will ask what situation it was designed to correct or promote, and what forces brought it into existence. The historian's whole attention is concentrated on the perception of its relationship with the physical and mental world to which it originally belonged. He looks at an object as a biologist might look at a fossil of an extinct species – as a fragment from which he hopes to create the complete structure of the creature to which it belonged. And both the historian and the biologist are able to do this for the same reason – that there is a logic in the forms of the past which requires that the parts fit together in a certain way and in no other. In a historical enquiry there is only one test of the importance of an event or an object: that is the number of ramifications which it suggests and the size of the area which it illuminates. The most insignificant object may have a greater power of illumination than the most splendid. In my own area of study a village charter may do more for us than Magna Carta; a single word in an obscure text more than many State papers. Importance in any other sense is unimportant.

Very often the first impressions are very discouraging. The words of the document in front of us may make grammatical sense, but their historical meaning may be entirely hidden. Then suddenly, perhaps from some single clue – the form of a name, or the identification of a person, or the appearance of a familiar formula – light dawns. It is an experience like that in childhood when we are lost. At one minute we are surrounded by meaningless objects conveying nothing except incipient panic. Then something, maybe a gate, or the shape of a curbstone, stands out as recognizable; a small area of intelligibility appears in the midst of chaos; it grows larger and takes in more objects; the scene fits together and we are safe. That is what it is like to have in its most primitive form the historical experience I am speaking of.

I think any historian must have had this experience of a sudden perception which gradually makes sense of a whole large area of the past many thousands of times. The extraordinary sense of peace and satisfaction that it brings is never diminished. Yet I cannot remember without emotion the first time it ever happened to me. It was in October 1927; I was fifteen. Like many thousands of our young every year I was facing the depressing prospect of writing an essay on King Henry VII. Acres of facts of intolerable dreariness and frightening unintelligibility stretched out in all directions, numbing the senses. Then suddenly, out of nowhere, the precious words formed themselves in my mind. I can see them yet. They were: "Henry VII was the first King of England who was a business man." Wrong, of course; or right only in a rather peculiar sense. But no words can now express the illumination they then brought with them. Tracks appeared in the jungle; it was possible to advance. Heaven knows the tracks were few enough; perhaps not more than the prongs of Morton's famous fork; but they sufficed. The thing worked. Crude and naive though it was, it was a historical experience as genuine as any I have ever had. So let me not blush to examine it more closely, for it had most of the characteristics which we shall find in the more important perceptions we are soon to examine. First, it was very sharp and vivid; secondly, it had a private and personal significance; and thirdly, it worked. All are important.

As to the first point, it is more important that the initial perception should be sharp and vivid than that it should be true. Truth comes from error more easily than from confusion. It is only by having a vivid perception that an energetic search can begin; without it, there is only languid and aimless confusion.

Second, the initial formulation must have in it some urgency of personal significance. My own poor perception about Henry VII came from a large hidden body of experience of daily life in a northern industrial town – Newcastle, no less, from a romantic picture of the unedifying expedients which keep life going in these surroundings, and from the sound of voices discussing the intricacies of a family business far into the night. Of course, I did not consciously associate Henry VII with all this, but I see now that such force as the perception had came from this source.

Then lastly, the initial perception must work – that is to say it must not break down when it is applied to a large number of apparently unconnected actions and situations. The best perceptions have many ramifications. They bring together, within a single system, many apparently disconnected and trivial acts or habits which have not been brought together before.

Even the thread of a single word as it is seen running through a period of time may provide a view of a changing scene perceived in a new way or with a new clarity. A few weeks ago for example my attention was drawn to the word "infallible," which had a portentous impact on the world in 1870 when it was incorporated in a famous doctrinal statement. The ripples of that impact have not yet subsided and there is a certain interest in observing the humble origin of this innocent word. The fortunes of words are among the least well-charted areas of the past, but it takes very little research to discover that the Latin world got along for many centuries without feeling the need for this powerful and unusual tool. It first appears as one of the novelties of the twelfth century to which we owe so much of our traditional intellectual equipment. The point of departure would seem to have been a single occurrence of the word *infallibilis* in the Latin translation of Aristotle's *Topics* which became current about the middle of the twelfth century. It is there used as an example of a false proposition in the phrase "a geometrician *cannot be deceived*"; and from this unpromising start it made its way, slowly at first, and then with increasing momentum in the thirteenth century, into common speech. At first it seems to have been used chiefly to describe the power behind the unvarying processes of Nature. It was in this sense that it was used by Gerald of Wales in about 1190 to describe the way in which dogs identify their masters by their smell, "as if Nature had implanted the whole infallible power of experience in the nose." Then the uses of the word were extended to describe the certainty of the senses, the truth of dogma, the conclusions of geometry, the attributes of God. Thomas Aquinas used the word in all these senses; and lesser mortals, historians and others, were beginning at the same time to use it for all kinds of events or expectations which were as certain as anything can be. Shortly it became established in the vernacular language; and finally – but perhaps not until the seventeenth century – it reached its peak as a uniquely emphatic way of expressing the highest power of the papacy.

Words are only straws in the wind, but as we follow this word's path, the new view of Nature which it expressed, and the various applications of the word in theology and common speech, it throws light on the search for fundamental certainty in the thirteenth century and later, which can indeed be seen in many ways, but is here unconsciously displayed in the slight and unregarded symptom of an immense desire.

To follow the ramifications of these simple things is one of the greatest pleasures of the historian. The difficulty is knowing when to stop, and it is better to stop too early than too late. So I will only observe that in all these ramifications we seek simply to extend the vividness and variety of the areas of intelligibility in the past. The intelligibility we obtain is not open to any demonstration by logic or experiment. The only guarantee of truth is the internal consistency of the evidence, and the converging support which each bit adds to the rest. We seek congruity between the various bits of evidence; we seek congruity also with our own experience of the possible. It must not be beyond our powers to conceive that we might ourselves have thought or behaved thus in the circumstances and under the pressures which our observations of the past have brought to light. There is no further certainty in history than this combination of coherence and intelligibility. And it must be confessed that in the end there is a frailty at the basis of history, a lack of logical robustness and systematic doctrine, which in an academic discipline would have shocked the founder of this lecture, and indeed any sensible man, who thought about the matter, almost until the middle of the nineteenth century. How then can we account for the rapid rise after this time of an academic subject that lacked the qualities previously considered essential for any important body of truth, and for academic studies especially? Why did a subject with such frail foundations succeed in taking its place alongside, and sometimes replacing, older disciplines that had long boasted their unshakable security?

II

The simple answer to these questions is that quite suddenly historical perceptions were found to have unexpectedly important consequences. This happened in many ways during a fairly short space of time, and the way in which it happened can best be understood by taking a few examples. It would be easy to give many more, but the four I shall give will suffice to define the wide area in which historical perceptions intervened with startling results in the decade from 1835 to 1845 – that is, in the years immediately preceding the introduction of history into our universities as a serious academic subject. In each of our examples we shall watch the way in which a simple historical perception overturned a whole set of previously firmly held assumptions and attitudes.

It is appropriate that we should start with a great Cambridge figure – Charles Darwin: appropriate not only for what he means in this place, but also because he is the central historical thinker of the period we are concerned with though no one would have been more surprised or outraged than he to hear me say so. Also, his private journals and diary, together with his autobiography and his published *Journal of the Voyage of HMS Beagle*, provide a perfectly documented example of the growth of a historical perception, and at the same time illustrate the transition from an old way of looking at the past to a new.[1]

The general outline of the story is not in dispute. Everyone knows that the voyage of the *Beagle* which lasted from December 1831 to October 1836 was the turning-point in Darwin's life. When he set out, he thought of the past as western Europeans had long thought of it, as a stable and, in its main lines, unchanging state of affairs going back to the moment of Creation some 6,000 to 10,000 years ago. Of course, no one had ever thought that the past was completely stable. All sublunar things were subject to mutability, and this mutability showed itself chiefly in a tendency to decay: "Change and decay in all around I see," wrote the author of "Abide with me" in 1847, and he might have written this at any time for a thousand years. On this view, it was a main task of all good men to arrest decay and corruption, and to restore institutions and doctrines to their primitive excellence. This was the human task; and recently geologists had shown that Nature provided evidence of a comparable divine task. Nature too had a tendency to decay. This took the form of species dying out and being replaced by new species broadly related to them. This discovery simply extended to Nature a phenomenon which had long been known in human affairs. It was reasonable to suppose that what men were required to do in human affairs, God by reformation and new creation did in Nature. The whole picture was perfectly consistent and reasonable. For Darwin, who was a seriously orthodox and pious Christian, the fossils of South America and the great variety of species he observed presented no immediate problem. He probably returned from his voyage with his outline of the past troubled yet unchanged. But when he got home and began to examine his notebooks, a new historical perception leapt out at him and changed all his views. We shall look at only three moments in the process, for they are moments in the growth of every new historical perception: first the moment of observation; then the new perception; then the moment of final commitment.

First, the moment of observation. Darwin later looked back to one date in particular as the source of all his later views. It was the arrival of the *Beagle* at a small group of islands, the Galapagos Islands, in the Pacific in September 1835. This was how he described what he saw:

> The natural history of these islands is eminently curious, and well deserves attention. Most of the organic productions are aboriginal creations found nowhere else... Considering the small size of the islands, we feel the more astonished at the number of their aboriginal beings, and at their confined range... Both in space and time, we seem to be brought somewhat near to that great fact – that mystery of mysteries – the first appearance of new beings on this earth.[2]

These words, though only published in 1845, probably express his first reaction to what he had seen ten years earlier. He was surprised by the large number of otherwise unrecorded aboriginal species in a small and remote group of islands. But what they at first suggested was not evolution, but Creation: the islands were a sort of little Eden "somewhere near" to the state of the original creation. His main task, however, was not yet to explain, but to measure and record what he saw. Like a historian examining and describing piece by piece the contents of a rich and uncatalogued archive, he was too busy noting the details of shape and size of beaks, tails, plumage, bone-structure, and so on, to have any time for new general thoughts. He catalogued and marveled.

Then came the second moment: the birth of a new perception. Darwin provides the date: it was in about March 1837 (in his cautious phase) that he was "greatly struck" by what he had observed in 1835.[3] The point that "greatly struck" him was that the many new species he had observed especially on these small islands could better be explained, not as the relics of a state of affairs somewhere near the moment of Creation, but as the result of an unimaginably long process of transmutation.

He got this new view in March; and in July he opened the first of four notebooks to follow up its consequences. These scrapbooks vividly reflect the turmoil of his mind as he turned his mind in all directions for objects that might bear on what he repeatedly calls, without defining it, "my view," "my bold view." In general he seems to have had no doubt that his view was right, that the whole of the past was a scene of endless movement and adaptation to changing conditions; but he could not yet understand either the mechanism, or the limits, or the driving force of the process. With all his growing certainty he suffered much from discouragement and exhaustion. In October 1838 he wrote:

> Frittered these foregoing days away in working on transmutation theories... all September read a great deal on many subjects; thought much about religion. Beginning of October ditto.[4]

It was in these seemingly empty and aimless days that his historical perception suddenly became clear and complete: "I first thought of selection owing to struggle," he wrote. And elsewhere he tells us where the thought came from: it came from reading Malthus's thirty-year-old essay on the limitations imposed on human population by shortage of food. As he read he saw that he had at last precisely located the driving force which he had been looking for during the last eighteen months. Then on October 3 he recorded his own leap forward from Malthus. His journal is mutilated at this point; but after a torn-out page, some final words from Malthus remain, with Darwin's comment: "This applies to one species – I would apply it not only to population and depopulation, but extermination and production of new forms – their number and correlations."[5] These hastily scribbled words signal the final formulation of his historical perception. His new view of the whole process of history, its chronology, its dynamism, and (despite Darwin's continued optimism) the horror of the methods it employed, was complete.

I have dealt in some detail on the stages of this development, partly for its intrinsic importance; but chiefly because it is the first occasion on which we can observe a historical perception coming into existence that transformed a large area of scientific and popular thought. Modern scholars, who have never seen the world as Darwin saw it in 1831, are often puzzled by Darwin's hesitations, and have doubted the accuracy of his account. But this is to forget how well-grounded the old view of the world's history was. It represented the efforts of many centuries in reconciling reason and Revelation, and sensible people could still find the result persuasive. Now we only hear the voices we understand, and those are the voices of dissent. We forget the silent multitudes who believed or acquiesced in the old view. We forget that even those who disbelieved did not encourage disbelief in their servants. We forget also how flimsy the grounds then seemed on which Darwin proposed to destroy this great creation. He would have liked to have had proof of a traditional kind – either from first principles or from experiment. In the end he had to be content with the only kind of proof a historian can have – the proof of coherence and plausibility:

> I am actually weary of telling people that I do not pretend to adduce direct evidence of one species changing to another, but I believe that this view is in the main correct because so many phenomena can thus be grouped together and explained.[6]

Here speaks the historian. This is all a historian can ever say, but it was flimsy evidence on which to destroy a world.

We must leave Darwin in October 1838 to work out the ramifications of his new historical perception, and turn to another example of a similar process at work in Oxford in the same years. We turn to John Henry Newman, not yet Cardinal, but Fellow of Oriel College, and Vicar of the University Church of St. Mary's. He too was torn between two conflicting views of the past. One of his friends described him in 1836 as being deeply impressed with the law of change:

> Coming out of St. Mary's with me on Good Friday, he was struck by the sight of very large flakes or feathers of snow falling into the black, swollen gutter and instantly disappearing. "So," he said, quoting the quaint language of the Oriel statutes, "are human affairs tending visibly to not-to-be."[7]

This simple remark summarized the old view of human history. Human affairs decay; Newman and his friends like almost all religious reformers since the eleventh century were dedicated to the task of restoring them to their pristine purity.

But very soon we find Newman beginning to entertain a quite different picture of the past: a past in which change took place, not only by a process of decay and restoration to their primitive state by human efforts; but also, and most importantly, by a natural and benign process of development from within. In 1838, the year in which Darwin read Malthus, Newman formulated the contrast in the form of two images of truth: the one "entirely objective and detached" from time and place, but needing constantly to be kept in repair; the other evolving from age to age under the pressures of enemies threatening its destruction, and of the faithful asking for more. The first stood for the Church of England, the second for the Church of Rome. Two years earlier, Newman had had no doubt on which side he stood. But by 1838 he was not so sure. He began to picture the Roman Church as a Madonna with the Holy Child: that is, as the Church with truth in its bosom waiting until the moment had arrived for its development and appearance in the world.[8] In this simple way the seed was sown for a new historical view which would shake Newman from his sense of security, and shake with him the whole English Church.

Newman's moment of historical perception came in the Long Vacation of 1839. In June he had settled down to spend three months in the study of the Monophysites of the fifth century. He wrote:

> It was in the course of this reading that for the first time a doubt came upon me of the tenableness of Anglicanism... My stronghold was antiquity; now here in the middle of the fifth century I found, as it seemed to me, Christendom of the sixteenth and nineteenth centuries reflected. I saw my face in that mirror, and I was a Monophysite... There was an awful similitude, more awful because so silent and unimpassioned, between the dead records of the past and the feverish chronicle of the present. The shadow of the fifth century was on the sixteenth. It was like a spirit rising from the troubled waters of the old world with the shape and lineaments of the new.[9]

The historical meaning of the face that Newman had seen in the mirror was that his old concept of a stable, unchanging past was no longer tenable. The Church which had claimed to be built on a primitive and unchanging model had turned out to represent only a peculiar and repugnant variant. Development, far from being a sign of corruption, now began to appear as the mark of truth; stability, far from being a sign of primitive purity, began to appear a symptom of infertility; and infertility was the symptom of heresy.

The choice, therefore, no longer lay between stability and decay, between the primitive and the corrupt; but between the main stream of development and a series of abnormal and infertile variants in an evolutionary process. There is a striking similarity between Newman in 1839 and Darwin in 1837: they both emerged from their belief in a stable past; they were both committed to history as an evolving process; but they did not yet know how it worked.

It took Newman another six years to work out the full consequence of his new vision of the past. It was to take Darwin twenty years. But when they looked back on their experience they saw everything unfolding inexorably from the initial moments of perception. Different though their tracks were, they had both perceived in the present what they believed to be the indelible marks of a long development in the past. They could never forget what they had seen. "He who has seen a ghost," wrote Newman, "cannot be as if he had never seen it." The ghost brought a new view of the past. This is how he described it in his last University Sermon on February 2, 1845:

> Meanwhile the work went on, and at length a large fabric of divinity was reared, irregular in its structure, and diverse in its style, as beseemed the slow growth of centuries; nay, anomalous in its details, from the peculiarities of individuals, or the interference of strangers, but still, on the whole, the development of an idea ... Wonderful it is to see with what effort, hesitation, suspense, interruption – with how many swayings to the right and to the left – with how many reverses, yet with what certainty of advance, with what precision in its march, and with what ultimate completeness it had been evolved ... And this world of thought is the expansion of a few words, uttered as if casually by the fishermen of Galilee.[10]

What is this but theological Darwinism, evolved out of a few vivid and personal historical perceptions?

But once more we must leave our subject on the threshold of decision and turn from Oxford to the Continent – to Bremen. Here, in September 1838, while Newman in Oxford was seeing his face in the mirror of history, we find an impressionable and rather likeable young man working in an office many hours a day. He is Friedrich Engels. He has just come from Wuppertal to learn his father's business as a cotton manufacturer and merchant. His home town Barmen is now often referred to as the Manchester of Germany, but for Engels it stood preeminently for the Lutheran quietism in which he had been brought up. He saw its industrialism only through the shutters of evangelical piety. The traces of this still clung to him when he went to Bremen. For two more years he retained a strong desire for religion. He still sang in the church choir, composed music for *Ein' Feste Burg ist unser Gott* and *Stabat Mater Dolorosa*, and played parlor games with the pastor's family with whom he lived.

But soon new influences became prominent in his letters.[11] He was swept into a much more strongly historical tide than either Darwin or

Newman. We find him translating Shelley and reading Strauss's *Life of Jesus*. He was enchanted by the new vision of the past which Strauss gave him. On June 15, 1839, he wrote: "Here we have the *Leben Jesu* by Strauss, an irrefutable book...I hope to see a radical transformation in the religious consciousness of the world – if only I were clear about it myself. Still, that will come in due course if only I have time to develop undisturbed and in peace." And on October 8: "I am now a Straussian; I, a poor, miserable poet, have crept under the wing of the genius David Friedrich Strauss...If you can refute Strauss – eh bien, I'll become a pietist again." And in November: "I am on the point of becoming a Hegelian. Whether I shall become one I don't know yet, but Strauss has lit up lights on Hegel for me which make the thing quite plausible to me." Then four months later, in January 1840: "Through Strauss, I am entered on the straight way to Hegelianism." A year later he was still on the same road, still a follower of Strauss, still translating Shelley; and more and more immersed in the heady poetry and politics of young Germany.

Undoubtedly Engels was an excitable young man – he was after all only twenty in 1840 – and coming from a quiet parochial background he had quickly caught the language of change and progress which was increasingly popular with the youth of Germany. He was already filled with an enthusiasm for the fluidity of history; but his ideas were all second-hand. He had had no historical perceptions of his own. Then, in November 1842, still as a trainee in his father's firm, he came to Manchester.[12] This was the great experience of his life, and it changed all his views. The streets, alleys, and courtyards of Manchester absorbed and stimulated his emotional and intellectual energies. Coming to the classic ground of English industrialism, with an imagination already heated by Shelley and Strauss, he looked at the scene at once with a historical eye. He measured the thickness of the walls of the workers' houses, examined the layout of their slums, noted the strata of the working class – the immigrants from the surrounding villages, the foreign laborers from Ireland, the women taking the place of men – he made notes on their morals and religion, their diet and their wages; and all this not with the eye of a moralist or a sanitary inspector, but of a historian. He saw in everything that lay around him the evidence of a historical process. In the streets and factories of Manchester he saw humanity afflicted by a plague, and he looked at what he saw to find its causes, its progress, and its likely termination.

In many ways he was very naive, and his critics say he often got his facts wrong and misused his sources. No doubt they are right. In identifying the source of the disease in the bacillus of the spinning jenny, and the tissue on which it fed as the avarice of the middle class, he was probably unfair both to the bacillus and to the middle class. But Engels too had seen his ghost. He had seen in the overcrowded streets and tumbledown houses of Manchester traces of a historical process from which there was no escape. We are not concerned with the rightness of Engels's vision but only with the way in which a historical perception suddenly came into existence which grew over the years until it embraced a whole society. He wrote:

> While I was in Manchester it was tangibly brought home to me that the economic facts, which have so far played no role, or only a contemptible role, in the writing of history are – at least in the modern world – a decisive historical force.[13]

This moment of historical perception, which brought a vision of the whole structure of the past, present, and future of industrial society, can scarcely be thought less important than the contemporary and equally intensely personal experiences of Darwin and Newman.

Now finally we must turn to Paris. Here, once more in September 1838, we find a young man – or rather a schoolboy of sixteen – who had recently arrived from the remote town of Tréguier in Brittany. He is Ernest Renan; clever, imaginative, deeply attached to the habits and traditions of his Breton community in which he had been a model of youthful conformity and virtue. His aim was clear before him: he was to be a priest. A local examiner had singled him out to be sent to the most famous seminary in Paris to complete his education for the priesthood. But, alas for human plans, he too became the victim of a historical perception which changed his life. What Manchester was to Engels, Paris was to Renan. He wrote:

> I beheld sights as new and as strange as if I had suddenly landed in France from Tahiti or Timbuctoo... My Breton Christianity was no more like the Christianity that I now discovered than an old piece of canvas, stiff as a board, is like muslin. It was not the same religion at all. Those old priests of mine in their heavy Roman copes were to me like seers with the words of eternity on their lips; but what I now saw was a religion of fancy drapery, a perfumed and beribboned piety, a religion of little tapers and flower vases, a theology of young ladies, without solidity... This was the gravest crisis of my life.[14]

The past opened out to him in a new way. He had been brought up to believe in an unchanging religion descending from antiquity, and he discovered that there were two religions under a single name – the one stable, the other fluid. Brittany represented the first; Paris the second. He clung to the first but was swept away with the second, and in this world of change the Catholicism of his youth was no more than a fossilized survival. It is quite unlikely that the full historical impact of the contrast was at once clear to him. At first it just made him ill. But very soon a new historical pattern began to take shape in his mind: "I saw that there were more things in the world than Antiquity and the Church. Ideas and sentiments...which were the germs that later bore fruit."[15] For the next seven years he continued in the seminary torn between two diverging paths: the one, the formal, systematic, stable road of scholastic thought which he loved and admired and never ceased to long for as the lost ideal of his youth; the other, the winding, uncertain, and many-tracked path through the widely differing forms of life, which, whatever name they went under, had developed under the stimulus of their individual circumstances.

After years of terrible conflict Renan chose the path of historical movement. He had had his first shock of a changing world in the same summer of 1838 when Newman had seen his vision of the two Churches, the one static, the other changing; he walked out of the seminary of St. Sulpice as a convert to historicism three days before Newman at Littlemore entered the Catholic Church. Faced with a choice between the grand but impossible stability of his youth (the only Catholicism he could accept) and the petty, shifting Catholicism of Paris, Renan chose to construct his own catholicism of the human spirit in history. He made his final decision on October 6, 1845, the day on which Newman withdrew all his charges of corruption against the Roman Church in preparation for the step he took three days later.

But though their destinations were so different, the essential choice was the same. It was the choice in favor of historical movement, development, and growth, against the unchanging stability of Antiquity; and the choice was based, not on logic or strict forms of argument, but on a perception of the present as the product of a long process of change and development. The movement which took Newman to Rome made Renan, in the eyes of Pope Leo XIII, the great example of "the enormous rebellion of the modern world." Yet, in the context of the historical movement Renan only expanded to its furthest limits the vision of the past which Newman deployed within the framework of the Catholic Church. As soon as Renan recovered from the shock of his conversion he wrote out a program for his future work:

> History is the necessary form of the science of everything which is in a state of *becoming*. The science of languages is the *history* of languages. The science of literatures and religions is the *history* of literatures and religions. The science of the human spirit is the *history* of the human spirit...that which seems stable at any one moment is not what is most essential: the variable and that which is characteristic of its own time is the most important.[16]

For nearly fifty years Renan explored the ramifications of this doctrine. A steady cascade of beautiful, lucid, and often illuminating words – some five million at a rough computation – poured from him. He tried to gather up and enshrine every manifestation of the human spirit, with its inherent powers shaped by the circumstances of every moment in the past. He cherished, as a collector of works of art, every phase and every symbolic figure in each phase. History was everything. The reader is crushed, and even Renan himself seems to have felt crushed by the burden of history. In 1848–9 he had written, "Goodbye, O God of my youth, though you have betrayed me, I love you still."[17] At the end of his life he might have said of his historical experience, "O God of my maturity, though I am faithful to you, I hate you." He predicted that his new faith would have a shorter life than his old one:

> The historical sciences and their auxiliary philological sciences have made great progress since the time when I gave myself to them with so much ardour forty years ago – but the end is in sight. In another hundred years humanity will know almost all that can be known about its past and then it will be time to stop, for it is the peculiarity of those sciences that they have no sooner reached perfection that they begin to demolish themselves.[18]

III

And so Renan brings us to our final question. What is the likely future of the historical experience at once so fragile in its logical and experimental foundations, and so powerful in moving men in different directions during the creative decade we have been studying? Are we to think, to quote Renan again, that "a hundred years hence, no one will trouble his head about the historical sciences, the little conjectural sciences, which are no sooner made than they have to be unmade"; and that "it is in chemistry, in astronomy, and above all in general physiology that we hold the key to the secrets of Being, of the World, and (if one will) of God"?[19]

The first thing to be said in answer to this question is that it is time we came back to earth. We have been moving on the heights of a historical experience which compelled four men – three of them very conservative by temperament – to take giant leaps into an unknown future. With Darwin, Newman, and Engels, the leaps, though breathtaking, brought them back to earth with a new purpose. With Renan, however, the experience took him into a stratosphere of complete historical relativity, with the curious result that he wished everything to remain unchanged in a sort of gigantic museum of historical experience. We have in Renan an example of what happens when any single experience takes control, and makes claims which cannot be sustained. From the unwarranted conviction that history is everything, it is but a small step to the further conviction that it will soon be nothing. If we look to history for a solution to the enigma of the universe we shall look in vain; and I doubt whether the other sciences to which Renan's imagination turned in his old age will have any greater success. It is time for a historian to show a little modesty, and to return, if not quite to the level at which we started, at least to something nearer this level.

As we descend we shall pass Darwin, Newman, and Engels whom we must salute with respectful admiration. But even to them we must say that they required their historical experience to do more for them than it is properly equipped to do. It was an accident of their time that some new vision was needed to break down the last defenses of a system of thought, going back in essentials to the scholasticism of the Middle Ages, which had once been a source of energy and understanding, but had by their time become moribund. History was at hand to provide this new vision, partly because the first necessity in the final work of demolition was the strictly historical task of destroying the traditional scholastic chronology of the universe; and partly because, when leaps are needed, perceptions are better than any arguments. The traditional modes of deductive or inductive argument had been carefully cultivated to produce the old answers. Historical perceptions produced new answers; and provided the liberating force. They made movement possible in many different directions.

This will not happen again. No one will now become Catholic because he sees himself as a Monophysite in the mirror of history; few will now become Communists because they see in the workshops of Manchester the evidence of an inexorable process, soon to reach its grand climax in a new Jerusalem. There are other grounds on which both religious and political questions will be settled. We must not expect too much of history. It will not tell us what to believe or how to act; it will not make us more tolerant or more ecumenical or more peaceful. But if we are any of these things – or even *per impossibile* if we are the opposite of these things – it will add a new pleasure and breadth to our understanding of what it is we are. History, emphatically, is not everything; but it is an aspect of everything. This is the great and lasting legacy of the experience we have been examining. As a necessary aspect of every subject it will continue to grow, and as it grows it will add a new pleasure to every subject. The historical experience is first for pleasure; but it is also a warning. It holds up to every science a warning finger with this message: "You too are a product of your time, reflecting all the limitations, preconceptions, and special interests of your time. The time will come when you too will be swept away into Renan's Grand Museum alongside the scholasticism which once seemed so solid and which you replaced." Pleasure and warning are the chief fruits of the historical experience which developed in the last century. Within these humble limits – and perhaps they are not after all so very humble – the historical vision is not, as Renan feared, at the beginning of its end; but only, as Churchill said in a different context, at the end of its beginning.

7

The Truth about the Past

The problem announced in my title is so pretentious that I must begin by cutting it down to keep it within manageable proportions. I shall start by considering why it was long thought to be impossible for historians to discover important truths about the past; why that doubt was dispelled in the last half of the last century; why this doubt has come up again; and what can be done about it. And it will be convenient to discuss all these questions within the context of the development of the History School in this University [Oxford].

So let me begin by reminding you, or perhaps in some cases by telling you, that it was not until 1850 that history was given a place in the university curriculum. The University had existed without it for more than seven hundred years, and if we ask why it was so long delayed, the essential answer is quite simply this: it was thought impossible for historical investigation to discover a body of systematic, reliable, and important general truth, which would qualify for placing it alongside those subjects which had long been recognized as having all these qualities. Unlike history they could all be studied in authoritative texts, discussed according to well-developed rules for purging Truth from error, and in the end produce a systematic body of doctrine with indisputable importance for the conduct of human life. The subjects which had the clearest possible claim to possessing all these attributes were, in the first place, theology, the law both Roman and ecclesiastical, medicine, arithmetic, geometry, music, and the arts of the so-called Trivium – grammar, rhetoric, and logic. All these subjects had been offered for study by Oxford University since the early thirteenth century, and any reasonable person might think that they offered enough for all important purposes of learning and for the conduct of life in this world, and in preparation for the next.

This did not mean that history was not a subject which could give much entertainment and grounds for reflection. But, as an intellectual discipline, it failed to measure up to the subjects of the university curriculum on several grounds. First, it offered no systematic or certain body of truth. As Dr. Johnson said: "that certain kings reigned and certain battles were fought we may look on as reasonably certain. But all the colour, all the philosophy of history is conjecture." So there it was: history might have many uses, but it had no place among the subjects which were capable of being studied as coherent and well-attested bodies of systematic knowledge.

All this seems so reasonable that the real problem is why history ever gained admission to our University at all. Had it suddenly been discovered that history had been maligned, that there was indeed a substantial body of systematic, important, well-attested truth to be found in it?

The answer to this question is complicated, but there are two main points which stand out. First, what gave history its opportunity in 1850 was not so much that its reputation had gone up in the world, as that other subjects had gone down. The whole view of knowledge promoted by the old syllabus – the view, namely, that reasonable completeness had been reached on most subjects, and that all that was needed was to transmit the body of ascertained truth from one generation to the next, to complete this huge body of knowledge in detail – had during the previous century been subjected to hammer-blows which left the whole structure in a state of ruin. It was the collapse of the old body of learning which gave history for the first time a claim to be no worse than any of the other subjects and just possibly much better. There were not many people in England who were convinced that history could produce anything much better, but there were many who thought that it was at least worth trying, and it was in this spirit that the new Honor School of Law and Modern History was created – law providing the ballast which would give a little stability to the new enterprise.

One reason why many conservatively minded people were willing to take the risk of launching this fragile craft was that, although few thought that the study of history was likely on its own to produce important results, history had always had an important place in European culture. Even in the great subjects which the University existed to promote there was a strong historical background. Not least, the queen of the sciences, systematic theology, was known to be a growth with many historical roots in the Bible, the Fathers, the Councils of the Church, and the vast works of critical and historical elucidation that these records of the past had been subjected to. The same was true of all the branches of the liberal Arts, which you can see displayed in the Canterbury Quadrangle [of St. John's College]. Logic, grammar, rhetoric, astronomy, arithmetic, geometry, medicine – had all taken shape as a result of a well-attested historical development. So the central idea of history, that the whole system of human thought and institutions has been molded in the course of a long historical development, was firmly embedded in all European sciences. To an extent which I think is unparalleled in other civilizations, history was a central feature of all the sciences.

But now you may think, I have gone to the other extreme: from saying that history had no place among the traditional sciences of European tradition, I now appear to be saying that it had always had a central position. But notice the distinction: historical development had long been regarded as an essential background to systematic knowledge, while it had no place as a study in its own right. Why was this? Essentially it was because the central substance of history came, not as a result of historical investigation, but from divine revelation. But what was important about this whole body of knowledge was that, though it had emerged through a long process of accumulation and refinement, the knowledge it contained was not a product of history, but of Revelation and Reason—and therefore absolutely unshakable: history could accumulate and refine, but God and reason alone could guarantee the truth of the whole system—including, incidentally, the truth of a whole system of universal chronology.

So for centuries a paradoxical position had existed: history was a central feature of all thought; but the study of history had no place in any body of thought. It was a study for the lighter moments of life—an entertainment; not a study for universities which were committed to the task of handing on the acquired body of Truth from one generation to the next.

We can understand nothing about the historical revolution of the last one hundred and fifty years unless we understand this paradox: the thought of Europe had been from its very beginning profoundly historical in that the whole body of knowledge was the result of accumulation through the centuries; but this accumulation owed nothing to historical investigation. Every branch of systematic thought could be pursued in peace under this great umbrella of historical stability.

This alliance between divinely revealed and protected history and rational scientific truth served all the main purposes of European life till the first half of the nineteenth century. Of course it is easy to point to many criticisms and doubts about this combination especially from about 1700 onwards; but for most people, and even for most intellectuals, the combination stood up to criticism without having to face any unanswerable objections. There might be doubts, but there was no plausible alternative. And then quite suddenly the doubts became quasi-certainties, and the first glimmerings of a new, vastly longer, chronology began to appear. It was really the breakdown of biblical chronology which ruined the whole system, and by about 1800 it had broken down for most thinking people; by 1850, the breakdown had become irreparable. As it penetrated deeper and deeper into society, the discovery that the fundamental chronology, on which the whole system of a divinely ordered and rationally comprehensible universe had rested, was profoundly untrue, not just in detail, but in its essential framework, gained more and more reluctant adherents. It is hard to think of a more deadly assault on the foundations of European thought and life than this. The prospect for the survival of any ordered view of the world seemed very bleak by 1850. I feel immense sympathy for those who were first exposed to the dreadful fall from certainty into a vast pit of doubt. The historical movement we are now to consider was a first attempt to climb out of that pit.

II

One might have thought that if, on top of the long tradition of depreciation of history as a serious body of human knowledge, it was now shown that divinely guaranteed historical knowledge was riddled with error, this discovery would have signalized not the beginning, but the end of history as a serious contender for intellectual respectability. Previously its intellectual respectability had been beyond criticism. Now it might have seemed beyond repair. But not at all. It was only now, from the ruins of divinely inspired history, that the study of history in its own right, without any supernatural credentials, came into its own for the first time. Why was this?

In the first place, I suppose, Europe had been so long accustomed to think historically about the development of knowledge that, even when the source of historical certainty had been swept aside, it was impossible to adhere to a system of knowledge without at the same time seeing it as emerging from the labors of a continuous stream of investigation over a period of two or three thousand years. This historical perspective could not be simply swept away.

Then too, the new studies of geology, language, and astronomy which had been chiefly responsible for undermining biblical history had one common feature: they all pointed to a new chronology which could be constructed, no longer on the basis of Revelation, but by building up a new general account of development based on detailed observations of fossils, linguistic forms, organic changes in living creatures, astronomical observations, and so on. These observations all suggested that perhaps after all general truths *could* be discovered by historical investigation. It was difficult to know how this could be done, and during the years around 1850 the air in Oxford was thick with pamphlets proposing ways in which it might be done. After several false starts it came to be generally thought that the best field for finding general truths of importance in the past was in the study of government, and more particularly in the study of the development of Parliament and common law, both of which seemed to offer themselves as local examples of the growth of freedom in institutional and permanently developing form. It came as a huge liberation from a prison of despair to discover that here in our midst there was something like a divine instrument for the enlargement of human life developing through the centuries from the earliest days—a kind of secular embodiment of that force which had in the past been particularly associated with the now derelict pattern of Revelation.

This vision, which had seemed so elusive in 1850, had by 1880 become the new orthodoxy of Oxford, and it was now enshrined, no longer in the Faculty of Theology, as it had been since the thirteenth century, but in the Faculty of Modern History. By 1850 there seemed good reasons for thinking that general truths about the development of human behavior, especially in the organization of government, in the development of doctrinal statements, philosophical systems, and potentially in every area of human life, were within the scope of human enquiry, and therefore eminently suited to university teaching. The idea was beginning to take root that there could be a study of history which was not just a retelling of an old old story in more elegant language or greater elaboration than before, but a creative subject based on documents and artifacts which only told their story when questioned by historians. Thus there arose everywhere a search for a new historical method, from which it was hoped that a new frame for human life might emerge, with a universal appeal. The search for this consumed more energy than any other intellectual activity in the University from about 1850 to 1920.

When we look at the historical syllabuses of our universities, they may seem a somewhat laughable result of all this effort, a strange product of a turbulent process of intellectual reconstruction. But it is important to see that this academic response was at the centre of a much larger intellectual revolution. Broadly speaking, the devisers of the syllabus tried to do three things: first to rebut the charge that there could be no substantial system in historical knowledge; secondly to devise a program of study which would have the strength to stand up to hostile criticism; and thirdly to devise a program of study of universal value.

Effectively, the strength of the system came from concentrating on English history, above all on the institutions of Parliament and the common law. The claim to a high degree of certainty came from the study of original documents such as Acts of Parliament, charters, and other official documents. And the claim to universal appeal came from the theme of the development of freedom within an institutional development. Whatever else might be said about it, there can be no doubt about the immense success of the program. Within fifty years of the introduction of the subject, about one third of all undergraduates, not only in Oxford, but throughout the whole country, and not only in Britain, but in about half the world, were reading history as devised primarily in Oxford. The usefulness of the subject seemed to be established beyond doubt, and the intellectual credentials of the subject were such that, as the historical sciences of documentary study gradually developed, it came to be thought that a new kind of knowledge of the past was within reach, richer, more certain, more capable of bearing a systematic form and having a practical relevance than any earlier historical knowledge.

Documents which – for lack of sufficiently powerful tools for determining their date and location in a historical process – had never before revealed their secrets, could now, as it seemed, become the carriers of information quite beyond the scope of their original intention. For example, documents concerning meetings of magnates, lists of those who were summoned, the subjects of their debates, the documents drawn up as a result of their debates, the actions determined on and formulated in authoritative formulae over a long period of time came to form the basis of a new historical science. It was hoped that this science, like any other, could gradually be extended by creating a science of comparative developments throughout periods of time that might embrace several centuries. Thus it was that a new vision of a body of historical truth, more profound, more certain, and more important for the conduct of our lives emerged as a new hope for the future.

I can speak on this point, not just in general terms, but with a vivid recollection of the thrill that this message gave an undergraduate of 1930 discovering – rather late in the day you may think – that charters could recreate the social and political life of the twelfth century of which the participants had only the dimmest, if any, conception. But if this discovery could still give a thrill in 1930, how much more to the real innovators two or three generations earlier? They fervently believed that a hitherto neglected body of scientifically acquired truth could be created with credentials comparable to those claimed by the body of scientific truth which had been so ruthlessly destroyed.

Then there was a further claim that could be made for this new body of knowledge. The old body of scholastic knowledge which the universities had come into existence to perfect and hand on to the future had not only aimed at systematic certainty; it had also aimed at providing rules for human life in all its branches. One of the chief complaints of its critics in 1850 was that, besides being manifestly untrue, the knowledge purveyed by the universities was patently useless. One of the chief claims now made for the new form of history was that, besides providing a new body of organized truth, it was in the highest degree useful for the conduct of life. It gave those who were to govern the world a preview of the kind of problems they would meet, whether they were ruling vast areas of India or devising laws and regulations for this country.

This may now seem pure moonshine. But it did not seem so even sixty years ago [i.e., around 1930]; and seventy-five years ago, it seemed to fit the circumstances of the time like a glove. Indeed, history had succeeded beyond all expectation in giving the university that central position in society which it had had in the thirteenth century and had gradually lost in the intervening centuries.

In the thirteenth century it had been the systematic study of theology and canon law which – more than anything else – had given the universities a dominant position in society. In the late nineteenth and the first decade of the twentieth century, it was history. And I need scarcely say that it was the study of the development of Parliament which in this country gave history its dominant role in providing a body of truth which was regarded as being both firmly established and universally useful. It had every quality that scholars had been taught to look for in a scholastic subject: importance in the formation of attitudes to individual and corporate life; applicability to other times and other societies than that in which the original developments had taken place; immense significance both for the contemporary world and for the future; and scientifically established truth.

It is almost impossible, now that the bright vision has faded, to appreciate the full beauty and importance of the discovery of this central theme for historical study, which evolved steadily and without any important opposition between 1850 and 1914. At the first of these dates, the subject scarcely existed even as an idea; at the second, it had reached the fullness of its development as a scientific body of knowledge. Like all important bodies of knowledge, it had drawn into its orbit a number of subsidiary studies: common law; economics; the consolidation of a national community; the apparently unlimited possibilities of extension of the parliamentary ideal – in time from the earliest Germanic invasions of the Roman Empire into an indefinite future; in space to all the races of the world, which had so strangely come under the influence of these remote events through the imperial expansion of the time. And not only was there a prospect of indefinite expansion in the area of influence of this new science, but there was the prospect of its continuing growth through the rapid increase in the number of students and teachers of the subject in schools and universities. By 1900, about one third of all undergraduates were studying history; and the greater part of them had the study of parliamentary institutions at the centre of their program of study. In central Africa and in the schools of India, no less than in the public schools of England and its colonies, the same program was coming to occupy a central place.

By the beginning of this century, a new historical science had been created which answered all earlier criticisms of the eligibility of history as a serious contender for academic study. In an astonishingly short space of time, history as an academic discipline had been made to provide an important body of organized ascertainable truth – truth not only well established in method and persuasiveness, but also of a hitherto unimaginably universal applicability.

History had taken the place of theology as the queen of the sciences. And of course the sciences which now ride so high scarcely qualified for serious consideration. Let me recall a single detail as an illustration of this: as late as 1935, the late Professor Lionel Stones, studying chemistry at Glasgow, was warned by his father that he must think of his future and turn to some more practical study: being compliant as well as clever, he turned to medieval history. It was a choice which met every requirement: large scope for intellectual discovery, and a field of study of wide general importance for the conduct of human life. He never regretted it; but he must have been about the last to experience the full force of this appeal. Within twenty years of Lionel Stones's conversion to medieval studies, history was one of the declining industries of this country, and the decline in medieval history was the most marked of all. What had gone wrong? In what way had history come to seem inadequate to the claims which it made? What scope is now left for it? And what is its importance likely to be? These are the questions I must attempt to answer in the time that remains.

III

First then, what had gone wrong? This is a question that can be answered at every kind of level, but we may conveniently start with the large number of manuals written for students around 1900. They were written by some of the leading academic teachers of the day, and several of them are masterpieces of compression and order. But with all their virtues, they also have all the weaknesses of the established academic subjects which the history syllabus had been invented to overcome fifty years earlier. The subject had accumulated a body of doctrine which could be learnt without reference to the sources from which it had distilled. Year after year attempts were made to remedy this state of affairs, to insist that the documents *must* be studied by all students; but the plain fact was that since the answers were already known, reference to the sources was unnecessary, even unwise, for wiser heads had already extracted from them all the important truths that they were capable of delivering. It could only muddy the stream of truth to attempt to draw new or different conclusions. It was the problem of scholasticism all over again: new answers were bound to be wrong; old ones were already known. The result was endless dullness and repetition.

Behind this fact of life there lay a more general cause of discontent, which I must now attempt to describe.

The main aim of the new historical method was to trace lines of development from one stage of institutional development to the next. The questions asked had to take the form: how does a statement in a document of 1215 relate to comparable statements in 1166, 1259, 1297, and so on, back to the Anglo-Saxons on the one hand, and forward to 1640, 1832, 1887, on the other? Now, in one sense, there is nothing wrong with this method: ideas and procedures are adumbrated in the earlier documents in a series, developed, become confused and are applied to ends for which they were not originally intended, and it is part of the task of the historian to disentangle and display these transformations. But there comes a time when all these permutations have been worked out, and there is nothing to do but learn as many of them as possible. And this is what had happened to a large part of the material selected for study in the history syllabus. Students discovered that – whatever critics might say – all they had to do was to learn the answers.

And then there was a more fundamental difficulty. All the "right" answers were developed along a single chain of development: the growth of ordered liberty in the community, and this line of development was envisaged as having reached a peak of development by the late nineteenth century, when it had become available for export to all parts of the world. It was this conception which gave nobility and universal value to the whole study, just as five hundred years earlier, the application of logic, grammar, and rhetoric to the mass of material handed down from the ancient world had given dignity and practical usefulness to the scholastic methods of the early universities. The consequences were very similar in both cases: first, there was no more scope for discovery, and yet the world did not seem much better for all that had so far been achieved. So the question began to arise whether there was not some mighty flaw in the whole system: were the threads of the past which had been unraveled during the past fifty years the right ones? Had they not simply been imposed on the past by the needs or prejudices of contemporary society? Or, worse still, as it soon became fashionable to say, had they not been imposed by the socially dominant class in contemporary society?

Then, alongside these questions there was, for the future of historical enquiry, an even more general and disturbing question: did not the whole method of drawing out from the documents of the past patterns of development, which gave a permanent significance to individual events, impose on the past modern ideas which distorted the whole picture?

The usefulness for the present, which history claimed to have, required that the principles of the present should be found embryonically in the past. It was this capacity of historians to see through the diversity of the past to principles of universal validity which gave their subject a claim to general importance. From this had arisen the claim of historical study to replace the outworn scholastic system which was in its last stages of decay in 1850. But if all that historians were doing was to impose upon the past the ideas of the present, they might do better to leave the field to economists and political theorists.

Disillusionment with the intellectual limitations of history as envisaged by our academic ancestors was beginning to be fairly generally felt when I was an undergraduate nearly sixty years ago. I do not think I speak here simply with hindsight, for (unless my memory misleads me) I can remember thinking and writing at a very early stage in my undergraduate career that the trouble with history was that it left out everything of importance in people's lives. This criticism was reinforced, and perhaps inspired, by a further and even more damaging discovery. The universal usefulness of the past as a guide and model for future development suddenly and catastrophically appeared to be outdated; the system of thought which held everything together was itself becoming a piece of the past: the broadening down of freedom from precedent to precedent, the slow emergence of democratic assemblies from the Anglo-Saxon Witans and the Anglo-Norman *Curia Regis*; the great providential growth of freedom, which Acton so inspiringly had seen as the key to universal history, began to appear, not as a universal rule of human development, but as the invention of the nineteenth century, nearer indeed to our own in time, but as remote – in some ways more remote – in thought and feeling from the present than the thirteenth century. When this happened, the historical program which had dominated the universities from about 1880 to 1930 was widely seen to satisfy neither the past which it had attempted to put at our service, nor the present which it had aimed at serving.

IV

As this happened, there came an increasingly powerful demand for change, or reform as it was inevitably called. The reform took one of two forms. The first, and most immediately powerful, was a demand for a more "relevant" chain of consequences to be traced through the historical material. Out of this demand there arose the broadly Marxist academic history of the period from the 1930s to 1950s. But this too in the end suffered the same fate of revealing itself in the end as both untrue to the past and irrelevant for the present and future. Indeed, it seems inevitable that thematic linear histories, whatever their immediate merits may be in tracing long chains of consequences from document to document, and from century to century, will have a similar fate. Whatever kind of truth they may exhibit, it is not truth about the past.

I do not say that great masterpieces of "linear" historical writing may not continue to be produced, and they may serve the aspirations of historians for a time. They almost certainly will. But their essential aim is to promote a cause, whether good or bad, in the present and future. As aids to understanding the past, their role is very limited. For a fuller understanding of the past, we must turn to another form of historical writing, which the new breadth of historical studies is bringing for the first time within our grasp. This is what I may call "situational" history, of which the whole aim is to bring the surviving material of every kind to bear on understanding the minds, imaginations, world-views, aspirations of individuals and groups in a single limited period. I do not think that the full consequences of this change of view have yet been realized, although there are everywhere signs that a change in this direction is taking place.

In contrast to the historical movement of a century ago, the emerging aim is breadth of understanding of the minds and imagination of a few, rather than the tracing of a single purpose through a long period of time to the present. For *that* purpose, the materials of greatest value were administrative and legal documents, and the records of "out-worn" modes of thought, such as scholastic distinctions or biblical symbolism, were consigned to the rubbish dumps of the past. It is significant that these are the sources which are now at the center of medieval inquiry. Everywhere the emphasis of historical study has moved from the practical and organizational, to the imaginative and artistic, literary, the liturgical and theological, and to the monumental records of the past. In the light of these studies, chronicles are returning to the scene with a new emphasis on what they can tell us about the beliefs and world-views with which they were written; and administrative documents too are read as products of minds rather than as steps in the development of a system. To recreate the minds of the past in all their aspects, and with close attention to times and places and personalities, is the aim of this latest stage in the study of the past. In pursuit of this aim, the historian abandons, or relegates to an inferior position, all attempts to relate the past with the present, seeking only to understand minds and wills as they present themselves to us in their original setting. All these links which were formerly valued as stepping-stones along the great road from past to present have become increasingly simply by-products of the contemporary scene in which they were produced, no longer links in the chain of events along the road towards the end to which the whole Creation moves.

This change from what I have called a linear to a situational historical view has been taking place slowly and intermittently over the past fifty years. Let me give you one example, from my own experience.

In 1933, I worked for a year with Ferdinand Lot, one of the greatest masters of the French school of historians. In that year his seminar was on the reign of Charles the Bald, who was the last of the important Carolingian emperors, for just two years from 875 to 877. Lot's teaching represented partly a development of, and partly a reaction against, the linear ideals of late nineteenth-century history. In Lot's youth, Charles's reign had been interpreted as the moment when feudalism – that is to say the breakdown of central political authority into a large number of local components – was showing its first signs of becoming the dominant social form of western Europe. This view had been brilliantly expressed in a study by Emile Bourgeois of the last great document of Charles the Bald's reign, the Capitulary of Quierzy. In this document Bourgeois had detected many of the familiar features of feudalism, which were (so he claimed) given an irresistible momentum by the arrangements made in this Capitulary for the government of France during Charles's absence in Italy for his imperial coronation in 875, from which he never returned. One of Lot's aims in his long series of seminars was to demonstrate the superficiality of this view. He did this – or rather, we did it under his direction – by a close study of the problems of the kingdom as they emerged year by year throughout his long reign: the devastations of the Vikings; the panic-stricken flights of monastic communities with their relics from the invaders; the family disputes of the Carolingian family; the final revolt of King Charles's son-in-law Boso. Boso was my task, and I look back on the experience as the beginning of intense concentration on global situations as they actually were, without regard to what was to follow. In a sense, the whole effort represented a new approach to the situation as it was at the time, without regard to any hypothetical chain of consequences.

From this point of view, it was extremely penetrating. But, looking back fifty-five years later, the most conspicuous feature is that it was not penetrating enough. There was, to be sure, no lack of subtlety or complexity, no lack either of penetrating criticism of sources or imaginative force in interpreting them. All that was lacking was the study of the minds of the main actors. The problems of removing relics from one part of the country to another, with all the military, economic, and transport problems these flights entailed, were not only understood but felt in all their intensity. But why the relics were the *one* thing the monks desired to save was a question that could only be answered with a shrug of the shoulders. It was all just part of the inexplicable inbred superstition of the time. Or again, the question why Charles should risk the destruction of his life's work in order to go to Rome to seek an imperial dignity which could confer on him no additional power, was never explored. It was seen as a question of power and prestige, not as a visionary ideal which, however impracticable, made life worth living. The furniture among which the actors moved was all old; but their aims, their desire for power, their fear of failure and death, were assumed to be what people at all times have experienced.

I can best describe the change which has come over historical studies since 1933 by contrasting my experience then with Michael Wallace-Hadrill's Raleigh Lecture of 1978 on Charles the Bald.[1] In his account, those things which are omitted by Lot occupy the foreground of the scene: symbols, liturgies, the theology of Christian rule, images of the past, the weight of Empire with its mixture of divine and human duties – all the wealth of thought and imagery of the time is concentrated on the single task of understanding the mind and personality, the personal world-view and the ideal of government of this strangely complicated individual, Charles the Bald, with a vision of the imperial past, of which he tried to be worthy – the story of the somber life of a spiritual being, a deeply thoughtful man, oppressed by many cares and carrying a weight of tradition greater than any of his predecessors or successors.

This imaginative leap, this appropriating of a distant frame of mind and being, is the first step towards understanding the European past in its own terms, and not in the terms of the present.

V

But here it may be objected that, seen in these terms, the whole *raison d'être* of the study of history as devised in the mid-nineteenth century, and still carried on in our university courses today, has been destroyed. The founders of these courses were engaged in making the past available for the purposes of the present. What other justification for its study can be given? They hoped to make the present more intelligible by tracing its origins and development step by step back into the past. This process was thought to be valuable because it showed how the apparatus of our lives – Parliament, the law courts, town and communal government, the organization of parishes, dioceses, counties, and kingdoms – came into existence and grew into the forms in which we see them today. It showed also how these institutions, with whatever aims they began, came to be the agents of tolerance and of government by consent. And it showed how, if they were transported to other lands, they could carry the same way of life with them. Seen in these terms, history provided a medium for reflecting on our present, a warning of the dangers which threaten the values enshrined in these institutions. It brought an understanding of ourselves and of the enemies of our civilization. It aimed at giving our lives a new depth by allowing us to see the past, and by implication also the future, in everything around us. It made our past an instrument for education in the values of our civilization. It could reasonably be claimed that whoever has eyes to recognize the landmarks of the past will have a greater depth of experience than those who see nothing of this recession through the centuries. The study of history was designed to encourage this recognition throughout the whole community. Is this linking of the present with the past to be abandoned, in order to understand the past for its own sake, to participate intellectually and imaginatively in ancient visions, ancient symbols, ancient systems of thought, ancient forms of art and architecture, of prayer and worship, of ceremony and status?

If we ask what the study of the past for its own sake and in its own terms can contribute to the present, I think the answer is that the interesting, perhaps the educative, thing about the people of the past lies in the ways they differ from us rather than in what we have in common. They differ from us in their sense of eternity, their wealth of images and symbols, their recognition of their powerlessness. Of course, no amount of understanding of the thoughts and symbols of the past can bring these lost parts of the human psyche to life again. But in understanding what we have lost, we take a first step towards our own regeneration. At least it is an experience which throws into high relief the emotional and imaginative poverty of the present. And this leads to a second point.

The greatest weakness of the historical thinking of the century after 1850 was its tendency to think of the present as a climax, with man in command of his destiny. Nothing has done more to impoverish humanity than this absurd delusion of self-sufficiency, which ultimately leads to despair as its falsity comes to be recognized. By contrast, in learning to understand the beliefs and images of the past, we shall not be brought into a believing or creative frame of mind, but we shall at least come to recognize our poverty in contrast to the wealth of the past. This imaginative participation is a first step towards taking seriously our own shortcomings. The mere thought of what we have lost is a challenge to explain, perhaps to replace, the defects of the present. We may come to look on the past as a treasury of unused wealth which is open to investigation, perhaps appropriation without any losers.

Put in these general terms, the strong effort which is necessary for this participation in the past may not seem either a very energetic exercise or a very useful one. But a little reflection will show that it is both demanding and educative. It is demanding because it requires a strong effort of mind and will to empty our minds of our contemporary presuppositions, to turn our minds upside down, to see a spiritual universe of which we now know almost nothing, and to think thoughts long submerged by the paraphernalia of modern life. We must take into our consciousness a whole range of thoughts and emotions which may be quite foreign to us: to begin with, a consciousness of a universe in which eternity is very near, in which there are hierarchies of heavenly beings, each having functions related to our activities on earth; in which there are heavenly spheres closely related to our lives on earth, and spiritual influences everywhere. The list could be greatly enlarged, but perhaps I have said enough to show that the new study of history in depth and for its own sake, seeking to understand the past in its own terms and with its own standards, is no easy option. But it is not quite such a formidable task as it appears from this catalogue. If I were to detail the steps necessary for making a loaf of bread, if you had never seen it done, you would declare it to be impossibly complicated. But as soon as you become familiar with the general idea, each new step becomes easier, and all are a pleasure. Or again, it's like looking at one of those complicated pictures of the seventeenth century – say, a Rubens. The further you look into it the more there is to discover: who is that winged figure walking along that country track? and why is the young man beside him carrying that enormous fish? and who is that old man supported by an equally old woman coming towards them? and why, and for whom, and when was it made? The questions are endless, and there are so many pleasures by the way that the journey is easier than you imagine.

Part III

Historians

8

Review of The Letters of Frederic William Maitland

It must be an almost unparalleled event for a collection of letters by a scholar, who made no mark on public life, to be collected and published nearly sixty years after his death. Nothing would have surprised the writer of the letters more than this careful and scholarly volume. He was not a great letter-writer; he was too busy a man to write unnecessary letters, and too self-contained and self-effacing to make his letters a vehicle for his deepest feelings. Only once or twice does he take the lid off his habitual reserve, as when he writes to his closest friend, Leslie Stephen, on the death of his wife: "I have an irrepressible wish, however foolish and wrong it may be, to touch your hand and tell you in two words what I think of you" (no. 157). The lid is at once replaced, and we are glad, for though Maitland was a man of deep and lasting affections, he did not easily write about them. Yet these letters have moved me deeply, and they have set me thinking again about his place in the great company of scholars who transformed the study of history in the second half of the nineteenth century. It is true that the letters tell us little about Maitland's work that we did not know already, but from first to last they are so fresh and distinctive in style and matter that they bring the man and his achievement before our eyes with a new clarity and a certain pathos.

Frederic William Maitland was born in 1850, the son of a lawyer who had been a Fellow of Trinity College, Cambridge, and later became secretary of the new Civil Service Commission. His grandfather was S. R. Maitland, a country gentleman and clergyman in Gloucestershire, whose book *The Dark Ages* (1844) was one of the most significant events in the revival of medieval studies in England. These family connections gave Maitland a setting which satisfied him throughout life; Cambridge, the law, the Middle Ages were the three great influences on his life. The only part of his inheritance which did not survive was the Christian religion. I can discover nothing about his father's religion, but Maitland from the first moment that he comes into our view had none. His daughter called him "a low-church agnostic." This was a not uncommon position for serious and high-minded Englishmen at this time, especially in Cambridge; but it was somewhat rare among medievalists, who were apt to be high-churchmen of one form or another, whatever their religious allegiance or lack of it might be. Having no religion, Maitland found some of the satisfactions of religion in human relations. No man was ever a better or more constant friend. He was entirely lacking in envy, pomposity, or self-seeking of any kind, and remarkably sweet-tempered and indifferent to the world's rewards. In addition, he was absurdly and unaffectedly modest about his own achievement, and seemed to find it necessary (perhaps as a direct result of his sense of religious deprivation) to people the world with father-figures like Henry Sidgwick, Leslie Stephen, and Paul Vinogradoff, to whom he ascribed a far greater share in his formation than now seems reasonable. To younger men and fellow workers, he paid a deference which might seem exaggerated if it were not so patently natural and unselfconscious. His letter to the young James Tait, whose review of *Domesday Book and Beyond* cut deeper than any other review of any other book of Maitland, should be read by every author on the publication of a new book.

It would be possible to continue at length to celebrate Maitland's personal qualities and to illustrate them from these letters, but we must turn to other things. His letters, after all, will be read not for his personal virtues but for the historical genius they display. From this point of view, it is a great loss that very few letters have survived from his formative years down to 1884, when his first historical work appeared. To understand his approach to history we must turn to the earliest essays in his *Collected Papers*, and, since the letters can only be understood against this background, a few words about the years which are scarcely represented in this volume may not be out of place.

Maitland took the Moral Sciences Tripos at Cambridge in 1872, and in 1875 he submitted a dissertation on *Liberty* for a Fellowship at Trinity College. In this he was unsuccessful, and in 1876 he was called to the Bar, where for eight years he practiced as conveyancer and equity draftsman. It was as a result of this work that he became interested in the Middle Ages. The work itself forced its practitioners into *some* attitude toward the medieval past: the land law of that day was so enmeshed in medieval principles and procedures that there was no escape. Among lawyers, two main attitudes were prevalent. The reformers, who included most men of sense, were impatient with the nonsense of the past and wished to sweep it away with comprehensive contempt. Their opponents, who cherished the intricacies of their profession, found reasons in the mythology of the constitution and the continuity of the body politic for retaining absurdities provided they were ancient. Neither attitude was historical: the one was anti-historical, and the other pseudo-historical. In practical affairs Maitland aligned himself decisively with the reformers: "no practical convenience, however small," he wrote in 1879, "is to be sacrificed on the altar of historic continuity" (*Collected Papers*, i, 195). He could scarcely have put himself more plainly on the side of the Utilitarians against the followers of Burke. Yet equally plainly he rejected the historical ignorance and shallowness of the Utilitarians, who saw the follies of modern procedure as proof of the inherent absurdities of a feudal past. What is absurd is feudal; what is feudal is medieval; therefore what is medieval is absurd. So ran the syllogism; and even after a hundred years of work, a surprisingly large number of people still think it is true. It was here that Maitland parted company with the reformers. He saw that what was absurd in 1870 was not necessarily absurd in 1270, and he set himself to discover the system behind the wreckage which choked the legal machinery of his day.

Anyone who wishes to understand his historical starting-point and to follow the development which these letters illustrate must read his essay on Real Property, published in 1879. It is brilliantly destructive; but through it all we can see that he has been laying careful foundations for his later historical mastery. He already knew the barbarian laws of Europe, he was familiar with Bracton, and he could judge the worthlessness of recent Bractonian scholarship. He could even commit himself to generalizations of remarkable assurance for a beginner, as for instance this:

> Were it necessary, we might easily show that for centuries past there has been one steady tendency running through the whole movement of our property law; a tendency towards the assimilation of real to personal property. Indeed we know not where to date the beginning of this tendency, for as far as our records reach we may see it at work. (*Collected Papers*, i, 195)

Maitland was already at work on the problems and sources which were to occupy him for the rest of his life. We must not be deceived by the legal language of this passage. What interested Maitland was the society behind the legal concepts. This remained his main preoccupation to the end.

By 1879, then, Maitland's main characteristics were already formed. In practical affairs he was a reformer, but he wished to reform the present without abusing the past. At this time and for a long time afterwards, he thought that the path to reform necessarily lay through the understanding of the past. In Germany, in particular, he admired the part which historical study had played in legal reform, and he seems to have thought that it might play a somewhat similar part in the Anglo-Saxon countries. But as time went on he spoke less of legal reform and more of the system of medieval law. He reserved his reforming activity for academic politics and turned his main energies to history.

Maitland's work in making medieval law intelligible as a system adapted to the state of society of that time is somewhat similar to the work of his grandfather on the religion of the "Dark Ages." There was a strong similarity between the two men. They both insisted on the rationality, in their time and place, of ideas and modes of action which most modern men condemned as inherently absurd. Even medievalists like Stubbs had little appreciation of the system of medieval thought and social organization; they simply hoped to detect a few rays of light in a scene of general ignorance, violence, and superstition. It was Maitland's first contribution to history that, though he rejected – much more completely than Stubbs – the beliefs of medieval men, he was willing to treat their thoughts and problems seriously and systematically down to the last detail.

Although there are few letters before 1885, the first two, written as a schoolboy at Eton, are among the best. It is astonishing to us that no one realized there was anything unusual about Maitland until he was twenty or more years old. He was no good at school, and he was nineteen before he scraped into Cambridge. He looked back with hostility to the classical education of Eton, and this too is odd, for he later showed outstanding linguistic abilities. At Cambridge he continued to drift intellectually until he met Sidgwick. Then he began to see his way ahead, but – and this is the oddest feature of all – it was the conveyancer's office which gave him the intellectual stimulus he needed. The contact with original documents and precise problems gave his powers of generalization a new purpose.

When he moved he moved quickly. His mind and attitudes were formed before he was thirty, and thereafter they did not change much. What the letters illustrate is the mature Maitland at work. Most brilliantly they illustrate his extreme virtuosity as a craftsman. He understood every side of the craft of the historian. It is common knowledge that he was an astonishingly rapid and accurate worker, that his eye fell effortlessly on what was significant, that he expressed the most recondite thoughts and described the most complicated procedures with sparkling lucidity. But what the letters bring out is his willingness to labor on tasks of grinding monotony. Few historians hold all the trump cards. Those who can generalize are often inaccurate in detail; those who can write well shirk the labor of transcription; almost everyone hates the task of indexing. Maitland loved it all and did everything – or almost everything – supremely well. He transcribed documents, till the corns stood up on his fingers. He taught himself paleography and medieval French grammar; he searched large quantities of disorganized records for illustrative cases. He would even make indexes for other men's books. No man has done more of the donkey-work of the historian. And on top of it all, he could write and reason like an angel. It seems unfair that one man should have so much. How did he manage it?

In the first place, his vivacity of mind was so great that he seemed not to know weariness, boredom, and fatigue. "I am enjoying it immensely" – these and similar phrases describe his invariable reactions to long and dreary tasks. Perhaps his constant illness made him dissociate himself from his body and look on it with a sort of amused detachment. It is a curious thing that it was only when he began to be very ill indeed that he began to experience the pleasures of physical well-being: "For the first time in my life I am feeling that mere existence is pleasant," he wrote from Las Palmas in the autumn of 1898, when his enforced winterings abroad began (no. 230). For Maitland this discovery, which most men make in adolescence, was a sinister one, for it meant that the machine was beginning to run down. He still continued to produce more than most men, but his marvelous fourteen years of unsurpassed achievement from 1884 to 1898 were over.

The secret of his productivity was certainly his speed of execution, and the letters give many illustrations of the rapidity with which he could plan and carry out original and ambitious projects. The range of his activity at full stretch is well illustrated in the letters from 1890 to 1892, when (in addition to a load of lecturing almost unknown to modern professors) he was planning and writing a great part of the *History of English Law* and *Domesday Book and Beyond*, editing the *Memoranda de Parliamento* for the Rolls Series and Court Rolls for the Selden Society, revising Vinogradoff's *Villeinage in England*, and generally keeping in the thick of everything that was going on in the medieval historical world. He could only have done so much if he had had a most accurate power of discriminating between essentials and inessentials. Indeed it is not so much his rapidity, as the judgment which made speed safe, that impresses the reader of his letters. He understood instinctively how historical problems should be tackled – not just in general but down to the most minute details. There is a letter of 1885 (no. 17) which shows this power most convincingly. At this time Maitland had edited only one short text, but he was able to give an account of the way in which a quite different kind of text (the Year Books) should be edited, which could scarcely be improved. Nothing escaped his notice – typography, proofreading, payment of editors, as well as manuscript *stemmata*, annotation, translation, and indexing, are all dealt with in a few words – and on every point he was right. Those who stand outside the game are apt to think it is easy to make the right judgment on comparatively trivial points, and correspondingly difficult on important ones. But the players know that the important points often solve themselves; the *trivia* are the cause of fumbling judgments and sleepless nights. Maitland never fumbled; he was never hypnotized by learned detail.

Perhaps anyone who is not a medievalist will be disappointed in reading these letters to discover that they are so much taken up with the details of the craft. But it is for this very reason that Maitland is still important. If we compare him with Sir Henry Maine, the only legal historian of comparable stature among his contemporaries, we see at once that in this matter of historical craftsmanship, Maitland belongs to the present, and Maine to the past. Maine had a widely ranging mind; he could step with ease from Powys to the Punjab and from ancient Egypt to modern Turkey, taking in Hindu ritual and Christian marriage on the way. He opened the eyes of a large public to the importance of comparative history, but he has no illumination for us. It was Maitland's good fortune to be only moderately successful academically as a young man, so he escaped the easy assurance of the eminently successful man looking at the world. He had to learn about documents the hard way, in a conveyancer's office. This taught him to keep close to the ground. He learned that the approach to history must be through drudgery, and that no amount of elegance, economy, and precision of mind can take the place of an enormous capacity for hard work. He had no successors. Yet in a sense all modern historical researchers are his successors. Maitland's virtues are the virtues we should all like to possess; his way of doing things is the way of all modern research.

We must ask two questions before leaving him. Why did he have no successors? And why is it that now, fifty or sixty years after his death [this was written in 1967], his reputation is growing among a wider circle than ever before?

On the first question we must distinguish between the short-term and the long-term causes. Among the short-term causes, it was unlucky that his chief pupil, G. J. Turner, turned out to be one of the world's most accomplished procrastinators. Maitland's last letter speaks of Turner's delays: "he knows and I know and you had better know that his name cannot be mentioned at the Press Syndicate" – and Turner justified this reputation by keeping the volume prepared under Maitland's eye in proof for fifty years before it was (posthumously) published. It was unlucky too that for a variety of reasons Maitland in Cambridge did not have the opportunities of Stubbs in Oxford for founding a school of history. But these are only temporary and local reasons for the weakness of Maitland's immediate influence on historical writing. Much more important was the decline of law, and the rise of economics, administration, and theology – in this order – as the sources of historical inspiration. To the generation after Maitland the approach to history through law came to seem too formal a way of getting at the central problems of society in the past. In medieval studies this situation has been changing in recent years with the rise of a new school of canon law, but even this grows more naturally from the theological, administrative, and economic interests of our day than from the kind of law that Maitland chiefly studied.

Why then does Maitland's reputation and influence grow? The answer lies in a single word: sociology. We have passed through the constitutional, legal, administrative, and economic phases of historical writing. Most historians are now in some way sociologists. That is to say, they are more interested in the structure of society than in constitutional or institutional development. Maitland, though he scarcely knew it, was a pioneer here. There is very little development in Maitland's history. Even his *Constitutional History* is a series of studies in static situations. His greatest work, the *History of English Law Before the Time of Edward I,* is in fact an account of the bonds of society during a single phase of feudalism between 1150 and 1272. Maitland died while he was still laying the foundations for a similar account of the next phase. What he achieved is one of the most masterly accounts of the intricacies of society during a short and manageable period that has ever been written. There are more recent examples of this kind of history, but none that rival Maitland in intellectual power and beauty.

Maitland was the antithesis of Stubbs: Maitland is the historian of situations, Stubbs of development. It is fashionable now to depreciate Stubbs and to praise Maitland, and it is easy to see why this has happened. Maitland's precise concepts and lucid exposition are attuned to modern scientific requirements; Stubbs's muddy generalizations and anachronistic concepts are correspondingly irritating. But it should be remembered that Maitland left out those things which elude definition: human character and deep-seated change. There are no portraits in Maitland's history and little sense of social development. All things considered, I believe that Stubbs was the greater historian, but Maitland has more to teach us now. His letters are a case in point. Stubbs's letters belong irretrievably to his generation; those of Maitland speak our language and deal with our problems. Their candor, integrity, and absence of cant make them a worthy memorial of the brightest scientific intellect among the historians of the last century.

9

Sir Maurice Powicke (1879–1963)

Frederick Maurice Powicke was born on June 16, 1879, the eldest child of the Reverend Frederick John Powicke and Martha, youngest daughter of William Collyer of Brigstock, Northants.[1] His father was a native of Kidderminster and had been trained for the Congregational ministry in Birmingham; as a young man he must have had some romantic impulse which caused him to add a final "e" to the old Worcestershire village name of Powick, whence the family took its name. In 1878 F. J. Powicke began his ministry at Alnwick and his first child was born there in the following year. He called him Maurice after F. D. Maurice, whose liberal theology had greatly influenced him, but Frederick was the name by which he was commonly known outside the family until his middle years. The historical associations of Alnwick always appealed to Powicke and he liked to think of himself as having an adoptive interest in the land of Thomas Hodgkin and Mandell Creighton, "a district not devoid of inspiration for a spacious survey of the strange movements of ecclesiastical history," as he once called it.

These associations, however, existed only in retrospect, for in 1886 the family moved to Hatherlow, three miles from Stockport. This move determined the course of Powicke's life in its main outline. He went to Stockport Grammar School, where he remembered with gratitude the help of a schoolmaster, Mr. Knowles, "an irascible, touchy, redheaded little man, sometimes very bitter in speech and even cruel, but with a genuine respect for learning," and he "owed a lot to Mr. Pemberton the headmaster, not for his teaching, which was absurd, but for his kind and persistent regard" for his welfare. Altogether Powicke must have been a strange little creature in this rough Dickensian society. He describes himself as a kind of bird of passage, arriving at school after a walk through the woods, playing no games, and being allowed to use the masters' room so that he could work by himself. Most important of all, he found his way to the local Free Library where in a side room – "a stuffy, smelling place" – during the lunch hour he made his first acquaintance with the monthly and quarterly reviews, and through them with politics, literature, and the existence of the wide world.[2]

In 1896 he got the school-leaving scholarship and his father "decided not to put me into business but to let me go to the university."

> My father thought of classics, and saw Wilkins, the Latin Professor at Owen's College. He thought I was not good enough (as I certainly was not) and advised history. So I had my first momentous interview with Professor Tout, in the old Freeman Library, a room on the second floor of the main building... I was waiting in the corridor when I saw a strange figure with a jerky nodding head and a shambling sort of walk come along. I thought he was a porter. He said with a frightful jerk and a sort of gasp in the throat, "Are you waiting to see me?" I said, "I am waiting to see Professor Tout." He said, "I am Professor Tout." Then he pulled out a bunch of keys, opened the Freeman room, and took me inside.

Once inside, Powicke made a slow start. At the beginning of the second term Tout was still not sure if he was good enough; then "I must have found my feet very suddenly, for though I was not aware that I was getting on so fast I carried everything before me at Easter." From this time all went well, though there was a slight hitch right at the end when "Bury (the external examiner) nearly refused me a First because my ancient history paper was so bad." The three years between 1896 and 1899 were a time of immense activity, "reading Ranke, Hallam, Macaulay, Gardiner, Symonds, Burckhardt, Creighton, Sismondi, Roscoe, &c., as well as Macchiavelli, Guicciardini, Commines, the Clarke papers," writing on the Levellers and John Lilburne (for a Shuttleworth Essay Prize), winning a Derby Prize which was to help to take him to Oxford, and so on.[3] "I am still living on the impressions which I got from all this stuff," he wrote thirty years later. His horizons had expanded very rapidly:

> When I first began to read, I read Emerson and Matthew Arnold, and then I got on to Shakespeare (I read him all through) and Macaulay and lots of things in my father's study. I knew where every book was at one time. Once I asked him about the philosophers – what Locke said, what Berkeley said, and so on. I do not think he knew much about it, but I went to bed deciding to know *everything*. It seemed quite easy to know everything.

Specialized books about history, however, long remained an object of distant veneration – far longer than they would have any chance of remaining nowadays. When he read Tout's review of *Domesday Book and Beyond* in the *Manchester Guardian*, he cut it out and treasured it, and "wondered whether I should ever read the book itself." This must have been in his second year as an undergraduate. In his third year he won an exhibition to Balliol, Tout's old college, and he went there in 1899.

Although Tout was no doubt responsible for encouraging this move, the main inspiration behind it was Ernest Barker. The Barkers lived near the Powickes and the young man used to come over the hill to have long talks with Dr. Powicke. His unbounded vitality and splendid success made a deep impression, and Powicke left for Oxford with this ideal before his eyes. On his first night in Oxford, during the scholarship examination, he went to visit Barker in Merton and he fell at once under the spell:

> I can still feel (he wrote many years later) the first impression of that beautiful quadrangle at night. It has always meant Oxford to me...and I can still smell the smell of the rugs with which Barker had covered his sofa and the chairs in his panelled room lit by fire and lamplight.

In December 1899, at the end of his first term, Powicke was promoted to the Brackenbury Scholarship, the highest honor that a Balliol historian can ever achieve. But this was the prelude to three rather disappointing years. Powicke lacked the self-confidence and physical vigor of Barker who had carried off his lowly origin and provincial background with such élan. He was too sensitive and too deeply a dissenter, socially as well as in religion, to mix easily with the dazzling youth of Strachan-Davidson's Balliol. Yet he was sufficiently conscious of his merit to resent neglect and to feel that his Balliol tutors had little to offer him after Manchester. Many of his Balliol recollections therefore were memories of slight injuries and small kindnesses: the chaplain was the source of some of the former; the Master and the Captain of Boats, who advised him to give up rowing (he must have been a man of infinite tact), the heroes of some of the latter. In his last lectures as Regius Professor, which he delivered in Balliol Hall, he spoke with admiration of A. L. Smith's lectures, but the occasion was a moving one and I cannot find that he ever spoke of them at any other time. On the whole, Manchester College and Mansfield College, then at the height of their influence, with their pulpits often filled by notable preachers, were places where he felt more at home than in Balliol. This unease was also reflected in his academic record. He got only a Second in Greats[4] in 1902 and only a *proxime* in the Stanhope Essay Prize in the previous year. Since the Stanhope was won by R. W. Seton-Watson a *proxime* was no disgrace. But Powicke did not know this at the time and he felt it deeply. A First in History in 1903 somewhat redeemed these setbacks, but failure in a fellowship attempt at All Souls College put him back once more into uncertainty. These are small checks to record in a distinguished career, but they are reminders of the strains and struggles of Powicke's early life. Success did not come easily to him and he knew nothing of effortless superiority. Disappointments were sharp and frustrations never far off. But, if he felt them keenly, he faced them with an inbred humor which brought a lightness to his distress.

It was left to Tout, his constant stay and support in these years, to come to the rescue. In 1902 Powicke's first publication appeared under Tout's auspices in the volume of *Historical Essays by Members of Owen's College Manchester*. Powicke's essay was on Pierre Dubois. It is not a very powerful essay, but it shows that he was already interested in the recently revived study of medieval thought, and it is rather surprising that after such a beginning he should have published nothing on any similar theme for another twenty years.

Tout's other good deed for Powicke in 1902 was to get him appointed as Langton Fellow at Manchester. This was a research fellowship for three years, and it meant that the failure to get a fellowship at Oxford was not disastrous. Powicke set to work with vigor and by the summer of 1904 he had finished an account of Furness Abbey for the *Victoria County History*. This was his first serious piece of historical writing – "my first-born, my fair one, my darling," as he ruefully described it in the following year when it emerged mangled from Tait's friendly criticism. All seemed to be going well at last and he wrote to his favorite aunt in June 1904:

> I have achieved all that I hoped to achieve ten years ago – the outlook was very narrow then, and ten short steps up the ladder have revealed vast plains beyond the high garden wall.

In fact, however, he was on the brink of what might have been a final academic disaster. The cause of this was a successful application for an assistant lectureship at Liverpool in 1905. Ramsay Muir in his *Autobiography* has left a lively though rather inaccurate account of the incident.[5] The professor in Liverpool was J. M. Mackay, described by Muir as having "the figure of an athlete and the shoulders of a prize fighter, crowned by the most magnificent head I have ever seen." It seems that Mackay's views on history and historical teaching owed more to his pugilistic shoulders than his fine head, and from the beginning he thought little of a lecturer so ill-equipped in this respect as Powicke. He betrayed (in Powicke's words) "a well-bred, courteous and not unkindly repugnance to my presence."[6] Whatever the reason, he decided not to continue the appointment after a probationary year, and the future – especially after an unsuccessful attempt at Bristol – seemed blacker than ever. "I was on the point of taking up a commercial career," he once said with reference to these days. Once more it was Tout who effected a rescue by the offer of an assistant lectureship at Manchester. This was the turning-point in Powicke's career. For the next few years he was carried along on a prosperous course and developed rapidly as a scholar and teacher. From being a struggling student with little encouragement outside Manchester he rapidly won the approval of such stern critics as R. L. Poole and J. H. Round. Poole's encouragement was especially important to him because it opened the *English Historical Review* (*EHR*) to him and gave him his first serious discipline in learned publication. But without Tout he would never have got started at all. Tout had watched over him with a fatherly eye for ten critical years, dealing out praise and blame with a rough honesty in letters which still warm the heart of a reader after sixty years.

In 1908, when Powicke was about to try for a Prize Fellowship at Merton, Tout wrote to him:

> The root of the matter for you is, I am sure, to get the successful lawyer's supreme gift of going straight to the vital point, and making it clear to all readers that you have arrived at the same vital point. Mind you I don't say you don't – and I'd not venture to pester you at all if I didn't think that taking you for all in all you are the best man of your years I've ever had anything to do with.

The field for the Merton Fellowship was a strong one, but the examiners saw the light – Tout took care to shine it in their eyes – and Powicke returned to Oxford for a year which he never ceased to look back on with a glow of pleasure. "The kindly influences of Merton, *domus placida*, of the Fellows' Quadrangle, and, most of all, of Bishop Rede's Library" softened the asperities of earlier experiences. He resided for only one year of his seven years' fellowship. In 1909, after failing at Birmingham, he was appointed to the Chair of Modern History at Belfast. Before leaving for Belfast in September of this year he married Susan Lindsay, the sister of his old Oxford friend A. D. Lindsay. In every way he was secure at last. It is probably not too much to say that till the day of his death his whole being depended on the support and security which he drew in daily replenishments from this marriage.

We may stop at this point to consider his early work as a scholar. As I have already mentioned, the Pierre Dubois essay of 1902 contained a promise of future development which was not at once fulfilled. It was in many ways immature, and Powicke may have realized that he did not yet have the equipment to deal with the difficult problems of medieval philosophy or political thought. In any event he turned to the better-trodden paths of Anglo-Norman feudal and political history and gave them a charm and distinction – they are paths not easy to beautify – quite his own. It was ironical that at the moment when Mackay was preparing to administer the *coup de grâce* to Powicke's academic career, his first article in the *EHR* on Roger of Wendover and the Coggeshall Chronicle was going through the press. His special gift for bringing intimacy and light into problems which in other hands would appear barrenly textual or drably political was here first displayed in public.

For the next ten years not a year passed without a substantial contribution from Powicke. It was these contributions which first placed him in the front rank of English medievalists, and R. L. Poole, the editor of the *EHR*, was the first Oxford historian to believe in him as a coming man. He gave him plenty of books to review, chiefly on French history, and Powicke grew rapidly in power and authority. He developed a quick eye for important details in long dull books and a high proportion of his very numerous reviews is still worth reading for this reason. The one criticism that can be made of these reviews is that the book itself is often a disappointment after the expectation aroused by the review. Powicke saw what was significant and the reader who follows in his footsteps often finds that the best things have been picked out and he is left with some very tedious matter on his hands. His articles too showed a growing power of seizing on an inconspicuous detail of geography or family alliances and giving it a central place in a brilliant reconstruction of familiar events. This ability, which became a characteristic feature of Powicke's writing, reached its full development in 1909 in the account of the murder of Arthur of Brittany. In its kind he never wrote anything better than this.

The results of this first phase of Powicke's activity were gathered together in the volume published in 1913, *The Loss of Normandy (1189–1204)*. This volume "based upon researches which I began some years ago as Langton Fellow in the University of Manchester" is a collection of studies rather than a single whole. Its scope is much wider than the title would lead one to expect and it shows a very vivid appreciation of the feudal arrangements of the late twelfth century. Some will regard it as his best book, and certainly as a craftsman working with complicated and intractable materials Powicke was never seen to better advantage. Even J. H. Round had to admit that in so detailed a study of the Norman baronage and its holdings of land "a much larger proportion of slips might have been expected." High praise indeed from the master detector of slips in feudal history.

II

I can find very little to report about Powicke's work at Belfast, beyond the facts that Miss Maude Clarke was his best pupil and outside the university he was active in promoting the work of the Workers Educational Association. In 1915 he joined the War Trade Intelligence Department in London. Before he could return to Belfast, the History Department in Manchester needed to be reorganized as a result of the retirement of James Tait and the partial retirement of Tout in 1919. Powicke was offered the Chair of Medieval and Ramsay Muir that of Modern History, while Tout continued as Director of Advanced Studies and Chairman of the History Faculty until 1925, when Powicke succeeded him in these positions. These nine years in Manchester from 1919 to 1928 were the most fruitful years of his life in the variety of plans and achievement which they inspired.

The central fact in these years is his own scholarly and intellectual development. For nearly twenty years he had immersed himself in the secular feudal history of the period from about 1170 to 1220. In his published work he had made very few excursions outside this field.[7] But now there came a change which may be associated with two events. The first of these was the action of Robert Fawtier, at that time an assistant keeper of manuscripts in the John Rylands Library, who called his attention to some theological collections of Walter Daniel, the twelfth-century monk of Rievaulx. This stimulated Powicke's interest and finally led to his discovery of Walter Daniel's biography of Abbot Ailred. He published the text of this biography with a long introduction. He had a long familiarity with Rievaulx and its neighborhood, and to anyone who knew him the similarity of temper between Powicke and Abbot Ailred was very striking. The subject therefore was naturally congenial, and he brought to it his bibliographical flair and his talent for constructing realistic portraits of men and events from flimsy and scattered materials. The result is a piece of work so suited to his talents and temperament that it has always been a mystery to me that he never followed it up with more work in the same field. The truth seems to be that he was not very interested in the details of monastic life and thought. He liked Ailred as a man, he loved Rievaulx, and he enjoyed bringing the pieces in the jigsaw together. He was glad when an opportunity arose, thirty years later, of making a new edition of his work. But he had said what he had to say, he had no desire to say more, and he was even a little impatient at the importance which later scholars came to attach to Ailred.

The other, and much more important, event in the enlargement of his scholarly work came from his connection with Merton. In 1920 the librarian at Merton, P. S. Allen, had brought together the catalogues and other documents relating to the medieval library of the college. He asked Powicke to help in editing them. Powicke agreed, but (to quote his own words) "as I worked upon these documents, the original plan changed." The plan which began to take shape was something more than an edition of the library lists with identification of existing manuscripts; it was a sort of corporate intellectual biography of the college during its first two centuries, reconstructed from the records and survivals of its medieval books.

The volume, which appeared in 1931, contains a vast amount of bio-graphical and bibliographical information about the college in its golden age when it had a distinctive place in the development of European thought. It may be objected that the result is in many ways incomplete. It is not a complete catalogue of books, nor is it a complete account of donors or authors. For Powicke it represented simply a beginning, and in a talk to the students of Royal Holloway College he gave a very candid account of his own and the book's limitations:

> When I first began to interest myself in these books (about 1920), I found myself at a loss. They meant little or nothing to me, and those which sur-vive, as I turned them over, seemed even more mysterious than the records of those which are gone. After ten years they mean more, but how little. I have read none of these particular manuscripts, and I am acquainted with the contents of perhaps a dozen. I never shall read them. I seem to be scratching away at the surface of a great mound, rather like an inquisitive fowl. Yet what worlds of learning and experience, old and new, have dimly and dis-tantly been revealed.[8]

Surely a distinguished author can seldom have spoken to a group of students more candidly about his latest book. He puts his finger on the book's weaknesses and strength. Powicke neither had, nor claimed to have, the equipment to deal exhaustively with scholastic thought or manu-scripts. But he saw the opportunities offered by a collection like that at Merton, and he rightly thought that he could do something to open these opportunities to others.

One of the first lessons which he learnt from this work was the need for better tools if the work was ever to prosper. High in his list of desiderata was a comprehensive catalogue of *incipits* of medieval scholastic treatises. At the International Historical Congress in Brussels in 1924 he urged the need for such a catalogue. The plan was approved and referred to the various learned academies. Although Powicke did not lose sight of the plan, nothing came of it. This was his first introduction to the planning of cooperative enterprises and to the frustrations which such plans entail.

The work on the Merton manuscripts continued slowly through the 1920s, and the enlarging of Powicke's interests began to be seen in 1925 in his article on Master Simon of Faversham and his reviews of the works of Haskins and Lynn Thorndike on medieval science. In the following year there appeared his essay on the *Christian Life in the Middle Ages*. This was the first example of the discursive essays of his later years. It was a kind of writing in which he excelled. He liked to take up themes as they presented themselves to his mind, to respond to their stimulus, and then to pass on as the mood, rather than the logic of the argument, led him. He always believed, whether rightly or not I do not know, that it was the reading of this essay that caused Baldwin to offer him the Regius Chair in Oxford three years later.

Before this event took place he had an opportunity to show the new direction of his interests on a large scale. About the end of 1925 he was invited to give the Ford Lectures at Oxford. He chose as his theme Archbishop Stephen Langton. Oddly enough he had at first no intention of displaying or developing his new interest in scholastic thought. He intended simply to study Langton's part in the struggle for the Great Charter and to sketch his later activity as an ecclesiastical administrator. It was almost by chance that the discovery of Langton's Parisian lectures changed the direction of his thoughts. The discovery gave him the idea of investigating the links between the practical politics and academic thought of the thirteenth century. In retrospect the combination seems an inevitable result of Powicke's development. All his previous work was, in one way or another, a preparation for the conflation of these hitherto distinct lines of research, and all his later work was a continuation of the discussion initiated in the Ford Lectures. As I have already hinted, he was not either interested in or equipped for an intensive study of medieval scholasticism; yet even his earliest work on feudal politics had shown his desire to step out of the rather narrow limits of earlier work on feudalism. He never forgot that feudal society could only be understood in the light of ideals and attitudes which had originated in the monasteries and schools. Stephen Langton gave Powicke a chance to draw theory and practice together into a single whole. The lectures, which had been begun in a spirit of retreat to the range of interests displayed in the *Loss of Normandy*, became the occasion for a new step forward. They were mostly written in a great burst of activity in December 1926. At the end of the year he wrote to Tout:

> It has been a most distracting and busy term, but I am grateful to God that I am better than I have felt for years. This vacation I have worked harder than I have done since 1906, and without much sense of strain. Five Ford lectures have been written since the end of November. Of course I have been poking about and meditating on them since the spring and knew what I wanted to say, but a year ago I simply could not have written them straight off like this. I have read them to Susie who says they are quite simple and clear, without too much detail, but not giving any impression of "slightness." She is a good judge, so I am not bothering about them any more. The sixth lecture – on Langton as archbishop – will be quite new to me, as I have not thought about it yet, but I think I ought to be able to do it in January.

He always looked back on these lectures with special pleasure and regarded them as his best book. Their publication in 1928 was certainly a notable event in English medieval studies. Never before had medieval politics and academic thought been used to illuminate each other as Powicke used them in these lectures.

> I have tried (he wrote) to describe a great man, with a clear, sensible, penetrating, but not original mind, at work in a time more important, more critical, more full of opportunity, than any other period in the history of the medieval Church. And above all I have tried to bring him into relation both with the common man in England and with the intellectual life of Europe, to break down the barriers which prevent us from considering as a whole, in the light of the influences which played upon them, the men and affairs of politics and religion.

This statement describes the whole tendency of Powicke's later teaching and influence. It helps to explain why the book gave an impulse to the work of others which has not yet lost its momentum. Yet (it may be admitted) Langton himself – laborious, conscientious, courageous though he was – could scarcely support the role of a central character in European affairs; consequently, the book itself, considered apart from its influence, suffers from the difficulty of making ends meet.

To say this, however, is to speak with the advantage of nearly forty years of continuous progress in these studies. It is more important to consider the immediate effect. The most important effect was to give a new direction, and to impose a new pattern, on Powicke's plans for co-operative research. We have seen that his plan for a catalogue of *incipits* proposed in 1924 had come to nothing. Since this time he had been directing his Manchester pupils to the study of proceedings under the Dictum of Kenilworth. This had been a plan suggested by Hilary Jenkinson, and most of Powicke's pupils took some share in the work. Stephen Langton opened up a new field, or rather two new fields, of impressive dimensions. The first of them was the intensive study of Langton's scholastic works, the second was the study of ecclesiastical administration and the reorganization which followed the general Council of the Lateran in 1215–16. Each of these fields was to be tilled by groups of workers under Powicke's general guidance, inspired by his initiative and vision. The first members of the "scholastic group" were Miss Beryl Smalley and Miss Alys Gregory; they were soon joined by Mgr. George Lacombe, and the group produced the series of studies and indexes of Langton's works which appeared in 1931. From the "administrative group" came the work of Miss Gibbs and Miss Lang, the edition of Langton's *acta* of Miss Major, and finally the plan for a new edition of Wilkins's *Concilia*.

In the year in which *Stephen Langton* was published Powicke left Manchester for Oxford. On the eve of his departure he wrote: "Most of my energy in late years has gone in getting the right people together and helping them to work together with confidence."[9] He was in high hopes. He had found the right kind of cooperative work: it was informal, friendly, intimate; everything depended on his inspiration; nothing was left to committees. Within three years of Tout's retirement he had given a new turn to the tradition of the historical research in Manchester. In these few years he had established himself as a central scholar in an international movement in medieval studies, and he had discovered his full powers as a teacher. Both developments had come quite naturally from his earlier interests. From Pierre Dubois and Norman feudalism to Stephen Langton and the Christian life in the Middle Ages, from the reading parties in Yorkshire and the Cotswolds to the groups of researchers depending on him for encouragement and inspiration: these steps represented the blossoming of Powicke's highly individual genius, and made him from small beginnings a scholar of world-wide fame and influence. To understand this development is to understand Powicke.

III

In coming to Oxford Powicke believed that he was being called upon to do in Oxford what he had done in Manchester, and he imagined that his new colleagues welcomed him for the same reason. This led to some misunderstandings. In his Inaugural Lecture on February 8, 1929, he spoke urbanely and appreciatively about the Oxford History School of his youth and the developments of the last thirty years. Then came a phrase which must have seemed ominous to some of his listeners. "In attempting this rough sketch...I have had a practical object." This object was to raise "the issue of the organization of advanced or post-graduate work." Powicke proceeded to outline his views on this subject. He advocated, among other things, a closer connection between undergraduate and post-graduate studies, and, as a measure tending in this direction, the division of the undergraduate course into two parts as in Manchester. The word "Manchester" was not mentioned, but his listeners were quick to supply without enthusiasm the omission. He drew a picture of undergraduate studies culminating in the third year in the "two kinds of experience which historical study can provide and which should not be separated, namely, the lessons suggested by the historical treatment of political science and of general historical developments, and the discipline implied in the careful intensive study of a special historical subject"; and he referred to his own experience:

> I have learned how much a group of people can get out of work, in itself rather dull or seeming to lead nowhere, when they are conscious of working towards a common goal... We want more country gentry and clergy, more

ecclesiastical dignitaries, more schoolmasters and mistresses, more lawyers, more public servants, more persons of leisure to be engaged in historical work. Hence, while I hope to see a systematic organization of advanced study...I venture to suggest that we should avoid the tendency to regard advanced students as constituting a separate post-graduate school.

These views may seem harmless enough now. Such things are said almost daily. But there was much in them in 1929 to displease the majority of Powicke's listeners among the senior members of the University, and their opposition hardened as the plan behind these sentences became clearer. They felt that the professionalism, which Powicke deplored in post-graduate studies, would simply be diffused throughout the whole course, they distrusted any move towards turning undergraduate studies into a training for historians rather than a general education, and they had no faith in the merits of post-graduate degrees. The conflict came to be concentrated in the single issue of the division of the undergraduate course into two parts. Powicke never gave up trying to carry through this change; he fought for it in committees, boards, and in congregation; he always hoped and he always failed. The failure cast a cloud over his years in Oxford, and he scarcely realized how much he had in fact achieved.

In Oxford, as elsewhere, Powicke expended a great deal of energy on organization and often got what he wanted by sheer persistence. But his greatest influence was felt in his dealings with individuals, and in small groups of his own choosing. It was less strong in addressing large audiences: his fluty, quavering voice was not easy to hear, and the course of his argument, sufficiently clear in conversation, was lost in lectures. On these occasions he was strangely unaware of his audience, as the experience of one formal lecture shows:

> The first and only time I gave a Rylands Lecture – on Gerald of Wales – I suddenly realized, when Guppy came to me and gently turned me round, that I had unconsciously turned the swivel-top of the reading desk and was speaking with my back to the audience.[10]

Crowds did not inspire him. But "groups" – a favorite word of his – and individuals called forth all his powers. Among his first innovations in Oxford was the "Medieval Group," an informal meeting of tutors and research students to read papers and discuss problems. Thus baldly stated nothing could sound more commonplace. But there was nothing commonplace about Powicke's creations. Some did not like it, but the "Powickery," as it was called, was a privileged circle, and I do not think that anyone felt that its meetings were quite like other meetings.

Powicke's talent for blowing the smoking flax into flame was exercised most conspicuously in the class on "Church and State in the time of

Edward I," a Special Subject which he introduced shortly after his arrival in Oxford. It was never a large class, but over the years it gave a large number of undergraduates a new idea of historical research. In form, it was somewhere between the Continental seminar and the Oxford tutorial, and it provided an atmosphere in which Powicke felt at ease. The elevation, the mixture of formality and intimacy, was just right for him. His mixture of courtesy and severity, of encouragement and sometimes unexpectedly sharp criticism, combined with the rarefied atmosphere of strange ideas, made a deep impression, and in these classes he really fulfilled, without any of the legislation which caused him so much trouble and frustration, the purposes that he wished to promote.

The same may be said of his relations with his research students. When Powicke came to Oxford research degrees had scarcely begun to win for themselves the place in the University which they now hold. It is fair to say that they were regarded with varying proportions of suspicion, contempt, and indifference by most college tutors. It was against this whole attitude that Powicke set his face. He felt himself the protector of all research students in modern history. He interviewed them all, he arranged their supervision, and supervised many himself. In this field he exercised an intensely personal rule. He had inherited an embryonic Faculty Library and he made this his special domain. He chose the books, determined the conditions of admission, and supervised every detail. I still recall the strange feeling of other-worldliness on entering it thirty years ago. It was like a shrine and had to be approached with care; and this feeling expressed in an extraordinary way Powicke's idea of advanced historical study.

Although disappointed in many ways by his reception at Oxford, and although he failed in most of his legislative proposals, he nevertheless made a contribution to the study of history in the University greater than any professor since Stubbs. He did this partly by the penetration of his personal influence through his pupils, and partly by the long-term efficacy of his ideals of historical training and research. He did not influence the structure and balance of historical studies as Stubbs had done, but he succeeded in exciting a more lively interest in Continental scholarship and especially in the rapidly expanding study of medieval thought. During his time Oxford replaced Manchester in general repute as a center of medieval studies. Like Stubbs, Powicke was disappointed by the appearance of failure where he would most have liked to succeed, and the extent of his success was hidden from his eyes.

Outside Oxford his influence in the historical world at large continued to grow during his years as Regius Professor.[11] Among his many activities there are two which deserve mention both for their importance and for the light they throw on the development of his plans for cooperative research. I have already alluded to the first of these as a distant outcome of the lectures on Stephen Langton, which had turned Powicke's mind towards the problems of ecclesiastical administration. When he was invited to give the Raleigh Lecture in 1931 he chose as his subject *Sir Henry Spelman and the "Concilia."* Like the Inaugural Lecture three years earlier it had a practical as well as a scholarly aim. He wished to draw attention to the work of the first collector of English ecclesiastical conciliar material, in order to recommend a project which had been forming in his mind for some time:

> Before very long some of us hope to get together and to plan a new edition of Wilkins, in continuation of the work of Haddan and Stubbs, from the Conquest to the reign of Edward II, perhaps even to the Reformation. It is a difficult task but the time has come to undertake it.

This lecture was delivered on March 18, 1931. In September there was the first meeting of the "Concilia Group," which continued to meet annually until the outbreak of war, and thereafter at irregular intervals. At the first meeting the scope of the plan was extended to cover the whole of the Middle Ages in five volumes, arrangements for publication were made with the Clarendon Press, the work was assigned to eight scholars, and a periodical bulletin was projected to keep the members of the group in touch with current developments. It was reckoned that the whole enterprise might take as long as twenty years to complete. This estimate has proved to be optimistic; but after thirty-three years the first two volumes, covering the period from 1205 to 1313, will have appeared before this memoir is in print.[12] The chief credit for thus bringing the main part of Powicke's original intention to a successful issue belongs to Professor Cheney, who has been a member of the "Concilia Group" from the beginning.

This was a far larger plan than any Powicke had so far conceived. He was influenced by the example of those groups of scholars in England and France who had moved mountains in the seventeenth century. Projects as ambitious as those of the Bollandists or the Maurists were not to be thought of in modern conditions; but at least works as large and fundamental as those which came from the circle of William Camden, works of the scope of Camden's *Britannia*, Spelman's *Concilia*, Selden's *Tithes*, Dugdale's *Monasticon*, ought not to be beyond the resources of modern scholars. This was the thought behind Powicke's plans, and to this thought he added his own way of doing things. His address to the first meeting of the Concilia Group ended with the words:

> Only a group of people, working as friends, and merging so far as this purpose is concerned all considerations of personal reputation, can do this

work. This is why I have ventured to invite you to this informal gathering, so that we can come together, not as representing interests, but as friends.

By the end of 1931 the Concilia project had been fairly launched and Powicke turned his attention to some wider aspects of cooperation. In December 1932 he initiated a discussion in the Royal Historical Society on "Modern Methods of Medieval Research," in which he made suggestions which had a considerable influence on the development of the society. He outlined a new policy for the society, which included the undertaking of a cooperative work on chronology, the concentration of resources on "major research enterprises" rather than semi-social and miscellaneous activities, and the building up of the library "not only as a centre, but as *the* centre of local record publications ... the centre for the student as distinct from the organizer and preserver of the records." These were very ambitious plans for revitalizing a society whose *raison d'être* had become obscured by the foundation of the Historical Association and the Institute for Historical Research in recent years. The need for some more positive direction of affairs was strongly felt by some and repudiated by others. Powicke's proposals made him the leader of the reformers, and in a contested election – the rarest of rare events on such occasions – he was elected President of the Society in 1933. He now had power to put his suggestions to the test.

The main results of his efforts may be briefly summarized. On the positive side, the society's drift towards obscurity was arrested. The library was built up into a well-equipped working library on local history. The volume on chronology projected in 1932 appeared in 1939. It was a work with many blemishes, as a contributor to it may freely admit, but at least it *appeared*, and this is more than can be said of the companion volumes planned by the impressively named "Commission des listes chronologiques" of the International Historical Committee. Beyond that it is difficult to speak. The "major research enterprises," however desirable they may be, have not yet materialized and the idea of "*the* centre of local record publications," always over-ambitious, has perhaps been rendered otiose by the development of the libraries of the Institute of Historical Research and other specialized societies. Nevertheless the plans which Powicke fostered in these years inspired an amount of work which no one but he could have elicited; and the passage of time has tended to emphasize the far-sightedness of his proposals, at least in their main outlines.

The flow of his own publications necessarily suffered from these growing preoccupations with the planning of many enterprises ranging from those of the solitary research student to the groups working on large-scale plans. Powicke's main publication in the ten years before the outbreak of the Second World War was a new edition of Rashdall's *Universities of*

Europe in the Middle Ages (3 volumes, 1936), in which he was responsible for the Continental universities and A. B. Emden for the chapters on Oxford and Cambridge. This work had been undertaken in about 1925, and it involved a great deal of minute research in the abundant literature since the appearance of the first edition in 1895. At the time probably no one but Powicke in this country could have done this work, but he often regretted having undertaken it. He was not good at refusing. Several years earlier Tout had written to him when he had agreed to write an appreciation of Vinogradoff for the *EHR*: "I admire Tait (who had refused) for his inhuman gift of refusal: but you would be wise to cultivate the habit as far as nature allows." But it was not in Powicke's nature to cultivate this habit.

Among other works which he undertook during these years was a volume in the Home University Library on *Medieval England*, and an account of the Reformation in England for a large cooperative history. The first of these is a personal and strikingly successful sketch of those aspects of the subject which interested him most; the second has some moving and imaginative passages, but as a whole it fails to give a balanced account of the unfolding of events. Besides these works there were numerous essays and reviews. Some of them are among the best things Powicke ever wrote.

It was not until the year of his retirement that another major work appeared: *Henry III and the Lord Edward* is not only the biggest of Powicke's books, it is also the one on which his permanent reputation as a historian must ultimately rest. His work as a friend and inspirer of others will slowly be forgotten; the importance of *Stephen Langton* will diminish as the change of emphasis in medieval studies which it both symbolized and helped to bring about becomes a matter of established fact; the *Loss of Normandy* will remain as a solid and lasting contribution on a well-worn subject, but it will scarcely mark an epoch. With *Henry III and the Lord Edward* the position is quite different. On any reckoning it must be judged a remarkable, highly characteristic, and personal book. Beyond that opinions are likely to diverge. It certainly has no "plot." The reader is taken through English history from 1216 to 1272 as through a piece of English countryside, intricately woven with footpaths, dominated by a great house in which there is much coming and going, with an ineffective and often indignant old gentleman pottering about at the center of things. There is a constant sense of the larger scene – France, Italy, the Holy Land, Wales, the Church Universal – which changes as the unfolding of English events requires. There are stirring events – a sister married by violence, troubles about a dowry, guardians appointed for the old gentleman, a frustrated heir, and so on. But in the end everything settles down, the heir goes off on a long adventure and all is peace. Despite every

trouble it is a scene of perpetual sunshine, like a tapestry. Those who wish
to hear the solemn sound of John Bull knocking on the door of political
privilege will not hear it in this book. There is no noise of rural industries,
no plows in the landscape, no bustle of trade, only the more distant
murmur of the schools and the most fleeting glimpses of monks and friars.
Instead of all this there is a small society going about its everyday business, entangled in family disputes, beset with follies, disturbed by its idiosyncrasies of personality, visited by tragedy. It is all entirely natural.
Although the book is stuffed with learning – that is to say with details
drawn from contemporary sources requiring critical footnotes, sometimes
of considerable length and complexity – there is nothing of the learned
treatise about the method of presentation; there is a minimum of institutional background and only occasional disquisition on "problems" and
"issues." Powicke wished to write a book which could be read by anyone,
the expert and the layman alike, and one that would be neither popular
nor recondite, but just like life. Above all I think he would have liked to
be intelligible to the men about whom he wrote. He had, as he sometimes
wrote, a great dislike of "stream-lined and neatly cupboarded history." So
even those sides of history to which he had devoted most attention in his
middle years – the history of universities, theology, and the religious life –
had in the end to go into the common melting-pot. What emerged was
history as perhaps Proust might have written it – episodic, fitful, haunting.
It is history for scholars and men of leisure who can stop and think and
savor. Least of all is it for students, or others, in a hurry.

Henry III and the Lord Edward was begun as a contribution to the
Oxford History of England. The rules governing that series called for a
volume of about 175,000 words. The editor allowed considerable latitude
to contributors, but *Henry III and the Lord Edward* was nearly twice the
length and covered only about two-thirds of the period required by the
series. Powicke appears for a long time to have been unaware of the exact
position. On Easter Day 1944 he wrote:

> I discovered not long ago that I had written two-thirds of a big book (not a
> bad book either) without knowing it and was hopelessly out of scale (or
> rather on the wrong scale), so I had to settle down to a second version to
> the right scale, as well as to finishing the big book to be published later –
> and not to make them too much alike.[13]

In the event, the "big book" *Henry III and the Lord Edward* was published first (in 1947), and the Oxford History did not appear till 1953.
Despite every effort at compression it was almost as long as its predecessor, and – as might have been foreseen from Powicke's own doubts in
1944 – the problem of bringing the material into conformable shape was

one for which he had neither inclination nor strength. The truth was that he was tired. He was seventy-three and though he had an astonishing fund of physical strength he was no longer capable of the intense imaginative and intellectual effort of a long book. The result was that, though there are some passages in the Oxford volume which show all his old fire, the weakness of structure, perhaps excusable in the "big book," has been accentuated by an attempt to work into the narrative long and often highly original discussions of the political and constitutional background. It is a difficult and sometimes bewildering book, but in its detail it contains a great amount of material to be found nowhere else, and much that could only have come from Powicke.

The appearance of this volume brought his active life as a scholar to a close. He continued to write reviews and recollections, and he spent much energy on a revised edition of the *Loss of Normandy* (1961), but there is nothing which calls for special notice here. For several years he cherished the hope of writing a book on Edward I, for whom he felt an inexplicable sympathy; but at last he resigned himself to the certainty that it would never appear. On his retirement in 1947 he was given a room in Balliol, and he continued to work there among the books which he had given to his old college. No detail concerning these books was too small to stir his interest; but he slowly relaxed his grip. In April 1963 he contributed his last review to the *EHR* and duly recorded it in his list of publications. A month later, in the night of May 19, he died after a brief illness.

IV

It remains to say something about Powicke's personal characteristics.

His great strength as a writer lay in his power of evocation. He could describe a personality, a stretch of country, or a situation, and preferably a mixture of all three, with great felicity. He was at his best in piecing together a few scattered facts, superficially of only casual or local interest, showing how they became significant when they were seen as local manifestations of great movements in European history. In whatever he wrote, the larger setting was always in his mind. Anyone who wishes to see what he could make from mere fragments has only to look at his essay on Loretta, Countess of Leicester: out of a handful of rubbish he creates a European scene of intense vivacity. He loved the ramifications of history more than its wide avenues. "I invite my reader to follow me along a bypath which gives access to wide prospects" is a characteristic sentence which catches my eye in one of his essays. The word "casual" often appears in his work, especially when he has something important and personal to say. A large part of his art lay in his power of relating the casual to the general, the unpredictable movements of personal feeling and impulse to the general pattern of great events. His art was the art of the magician who brings about unexpected combinations, rather than that of the system-builder.

He had an imaginative power of striking individuality. This was harnessed to the discipline of history, and the best pages he wrote were the result of a subtle combination of personal imagination and external circumstance. It was essential to his success that the material should not be too abundant, that the scope for reflection and for the play of his personal vision should be ample. There was nothing commonplace about the world as he saw it. This led to a certain element of fantasy creeping into his judgment on practical affairs, as if his faculty of imagination had to find an outlet. He was apt to think that the people around him were more inspired than they really were by benevolence, loyalty, and gratitude, or by malevolence, treachery, and ingratitude. He read into their personalities a fuller reality than they possessed. This caused him a great deal of suffering, but it gave his history a special quality. To most people, whose sense of the personalities of others is not highly developed, the personalities of the past are almost non-existent. With Powicke the focus seemed to be about right for the distant view: in the past he was entirely at home and unharassed, and he treated the characters of the thirteenth century as friends. As A. G. Little wrote in a review of his essays:

> Dr. Powicke lives on terms of intimate affection with the Middle Ages, and can even play with them...Such intimacy has its dangers. The talk of friends is sometimes mystifying to outsiders.[14]

The talk of friends indeed meant very much to him. He was a most courteous and gracious host. For several years it fell to him, as steward, to preside in Common Room at Oriel and generally to look after the comfort of the guests.[15] He did this with grace and dignity. He was alert to the needs of others and he exercised a natural and undisputed authority in an informal way; yet he seemed, because of his deceptively fragile appearance, to solicit protection. The combination was irresistible, and there are men with few other things in common – often those whom Oxford somehow left in the cold – who still speak of an evening in Oriel under Powicke's eye as a unique experience of the warmth and dignified ease which they had looked for in Oxford, and too often looked for in vain. But for the rough and tumble of a crowded social life he had neither taste nor aptitude. Like many men of vision he did not like controversy. He could inspire more easily than he could convince. He seemed to be subdued by confident men with firmly rooted habits and prejudices to which they could appeal, and I fancy that in contact with such men he felt the smallness of his physical stature. In familiar, allusive, unsystematic talk he showed himself most completely. Such talk was the real source of his influence as a teacher. There was a quality of the unexpected, the entrancing, that gave it a peculiar charm and excitement. Quite casually in talk he could open up prospects of historical understanding which cast a spell on the listener. This talk was very desultory, and moved about among memories of people and places and writers without much of the apparatus of scholarship. He did not, as some scholars do, pour out a wealth of learning from which lesser men could fill their pouch at pleasure. It was not easy to remember just what had been said, but it somehow whetted the intellectual appetite. He had an instinct for introducing people to the right books at the right time. Nor were these only, or even chiefly, scholarly books. I can still remember the books he used to bring me when I was ill a good many years ago: *Le Grand Meaulnes*, Henry James's *Sense of the Past*, the letters of Fitzgerald, an essay of Keynes, something on eighteenth-century London... they made a lasting contribution to my stock of ideas. He had a remarkable grasp of what was going on in the historical world and his most fragile remarks were signposts for those who could recognize them. He looked at everything, not least himself, with awe, and this gave an emotional consistency to his work over a period of sixty years. I find these words in an undergraduate essay on the poet Cowper, which might have been written at any time in his life:

> This shy retiring man, with his gossip about books and his tattle about hares and fish, confirms us in our noblest prejudice and stirs our strongest passion. He had been in some mysterious way behind the veil and comes forth halting like the patriarch from a strange encounter. Deep down in the hearts of all lies the sense of an experience which knows no limits of time or space; and it is from the threshold of this dark secret that we start upon the great journey of social life, reading meanings of strange import into the duties of common life and feeling a strange thrill in the commonest calls to seek the welfare of our native land.[16]

Powicke might have been talking about himself. Perhaps he was. Anyhow these words contain the clue to his own influence and his own approach to history. He too gave the impression that he came from some strange encounter. Even his practical plans were different from other men's, because they preserved something of the secret experience in which they had their origin. To some this gave them a compelling force; to others it made them quite impracticable. To some the dream behind the plan gave the plan its point; to others it simply clouded the whole issue. In a sense both were right, and men were sharply divided on the lines of their instinctive reactions. But there can be no doubt that the visionary impulse got things done when clarity and caution would have left them where they were. And the secret of Powicke's power to set large projects afoot is also the secret of his power to inspire beginners. He made them feel that he approved of them, more than perhaps he really did, that he saw beyond the inadequacies of the present to some distant achievement. Doubtless he over-estimated the powers of his pupils, but by doing so he helped to create them, and thus to vindicate his judgment in the end. In return he was the object of a warmer personal devotion than most scholars can hope to receive.

There was one conspicuous talent which may seem somewhat at variance with those already mentioned: he would have made a good and perhaps a great librarian. Libraries exercised an extraordinary fascination for him. They were a secret refuge from the present and a romantic storehouse of wisdom. Especially if they had associations with his favorite scholars like Selden, or even with his less favorite ones like Freeman, he savored their delights to the full. In later years his best-loved afternoon walk took him (through doors and paths denied to ordinary men) to the old library at Merton where he walked sniffing the musty air as Gibbon might have walked in the Forum. This instinctive attraction to libraries went back to his discovery, as a schoolboy, of the joys of the old Free Library at Stockport. Then later, of his undergraduate days in Manchester, he wrote:

> When I began to work seriously at history, I studied much in a room which contained Freeman's books, which had been brought together after his death and presented to the Owen's College, now the University of Manchester. At first they were merely a lot of books in a dusty room; then one day I began to read Froude's *History of England* in Freeman's copy. The ferocious marginalia in Freeman's unpleasing handwriting shocked while they delighted me, but they did more than this. They made me realise where I was...These were Freeman's books. He had collected, he had used them. This was a historian's workshop.[17]

Strangely enough Bishop Gray's library at Balliol made no impression on him; but at Merton there was the library of Bishop Rede:

> I know few places which give me so intimate a sense of the living past. Its ever-present beauty, its self-revealed transitions from one period to another, link today with innumerable yesterdays. It might so easily have become a mausoleum. With how gracious a persistence has it eluded this melancholy destiny.

Later still, in Manchester, there was "the delightful secrecy of Humphrey Chetham's library," and finally the library of the Royal Historical Society for which he dreamed of a great future, the Faculty Library in Oxford which he made his personal sanctum, and the Bodleian, of which he was a very active curator at the time of its great expansion. This was work which he enjoyed. It appealed to many of his instincts – his enjoyment of the past, his imaginative pleasure in making plans, his sense of the sanctity of books, and his love of having secret access to places which were full of memories. He liked secret places and special knowledge. I remember him once expressing some indignation at finding that the clerks in a large railway office used the same timetable as that available to the general public. He had expected to find some more spacious works of reference in familiar use at Headquarters. Doubtless he was not quite serious, but his sense of the privilege of having access to the best authorities was offended by this indifference to a great opportunity. He looked on books as extremely precious things, and he treated his own collection with a fastidious care which warred against his liberality in lending and harassed his borrowers with a sense of guilt.

He was a surprising mixture of fragility and toughness, both emotionally and physically. Physically he was very small – I suppose rather less than five feet tall – but he did not seem small to those who came under his influence. He had a fine large head, features which changed with extraordinary rapidity with his passing moods, an unexpectedly boyish smile, small dark lustrous eyes, a wispy moustache in the manner of the 1890s, and as long as I knew him he was bald with few white hairs. His voice, though not strong, had an emotional quality, especially when reading aloud, which was strangely memorable. In middle age he lectured with trembling hands and a quavering voice which seemed to betoken no long continuance; yet he would think nothing of walking twenty miles and he kept his strength almost to the end of a long life. Similarly, the least frustration or opposition would sap his strength, but the greater the trial the greater his power of meeting it. To the casual eye this seemed most evident in the greatest private sorrow of his life, the death of his only son in a road accident in 1936. Many then were astonished at his fortitude. But this was a wound too deep for the therapy of emotional expression, and it was one from which he never fully recovered.

I have already mentioned his upbringing in a liberal tradition of Congregationalism. This background gave him great satisfaction. In a general way he liked what it stood for, both spiritually and socially, and he had no doubt that this was where he belonged. But he was irked by the limitations of this, as he might have been by any other, tradition. After his marriage he became a member of the Presbyterian Church, of which he was an active member and finally an elder till the end of his life. He appreciated the security and order of Presbyterianism, but dogmas, doctrines, and systems sat rather lightly on him. His inclination tended to appreciation rather than systematic acceptance or rejection, and his lectures on History, Freedom, and Religion express this attitude. I confess to finding the doctrine of these lectures rather opaque, but his views on current religious problems were capable of exact and vigorous expression. At the time of the defeat of the Prayer Book Measure of 1928, he wrote a letter to the *Manchester Guardian* signed "Free Churchman" which will show his attitude to questions of ecclesiastical organization:

> Most of your correspondents seem to assume that a Church is "split from the top to the bottom" because it comprehends violently different schools of thought, and that the loose agglomeration which is called the Free Churches is more united than the Church of England because these violent differences of opinion do not exist within it. This seems to me to be a most curious view, even if it is based upon fact and not upon illusions. The Church of England has won the sympathy and admiration of many Free Churchmen simply because of its gallant desire to explore the meaning of comprehension, partly, and in their judgement unwisely, forsaken in 1662. In spite of the unhappy vote in the House of Commons, the Church has displayed a healthy and triumphant unity, an increasingly democratic organisation capable of comprehension, a living system gradually shedding the social obscurantism and its snobbish elements, ready for the next step forward towards unity with other Churches in the country.[18]

Outside his work and his family, Powicke's deepest and most lasting satisfaction came from his cottage in the Lake District. In his early years the part of the country to which he was bound by the strongest ties of affection was Northamptonshire, and especially Brigstock where his mother's family lived. In 1902 he wrote:

> I left Brigstock yesterday...Everything seemed almost to belong to me, and I recognised scenes familiar to me through my ancestry everywhere. It is very curious but it is in those flat wooded midlands that I feel most at home: the charm of Oxford and the loveliness of the Lakes are artificial in comparison.[19]

Later, as a lecturer in Manchester, he was in the habit of taking reading parties to various places in the Cotswolds and the Yorkshire wolds; but he was finally drawn to Cumberland. The article he wrote in 1904 for the *Victoria County History* on Furness Abbey was the beginning of his intimate knowledge and long devotion to this neighborhood. The impression that the Furness sheepwalks on the Fells made on him was never obliterated. "Shepherds have kept their sheep in all ages: why am I stirred so deeply because I can trace the very sheepwalks of the monks of Furness?" he wrote in his Oxford Inaugural Lecture, and nearly twenty years later in his Valedictory Lectures in Balliol Hall he returned to an allied theme:

I know no more touching, and at the same time more satisfying, instance of the union of man and nature than a lonely drystone sheepfold in wild country. I can picture several – one built like a little fort on the top of a steep bank above a river, another on a fell side where the heather merges with rock, another in a dell where two streams meet, two, my favourites, circular in shape, near the shores of upland tarns.[20]

In about 1927 he leased, and later bought, an old farmhouse, Christcliffe near Boot in Eskdale, from a local farmer. From that date he and his family spent most of their holidays in this (as it then was) quiet spot. He never tired of it. Hardknott, Butterilkel, Birker Fell, were scenes on which his eye and mind dwelt with most contentment. He was a vigorous walker and he knew, as the phrase is, every inch of the nearby fells, as well as the more distant slopes of Scafell and Great Gable. He saw the whole scene bathed in a historical light: the houses and fields, the church and the paths along which the dead were brought from outlying settlements, the Roman camp and the network of roads and defenses of which it formed part, provided him with endless opportunities for reflection. And in the evening, with the tick of the grandfather clock, the lamplight, the boots and walking-gear round the fireplace, and the shabby row of Dickens's works from which he was in the habit of reading aloud, he was completely happy. These were the golden hours of his life.

10

Vivian Hunter Galbraith
(1889–1976)

Vivian Galbraith was born on December 15, 1889, the youngest son in a family of four sons and a daughter.[1] His father David Galbraith, and his mother Eliza Mackintosh, came from Belfast, but in 1889 they were living in Sheffield where David Galbraith was secretary at Hadfield's steelworks. Two years later David Galbraith became the representative of his firm in London, and the family lived there from 1891 till 1906. Very early in this period Vivian formed a lifelong friendship with James Gray, later Professor of Zoology in Cambridge, who will appear on more than one occasion on the following pages. From 1902 to 1906 he went to Highgate School, but in the latter year his father was offered a job in the British Westinghouse Company in Manchester, and the family moved once more. Since it was too late to start at another school, Vivian began to attend T. F. Tout's lectures in the History Department of Manchester University when he was only sixteen, and he was formally enrolled as a student in 1907. The Manchester History School was then at the height of its influence and reputation under the powerful leadership of Tout, assisted by the personally less powerful but intellectually impressive figure of James Tait. These two scholars were to be the main influences in Galbraith's life and work. In addition, F. M. Powicke was an assistant lecturer from 1906 to 1908; although he never exerted the same influence as Tout and Tait, he remained throughout his life an admonitory figure in Galbraith's life, each exasperating but never deserting the other. Without any doubt, this group was the most remarkable combination of historical talent in England at that time, and in due course Galbraith became the main representative of their historical views and teaching.

At the time of their meeting Tout was in his early fifties, and in Galbraith's words "a PRODIGIOUS personality." Tout recognized in Galbraith, as he had earlier in Powicke, a potential historian of the highest ability, and he quickly became the main guardian of his career and his chief adviser in every crisis. Beside him, James Tait seems a remote and withdrawn personality, yet in the formation of his historical interests Galbraith probably owed more to Tait than to Tout. Tait was a man of an integrity which was matched only by his reticence. As an undergraduate, and perhaps earlier, he had quietly and without a word of either despair or joy abandoned the faith of his fathers, and he retained throughout the rest of his life an austere and isolated independence of mind. He could always be relied on to judge correctly about any problem which was brought to him. If the evidence of their correspondence is to be trusted, Galbraith relied on Tait mainly for scholarly advice, and on Tout for moral support. He wrote about both men in the *Dictionary of National Biography*. Of Tout he said: "Tout's highest gifts lay in his personal relations with his pupils...he met them on a footing of equality, not less interested in themselves and in their future than in their work." Of Tait he wrote: "The key-note of Tait's life was his consuming interest in historical research...Alike in nothing but their common devotion to research, Tout and Tait imparted to their school a new quality of exact scholarship which slowly but surely won for it an influence out of all proportion to its size." Almost the whole of Galbraith's later career is a commentary on these remarks.

At Manchester he twice attended (probably on the first occasion in his preliminary year) the series of Tout's general lectures on European history, and ten years later in Palestine he wrote that he relied on his recollection of these lectures to give a historical context to nearly everything that he saw. For his Special Subject on Richard II – a subject to which he often recurred in later years – he went to Tait. It is clear that from an early date Tout had picked him out as the outstanding student of his year. But when it came to the final examination in 1910, Ernest Barker, the external examiner, disagreed and selected A. E. Prince (later Professor in Kingston, Ontario) "as the person of best quality of mind in the year." Tout defended the claim of Galbraith and prevailed. Barker, slightly aggrieved, wrote to Tout, "I do agree with you about the eminence of Galbraith (but) ought not Galbraith to appear and have a chance to defend himself against my championship of Prince?" In the event both were given Firsts, but Galbraith was and remained Tout's man. Earlier in the year, no doubt at Tout's instigation, he had been a successful candidate for a scholarship at Balliol, Tout's old college in Oxford, and he went there – like Powicke before him – as Brackenbury scholar in the autumn of 1910.

The next four years brought a mixture of calamity and success which left a deep mark on Galbraith's later career. The Balliol of that time exhibited to the fullest extent the success of the policy, instituted by Jowett, of recruiting young men from the ruling families of England, and scholars from wherever they could be found. Galbraith belonged to the latter class, and his later reminiscences show that (unsure of himself and his scholarship) he felt his insignificance in the midst of this concentration of birth and talent. "Balliol in those days," Galbraith wrote late in life, "consisted of a large number of small social cliques which overlapped but never coincided. Looking back today, I think Balliol was very snobbish, but also had more able people than the rest of the University put together." The worst feature of his new situation was that he was expected to read *Literae Humaniores* – "Greats" – and for this he was in no way suited, either by preparation or habit of mind. At the end of his first year he wrote to Tout: "Now that my first year in Oxford is over I feel I should like to write and tell you what sort of a time I have had. I have found Balliol much more agreeable than I had ever expected. The men are older than I imagined, and there are besides quite a lot of post-graduate men in our year who are congenial company. I have had very few dealings with the dons except Mr. Davis who has been extremely kind throughout, and Mr. Lindsay, who is my tutor. I am rather lost in the wilderness doing Greats which is due, I think, chiefly to my own unphilosophical sort of mind, but partly too, I think, to Mr. Lindsay. He has been an awfully good tutor but he is very apt to talk over one's head. He has all the unintelligibility of the philosopher."

In addition to the uncongenial study of Greats, there was the further problem of a steep decline in the family fortunes. Characteristically the best source of information about this is a letter written by Tout some ten years later recommending Galbraith to an evidently reluctant prospective father-in-law. He wrote of V. H. G.'s father: "Mr. Galbraith was a Northern Ireland man, rather quiet and retiring but quite nice and very much a gentleman. An engineer by profession but rather given to the business than to the mechanical side of his profession. He came to Manchester somewhere about 1906 to be director of the Castings Department of the British Westinghouse Company. He had a good salary which I think went into four figures. After a few years Westinghouse found they could buy castings cheaper from the Americans and Germans than they could make them, so in true American spirit they cut their loss, scrapped the department and left him (Galbraith) in the cold." As a result of this dismissal the family returned to London during Galbraith's first year at Oxford, and in July 1911 Galbraith wrote to Tout: "My father, mother and sister have all come back to London and we are fairly settled down again. The padre I think was not very glad to return, for his own little business is not very flourishing and cannot absorb his energies sufficiently. I have got a coaching job for the Long Vac. to help matters." It cannot have been a very cheerful Long Vacation; but, besides coaching, he must have been writing his Stanhope Essay on "The Abbey of St. Albans 1300 to the Dissolution of the Monasteries." This won him the Stanhope Prize for 1911 and provided the main success of these rather dismal years.

In the long run the Stanhope Essay had a considerable importance in turning his attention to the historical writings of St. Albans, a subject to which he returned in several of his later publications. But in the immediate future the success was swallowed up in a calamity, which in the academic circumstances of that time assumed quite gigantic proportions – he got a Third Class in Greats in 1913, and it took him several years to recover from this disaster. As late as 1919, when he was a candidate for a fellowship at Oriel College, the Regius Professor C. H. Firth, who was also a Fellow of Oriel, wrote to Tout: "Galbraith stayed with me for a couple of nights. I found him interesting and liked him. I took him to Oriel and he made a good impression, but the fellows in general have a rooted objection that a man who obtained a Third in Greats is a person of an inferior intellect, and that a First in that school is the main qualification for teaching Modern History. I'm afraid his candidature will not be successful." So the disaster of his Third in Greats clouded his future for a long time to come.

As a first step to recovery he decided to take a second degree in History. He did this in one year, "and I only did it at all (he wrote many years later) because in 1913 I had got a Third in Greats. I remember feeling almost suicidal, and such was the worship of 'Firsts' at Balliol that no one would have been surprised if I had cut my throat. They were black days indeed for me 1913 and 1914." He worked during this critical year with Andrew Browning (later Professor of History in Glasgow) as his companion, and with A. L. Smith and H. W. C. Davis as his tutors. For Browning as a character, a scholar, and a golfer, he developed an almost reverential respect which remained with him to the end of his life. As for his tutors, he recalled that "H. W. C. Davis took me down to Hastings for the Easter Vac. of 1914, and every morning crammed me with a total survey of the whole of English History." The effort – worth recalling as an illustration of the tutorial system at its zenith – was not wasted, and after the examination he was able to write to Tout on August 6, "the viva was more amusing than formidable. They complained of lack of detail in my papers, but showed themselves very ready to be convinced. More than one point from Vinogradoff they shook their heads at, while the Chairman of the Examiners, when I quoted Petit-Dutaillis, replied with infinite scorn, 'I don't read such new-fangled people.'" The chairman was C. R. L. Fletcher, who was luxuriating in the success of his *History of England for Boys* written in collaboration with Rudyard Kipling, a very notable work in its own way, but far from new-fangled in its views. Despite Fletcher's "scorn," Galbraith got his much needed First Class degree, and even before the results appeared, Tout had persuaded the Senate of Manchester University to appoint him to the Langton Fellowship, which was the chief research award in the Arts Faculty, for three years. So his immediate

academic future was secured, only to be abruptly interrupted by the unforeseen outbreak of war on August 4, 1914.

Galbraith's letter of August 6 to Tout does not even mention the war. So
far as he noticed it, he was against it. But the older dons soon began to
feel a morbid anxiety about any young man whose desire to "do his bit"
seemed less than wholehearted. Several of them were worried about Galbraith. He seemed "unsettled." On September 27 Davis wrote a long letter
to Tout on the subject:

> Galbraith is a problem. I hope he will settle down, but he is an excitable
> creature, and I dare say private worries and public events have upset him
> this summer...I hope for the good of his soul you will induce him to take
> up some work which is not self-regarding; looking after University Clubs, or
> helping a recruiting agency, or doing anything which is not to his immediate
> profit. At present there is too much Ego in his cosmos, but he is by nature
> sympathetic enough. He needs to live in an atmosphere of public spirit, and
> then he will come out of his shell.

Tout did not interfere, and for some months Galbraith explored monastic cartularies and registers in the British Museum and the Public Record
Office. He was still acutely conscious of the gaps in his intellectual make-
up, and his association with Andrew Browning during the previous year
intensified his self-doubt: "Looking back, I am reminded powerfully of his
commanding intelligence and outlook, which won my lifelong conviction
of his amazing precocity when we studied together under A. L. Smith. His
outlook and even his literary style were already fully formed then, when
I was still trying to find my feet, and to learn not merely what I thought
about the Past, but how with my immature intelligence I could get it
down onto paper." With these self-doubts still unresolved, the war took
second place in his thoughts for several months. He kept his hostility to
the war largely to himself, but in the course of the Christmas vacation the
pressure on him became irresistible. On January 8, 1915 he wrote to Tout,
"I cannot pretend to explain how it has come about, but an increasing
uneasiness as to whether I was doing my bit during the last month or two
has grown into a determination to join the army in some way or other.
I fancy my work (which was very pleasant after the long drudgery) kept
me from honestly facing the question in my own mind. I could hardly
imagine myself becoming a soldier, but in the Christmas holiday I thought
it out and my mind is made up...The few people to whom I have spoken
of it seem to find any connection between me and war a huge joke. It is
scarcely flattering to me!" To Tait he opened his mind rather more freely,
in words which show that Mr. Lindsay's teaching had something to
answer for: "I have decided to join the soldiers. This resolution is the

result of an inward compulsion against tastes, inclinations, and (almost) private convictions. I have no wish for military glory, and shall look merely ridiculous in a uniform, but have learnt to believe from Aristotle that when everyone puts private feelings before the best common ethos, as it were the common ethos of the cabinet or the Labour party, the state must suffer. As soon as I looked at the question from the point of view of the real state, and not from that of the individual, I was certain I should have to join. I wrote to Powicke, and when he turned recruiting sergeant that settled it!"

The thing was no sooner settled than it was done. On January 19 Galbraith wrote to Tout, "By great good luck I have got into the Queen's at once, and am now waiting to be gazetted. Gray (his old friend from childhood) mentioned my name to the colonel – there were vacancies. I had to interview the colonel, and he took me on. As soon as gazetted I am to go to be trained at Windsor where I hope to be billeted with Gray and to profit by his experience. Meanwhile I mean to drill with the Artists or the Inns of Court in town."

The story of the next two years in the army was a tale of the usual succession of unforeseen and inexplicable moves: from Windsor to Tunbridge Wells, from Tunbridge Wells to Chelsea and back, and then to Ramsgate. Galbraith discovered, like many others, that "training is concerned almost exclusively with square-drill, which they regard as the one essential in the training of troops." Then in December 1917 his battalion went to Palestine to take part in the final stages of Allenby's campaign. Here he saw his first action, and in March 1918 he reported to Tout:

> operations on a minor scale are incessant here, and, as our division has been continuously in the line since I joined it, life has been interesting and energetic. I am bound to say I have found practical war (as here conducted) a most fascinating study, and I can scarcely imagine the monasteries interesting me hereafter. For one thing I shall want to know a lot more about the Crusades...I would rather have the *Itinerarium* (of Richard I) here than all Hardy and Meredith...The places I have seen – Ghaza, Beersheba, Hebron, Jerusalem, Jericho, Ludd (not to mention Cairo and Luxor which I saw on leave) – have taxed my "history" severely, and generally found it wanting. Prince and I (when we met in Cairo) agreed almost in a breath that we had to rely on the recollections of the "general European" lectures which, you may remember, I was fortunate enough to listen to twice...We could not help remarking that – with Moffatt – we are the sole male survivors of our small circle in Manchester.

Shortly after this letter was written his battalion was shipped back to France to fill some of the gaps made by the German spring offensive. He was in France in July 1918, and in the fighting near Soissons he won the

Croix de Guerre and was involved in an incident which might have had a ghastly ending. A survivor recalls that Galbraith, "leading his company with his accustomed incredible courage against a heavy barrage," called to a sergeant, who was sheltering with his men in a shell-hole, to advance. The sergeant refused and was later court-martialed and sentenced to death for refusing to obey an order in face of the enemy. The sentence was later commuted not without some unhappy publicity in *John Bull*; but the end of the war soon obliterated the incident in everything but memory. In September Galbraith was wounded, and he was back in England when the war ended.

The end of the war brought only one thought: how to get back to medieval history with the least possible delay. In December 1918 he was stationed in Oxford, training "either to be converted into an education officer or sent back to France." Getting out of the army threatened to be almost as confusing a business as getting into it, but, as before, the confusion was dispelled by personal contacts. On January 2, 1919, Galbraith reported to Tout, "I had lunch yesterday with Gray's friend in the War Office, and he tells me I can apply for demobilization immediately as belonging to Group 43. My procedure is simply to inform the colonel that the University has applied for me, and to quote the army order. Could I trouble you for an official chit stating that the University has applied for my demobilization as I hold a University appointment? I can then attach this to my application." Once more Tout set the wheels turning. On January 13 Galbraith was appointed a Temporary Assistant Lecturer for the remainder of the academic year, and on January 16 his Langton Fellowship was renewed for the remainder of his term of three years – that is until the middle of 1921. On January 23 he reported to Tout, "I am now a civilian. Last Tuesday the army demobilized and disembodied me at Ripon in the same casual kind of way as I enlisted in 1915."

II

For the moment all was well; but Galbraith was now thirty, and the position at Manchester was no more than a stop-gap. Tout advised speed, and Galbraith undertook "to try to collect the raw material of a book in the next six months." He continued to live in London throughout 1919, spending most of his time in the British Museum. His first step was to return to the work that he had been doing in the autumn and winter of 1914. To understand the direction which this work was taking, it is necessary to look back to the letter which H. W. C. Davis had written to Tout in September 1914. Davis is describing the advice he had given to Galbraith about continuing to work "on the sort of material which he has already worked at in Finals." He then continues: "The Bury St. Edmunds material is tolerably voluminous, and has hardly been touched. To write about decadent monasticism would be a waste of time, but I hoped that when he began to read the fourteenth-century documents he would discover that they are useful for secular history." This abrupt distinction between secular (useful) history and decadent monastic (useless) history was not the aberration of a moment or of a single man. It expressed a view of history which even Stubbs, the common master of all of them, had in large measure shared; and there is no sign that Tout dissented from it. It was the central point in Davis's historical creed that "history is past politics," and in a broad sense this view was held by the Manchester school. It was also Galbraith's point of departure.

He had already made considerable inroads into the Bury St. Edmunds material before he joined the army. Building on this, he was able to produce three articles, which appeared in the *EHR* in rapid succession in October 1919, July 1920, and January 1922. The first was an edition of some *articuli* in a Bury St. Edmunds cartulary, which were laid before Parliament by two friars in 1371, proposing the disendowment of the monastic orders to meet pressing national needs. The second was an edition of a fine collection of royal charters of the late eleventh and early twelfth centuries drawn from Winchester cartularies. The third was the text of a Visitation of Westminster Abbey in 1444 from a Bury St. Edmunds register. Galbraith's editions of these documents were businesslike, vigorous, and perceptive, and they at once marked him out as one of the most able and active of the younger medievalists. During the years 1919 and 1920 he was full of further plans for work in monastic cartularies and registers, but the main piece of work which emerged was an edition of the Chronicle of St. Mary's, York, to which his attention had been drawn by Robin Flower at the British Museum in 1920. The work on this chronicle was in full swing in 1921, and in June he wrote to Tout: "The text is progressing steadily...I have at last managed to relate it to the 'Brute' Chronicles in French, and have been lucky to find another copy of the same chronicle up to 1307." It took another six years before the edition appeared with the title by which it has become known to all medievalists – *The Anonimalle Chronicle, 1333–1381*. Its appearance established Galbraith's reputation as a major scholar. Meanwhile, however, his life had become complicated in a number of ways.

The letter of June 1921 which reported the beginning of substantial progress on this work also provides evidence of two further important steps in his career. In the first place it was written from the Public Record Office [PRO], which he had joined in February 1921. On the 10th of that month, the Deputy Keeper Sir Henry Maxwell-Lyte wrote to Tout giving him the news of Galbraith's appointment, and asking him to release him from Manchester "as soon as you can do so without great inconvenience to yourself." At about the same time R. L. Poole also wrote to Tout expressing his conviction that Galbraith would be an important acquisition to the Office. He was right. In that rather staid and still Victorian institution, his accessibility, his wit, and his power of laying his hand on significant documents became legendary. His free access to the whole range of medieval royal administrative documents gave him a view of government and of the technicalities of administration which he could have gained in no other way. We may compare these years "at the coal-face," to use a favorite phrase of his, with Maitland's years drawing up conveyances in a lawyer's office. Both men needed physical contact with documents to elicit their most fruitful and imaginative work. Certainly Galbraith always needed a document to excite his interest in a problem. Nearly everything that he wrote began as an attempt to unravel the complexities of a document. His greatest historical talent lay in drawing a lively and convincing picture of a complex world from the dry and unpromising language of clerks attempting to give a precise formulation to legal or administrative acts. It was fortunate for the range of his interests that he had already started work on the *Anonimalle Chronicle* before entering the PRO, for this work kept up his interest in medieval historical writing when the public records of government were his daily task. The combination of the study of chronicles and of administrative records stamped all his later work.

The nature of his daily task at the PRO is vividly brought to our attention by the entries in his official journal which has survived. It begins on March 12, 1921, and the record of his first week's work provides a good illustration of the material with which he had to deal:

12th March. Joined the office. Chancery Miscellanea $\frac{29}{5(2)}$ copied.
(*Indentura de rebus liberatis . . . cancellario* Oct. 30 1302).
14th March. Ministers Accounts $\frac{1147}{7+9}$ Lands of Roger Damory.
15th March. Enrolled Accounts Misc. (L.T.R.) 14. 15. 16. Enrolments of $\frac{1147}{2.9}$
17th March. Lakenheath Court Rolls $\frac{203}{94, 95}$. Farley deeds (system of calendaring used by the Abbey discovered).
18th–19th March. Pipe Roll and Memoranda Roll 49 Henry III (K.R.) compared in detail: Communia: nova oblata: Sheriffs compoti. Mem. rolls of this date still very "undifferentiated": also "action to be taken" obviously filled in in court – orally.

The record continues in this seemingly desultory way for several months: if there was a plan, it cannot now be detected. It seems as if he was free to roam over the whole range of Chancery and Exchequer documents in his own way, and he made good use of the opportunity. Occasionally small pieces of detective work came his way. We find him tracing licenses for the production of stage plays in the period between about 1590 and 1610, or searching for Chancery warrants for the Deputy Keeper or for references supplied by H. H. E. Craster of the Bodleian. For May 6 and 7, 1921, there is a single entry: "D. K.'s proofs," and this entry becomes increasingly common as time goes on. The explanation is to be found in a letter of June 9, 1921, to Tout, which gives a good idea of how he spent his days:

> Johnson and Crump are both taking great pains with my education. Indeed the Deputy Keeper is now lending a hand himself. At present my whole time is employed in correcting his proofs and I can only say that if he means to hang on until his magnum opus is finished there will hardly be a vacancy for a D. K. here for 10 years to come.

The D. K. was Sir Henry Maxwell-Lyte who had become Deputy Keeper in 1886, and was then engaged on his *Notes on the Use of the Great Seal of England,* a work of blindingly intricate detail on every aspect of the process of affixing the Great Seal to every type of document down to the seventeenth century. Work in the Office stood still while the officers, whose cooperation was somewhat meagerly acknowledged in his Preface, toiled at checking the multifarious details in the footnotes. Galbraith's rise to favor was the direct result of a brilliant (or, as he maintained, fortuitous) discovery which is recorded in his journal on June 3, 1921:

> Jerveys found (1547) and transferred to Privy Seals 883, 15667A – the P.S. to which it had formerly been attached.

The inwardness of this is that the D. K. had lost a letter of John Jerveys petitioning for a change in the terms of his appointment as chief joiner in the Tower of London in 1482. The letter was a key document in illustrating the progress of a petition through the Privy Seal office to the Great Seal, and the loss was a cause of great dismay. Galbraith, browsing (it would seem) among Chancery Warrants, found it misplaced and was able to restore it to its proper home and to the D. K.'s footnotes (see *Great Seal*, pp. 99n., 232–3nn., where the domestic crisis is of course not mentioned). Henceforward Galbraith was the D. K.'s favorite assistant. Unrewarding though it was, working for the great autocrat of the office had its compensations. It saved Galbraith much laborious labor of copying, which would otherwise have fallen to his lot, and it gave him a chance to browse among documents of every department of the royal government. Besides, the unconventional character of the old man made a strong appeal to him.

Indeed, he was singularly happy with his colleagues. The PRO was a repository, not only of documents, but also of characters who became Galbraith's friends for life. Among them, C. G. Crump and Charles Johnson were men of remarkable gifts and learning, and Johnson's name is the one which appears most often in the pages of the journal. It was to Charles Johnson and to H. C. Johnson, who arrived at the office shortly before he left, that Galbraith most often turned for information about the records in later life. He even inflicted his pupils on his old colleagues. I remember, when I was a second-year undergraduate and Galbraith was my tutor, he sent me to see Charles Johnson, who showed me the typescript of the *Regesta Henrici Primi* fifteen years before it was published, and entertained me at his home in Hampstead with a grave courtesy that seemed to belong to an earlier age. In his vast and leisurely learning he was the embodiment of the PRO of those days. Galbraith was never leisurely, and perhaps in the long run he would not have been an ideal keeper of the Public Records; but his years at the PRO had a greater influence on his development as a historian than anything after Manchester. In return, he brought to the PRO a more vivid sense of history than any of the officials whom he found there, and it was in the stacks that he discovered his personality as a historian.

III

A new note is struck in the journal in the entry for April 21, 1921:

> 21 April. Chancery Warrants filed. Edward I's Roman Itinerary. Marriage leave sanctioned. Fine example of Treasurer's seal found in Chancery Warrants I File 15? 51–3 (another 1596).

Other relevant entries followed in due course:

> 7 June – D. K.'s proofs. Ena in town: flat at Hampstead taken.
> 23 June – Vacation (Marriage).
> 28 November (1922) Arrived 10.30. Jane born: halfday.

The earliest of these entries is explained in a letter to Tout on June 9: "My marriage arrangements are now complete. The date is July 1st, and we are crossing to Cherbourg by the mid-day boat from Southampton with two bicycles and two Jerusalem baskets attached – nothing more. The proposed itinerary will include Mont St. Michel, Vire, Avranches, Domfront and Caen ... Yesterday I looked at a small flat in W. Hampstead which we can have for £2-2 a week and unless there is a hitch I think I shall settle on this." Thus began the marriage on which the whole of his later life was centered. He had met Miss Cole-Baker in 1919 at Manchester, where she was a research student working with A. G. Little on a thesis which was later published as *The Constitution of the Dominican Order, 1216–1360*. The letter of May 19, 1920, in which Tout recommended the bridegroom to an apprehensive father-in-law has already been quoted for the light it throws on Galbraith's family background. It also contains some echoes of the contemporary academic scene which should not be passed over:

> I was mystified (Tout writes in his most reassuring tone) by half-heard tele-phoning last night, but I have seen Galbraith today and things are made clear. I am much delighted with the news, for rather short acquaintance has given me a particular belief in and regard for your daughter, and Galbraith has long been one of my best pupils. I would send her gladly my heartiest congratulations, but feel that, before I do that formally, I must fulfil my promise to Galbraith to tell you what I know about him and his people. He has, perhaps, already put his financial situation before you, but he seems, in his chivalrous way, to have stressed his immediate impecuniosity rather than his really excellent prospects in a career which doesn't bring wealth to any of its votaries, but will, in his case I feel sure, soon land him in an assured position, a certain reputation in his line, and a modest but not insufficient competence which is all that can be hoped for practitioners of my trade of the academic teaching of history...He is going to do well as a teacher, and I shall be more than surprised if within half a dozen years he didn't get a good professorship somewhere which could hardly bring him less than £800.

It is interesting to see that Tout, the great architect of his career, was already looking beyond the PRO to a university post, to teaching, a pro-fessorship, and £800 a year. It was six years before even the first of these prophecies became a reality. The first hint of the change is to be found in the Minute Book of the Governing Body of Balliol College:

> 16 March 1926. The Master was authorised to ask Mr. Galbraith to assist with History tuition next year...to be paid £50 for his assistance, this to cover (also) his travelling expenses.

Under the same Minute, £10 was to be deducted from the stipend of Mr. K. N. Bell, one of the history tutors of the College. The reason for these canny proceedings was that Bell had become Senior Proctor for the year from March 1926 and a substitute was needed without delay to do his College teaching. Consequently, Galbraith went to Oxford every Tuesday evening for the next three terms and spent the following day tutoring undergraduates. We may leave it to Professor H. A. Cronne – no giddy undergraduate but a mature student who, after graduating at Belfast in

1925, had gone to Balliol to re-read History – to describe the effect of
these excursions:

> The real turning point for me at Balliol (he writes) came in 1926 when
> Kenneth Bell became Senior Proctor and a deputy was required to undertake
> much of his burden of teaching. This was Vivian Galbraith, then an Assist-
> ant Keeper of the Public Records, who came up from town once a week and
> stayed overnight. His figure was slight but full of the most intense vitality.
> Beneath a mop of unruly prematurely white hair and dark eyebrows were
> eyes that twinkled with amusement, shone with sheer delight of historical
> discovery, or flashed with righteous anger, or pinned one like an assagai as
> he probed one's mind, or expounded a fundamental truth, or denounced
> some intolerable wrong. The face was pointed and the features good, and
> they vividly mirrored his varying moods: often quirkish, sometimes sardonic,
> occasionally choleric; but there always lurked around the corners of his
> mouth a beguiling and radiant smile, which lit up his whole face. A first
> tutorial with Galbraith was, for most undergraduates, an astonishing experi-
> ence for which no other teacher could possibly have prepared them: it was
> rather like being immersed in a bath of gin-and-tonic, from which one
> emerged relaxed, refreshed and tremendously stimulated. In fact the next
> best thing to Galbraith that I ever discovered was the hot brine bath at
> Droitwich which had something of a similar effect. He began by commend-
> ing me for having based my essay on sources, but it was soon clear that my
> handling of them had been less than adequately perceptive. This led Vivian
> to expound forcefully, in informal and uninhibited terms, the importance
> and the nature of documentary study. He went on to speak of historians,
> living and dead, with the most intimate knowledge, of some with deep
> respect, of some with an impish lack of deference to them or to the existing
> "Historical Establishment." Undergraduates were delighted by his back-stage
> view of history, but it is to be remembered that back-stage is where the
> serious work of production goes on. One left a tutorial with him without
> having assimilated much precise factual information, but with new and sig-
> nificant insights and a clearer idea of how to pursue one's studies and, above
> all, with a good dose of Vivian's own highly infectious enthusiasm.

Like many others I can substantiate everything in this account from my
own experience four years later. Galbraith's tutorials were in a remarkable
degree intoxicating. They always started later than the appointed time and
finished much – sometimes very much – later: he was probably unique
among tutors in his generosity with his time and I have no doubt that we
exploited this generosity. In all his talk he showed his passionate zeal for
the study of documents, and his equally passionate contempt for all who
wrote history without applying themselves to this discipline. He was
proud to combine the alleged mustiness of the PRO with an almost reck-
less breadth of sweeping generality, colored with the warm humanity

which reflected Tout's contribution to the Manchester School of History. He put everything into his teaching. He often said that he had no private life, and this was true in the sense that he exposed his foibles, his prejudices, and his personal feelings to almost anyone who was young enough or congenial enough to suspend criticism and enter into the spirit of his sincerity. He poured himself out in his talk, whether in his tutorials or in casual encounters with a profusion that must often have debilitated him, but it aroused his hearers to a high pitch of excitement. When I first heard this amazing flow of vivid and picturesque historical discourse, I rushed away to write down what I could remember of it; and I was surprised to discover how often in the cold light of recollection it appeared to be wrong. The immediate reaction to this discovery was disappointment, until I discovered that the greatest gift of a teacher to his pupils is to lay himself open to criticism and dissent. He kept nothing back, he was never pompous, never self-important, and – unless some irritable nerve was touched – he was generous to excess and deeply perceptive of every quality in others except those of formality and a prudent reserve.

A characteristic remark of his was that he had never had any pupils. In saying this he was contrasting himself with his own great teachers, notably Tout and Powicke, who always seemed to see their pupils as agents in a grand scheme of historical research. Galbraith by contrast lived too close to the "coal-face" to have any broad view of what needed to be done, beyond trying to understand the records of the past. For him, the pursuit of history was a personal encounter between the individual scholar and the material. Nothing more; nothing less.

In recalling these experiences, however, I anticipate. The year's substitute teaching for K. N. Bell ran out in June 1927 and it was not until the following year that the move was made which would have seemed wildly improbable ten or twelve years earlier: Galbraith returned to Balliol as a tutorial Fellow. The immediate cause of this was his appointment as Reader in Diplomatic at Oxford in succession to R. L. Poole. When this became imminent Balliol offered him a College lectureship to be held jointly with the University readership. After some haggling, this offer was raised to an Official Fellowship at £400 a year. On October 8, 1928 his PRO journal closed with the words "Res. from P.R.O.," and three days later he was admitted to his Fellowship. The family had already moved to Oxford, to the house in Garford Road which became a center of warmhearted and hilarious social life for several generations of undergraduates.

The most important publication of his nine years at Balliol was the edition of the St. Albans Chronicle from 1406 to 1420 which was published in 1937. The general importance of this work lay in clearing up the whole bewildering question of the succession of St. Albans historians from the death of Matthew Paris in 1259 to the early fifteenth century, and in putting the complicated manuscript tradition of historical writing during this period into an intelligible shape. In Galbraith's scholarly development, it continued the series of studies of medieval chronicles which he had begun as an undergraduate in his Stanhope Essay and resumed in his edition of the *Anonimalle Chronicle*. Work on the new text had started as early as April 1930, when he wrote to Tait announcing his discovery of the "common original" of the work of the last great medieval chronicler of St. Albans, Thomas Walsingham, in Bodley MS. 460. Here again we have an example of the discovery of a manuscript providing the impetus for a long and arduous enquiry into the sources and ramifications of a large body of historical material. The work had to be carried on in the midst of his complicated activities as tutor at Balliol and Reader in the University, which he combined with a weekly visit to lecture on paleography and archives at University College, London. His research had to be fitted into fragments of spare time in the vacations and rare moments of leisure during the term. Not surprisingly it gave him a great deal of trouble to put his material into shape, and he was not very satisfied with the result. "The introduction (he wrote in the Preface) as finally presented is not, I'm afraid, very satisfactory. In so far as it is intelligible it is due to the patience of Dr. G. R. Galbraith, as I may here call her, who has read it in perhaps as many recensions as the Chronicle itself." The number of proof corrections led to some acrimonious exchanges with the Secretary of the Oxford University Press, but in the end it was completed. With whatever faults of presentation he might detect, he had cleared up the main questions of authorship and manuscript transmission, and made accessible to historians a new body of material for the years when the long tradition of monastic chronicle writing was petering out.

In 1937 he moved to the Chair of History at Edinburgh in succession to Basil Williams. The change did him good in giving him a new impetus and a flow of new ideas; but perhaps he now found it almost too easy to make an impression. Moving into a society where professors were accorded all the reverence that had once been reserved for the clergy, he took pleasure both in the absurdities of the veneration, and in the delight with which his bubble-pricking was greeted by his students. The stories of his picturesque formulation of historical problems are part of the stock of good stories still circulating among those who were in Edinburgh at that time. One of his colleagues writes: "His popularity with students may be gauged from the fact that a Law examination had to be moved from his vicinity on account of the stamping and laughter which accompanied his lectures." But it must not be thought that all this clowning meant that he had not given a great deal of thought to the preparation of his lecture. In 1941 he wrote: "The necessity of keeping all one's energy to lecture on the Outline of British History from Bodicea to Mr. Chamberlain three times a week to

150 raw but good Scots – this, in war-time, just degutted me *daily*." It was done with a broader brush and a more liberal sprinkling of expletives than had been necessary in his Balliol tutorials, but the effect was the same on the large numbers of students who – to quote the words of one of their number – could write: "How can I explain what an impact the Professor made on my life... He played on his first year students as on a musical instrument, having us stamping or scuffling at will"; or as another writes, "He was the first and greatest mindopener in my little suburban world. A dazzling light seemed to shine in my life after I had listened to him." The Edinburgh tone is subtly different from that of Oxford, but the message is always the same.

With the exception of the first two years, the whole of his time in Edinburgh was passed under the conditions of war, and this took up more of his thoughts than he cared to admit. In April 1942 he wrote:

> A sort of paralysis lies upon one here when you take up a pen, for every right-minded man has, *au fond*, only one thought – to win this war. Outwardly, all goes on as usual. I even "research" and publish: but the supreme moment in every day (however loath one is to admit it) is the nine o'clock (p.m.) news... The University goes on outwardly as usual. Our numbers each year show little decline in the Arts Faculty – but of course none of the men ever *finishes*. So history teaching consists of an eternal round of elementary, first year work; a little second year Honours, and a few third year (women), and still fewer to the Final. It is just a question of carrying on.

Nevertheless, it was in these years that the two most ambitious projects of his later years took shape. The first was a growing commitment to a new fundamental review of Domesday Book; the second, a plan for a series of editions of medieval texts in Latin with an English translation.

IV

The first of these projects had its origin in a discovery made as long ago as 1930, when he found in Balliol College Library a twelfth-century manuscript containing a transcript of the Domesday Book entries for Herefordshire. The main interest of the volume was that it represented an attempt by some royal clerk in the reign of Henry II to bring up to date the information which had been collected nearly a hundred years earlier. More interesting still, the attempt seemed to be connected with Thomas Brown, the well-known clerk at the Exchequer who had already had a career as an administrator in Sicily. This combination of circumstances suggested the possibility of getting new light on the way in which Domesday Book had actually been used throughout the Middle Ages. While he was in the PRO Galbraith must often have seen the two volumes of the original survey displayed in all their disconcertingly pristine beauty, looking as if they had seldom been looked at until they were displayed in the Museum of the Public Record Office, but they did not stir his imagination into active enquiry. Even in 1934, when he summed up his experience of the PRO in his *Introduction to the Use of the Public Records*, he had nothing to say about Domesday Book except that the edition of 1783 was "so well done that it has never been superseded." It was the Balliol manuscript that inspired his Domesday studies; but it was not until he had left Oxford that he started serious work on it. It was in July 1939, on the eve of a tour round the archives of Normandy just before war broke out, that he began transcribing the Balliol manuscript. In November he reported from Edinburgh to Tait, "I have copied out everything in the way of notes and marginalia (in the manuscript)...It seems to me full of interest, though I soon get lost in it all." He began to feel overwhelmed by the mass of genealogical detail which the Balliol manuscript contained, and it was soon broadly agreed that Tait should work out the genealogies, while Galbraith concentrated on the manuscript and the administrative background of its compilation. By the end of 1939 he envisaged a joint article with Tait which would draw attention to the manuscript; and this was to be followed, if (as was not at all clear at that time) there was any future to follow, by a full commentary and edition of the whole manuscript.

Galbraith was still writing to Tait along these lines in November 1940, when he received an unexpected invitation to deliver the Ford Lectures in Oxford in the following summer. It was alarmingly short notice, but on December 1 he wrote to Tait: "I am going to give the Ford Lectures next Summer Term, Robin Flower having suddenly gone sick. This raises a difficulty viz. what can I scratch up in such a short time to talk about? But beggars can't be choosers, and the money will just about pay me for setting up my brother Dudley who has just been bombed out of hearth and home in Croydon. I shall have to take refuge in 'Our Public Records' in some form or other. I have long intended to write the history of their custody and have made some collections to this end. So I think I shall manage."

In fact, the *custody* of the Records was soon forgotten, and the main interest of the Ford Lectures is that they gave Galbraith an incentive to develop his ideas about Domesday Book. We must, therefore, examine the way in which his ideas had been developing under the influence of the Balliol manuscript. The first point to notice is that the purpose of the compilation of Domesday Book had been a mystery to scholars since the beginning of serious work on the subject following the celebration of its eighth centenary in 1886. The celebration prompted J. H. Round's first important contribution to Domesday studies, his paper on "Danegeld and the Finance of Domesday," from which all later discussion of the purpose of the survey flowed.[2] Briefly, the problem was that Domesday Book contained more information on more subjects than could have been necessary for any well-defined purpose; and there were too many gaps in the information on almost any topic to make it satisfactory for any purpose whatsoever, however narrowly defined. In a word, it may all have been a bit of a muddle, and rather useless from the start. But this was not a conclusion that anyone, least of all scholars in the hey-day of administrative history, could readily accept. As we shall see, Round had by 1895 developed a very clear view of the purpose of Domesday Book, and had supported this view with a convincing account of the method of its compilation. Galbraith, who had imbibed some morally well-justified hostility to Round in the PRO, was not sorry to find that he was wrong, but he only slowly came to realize the extent of his disagreement.

It was the Balliol manuscript which suggested a new approach to the problem. With its help, he hoped to discover the purpose of the survey of 1086 by studying the way in which it had been used throughout the Middle Ages. The Balliol manuscript provided evidence of its use in the reign of Henry II; in the PRO there was another abbreviation of Domesday, written in the Exchequer in the reign of Henry III, which illustrated its use a century later. From these, with the help of the Pipe Rolls, he hoped to build up a picture of the continuing use of Domesday Book, and so to work back to 1086 and solve the problem of its designers' intentions.

It was a good plan, but it came up against a number of difficulties. First of all, if the purpose of Domesday Book itself was obscure, the purpose of the later abbreviations and annotations was scarcely, if at all, less puzzling. There were signs indeed that the annotations and additions to the Herefordshire Domesday had a financial purpose, but the precise nature of this purpose and its practical effect, if any, were not clear. As for the later abbreviation in the PRO, Galbraith wrote that "it is so clean and unthumbed that we can be sure it was never used." In the face of these difficulties, this line of enquiry soon began to fade out, though it was still given a place of honor in 1950 when the text of the Balliol manuscript was finally published:

> This Balliol manuscript and also the abbreviation of Domesday are surely our best guides to the broader motives behind the Domesday Inquest. The Inquest was after all a strictly financial matter which was carried through by the Treasury. Its essential purposes are best approached through the later record of the Pipe Rolls, which are in fact a running commentary upon it.

This passage contains the most extreme expression of the point of view which dominated the first phase of Galbraith's Domesday studies. But by the time these words were published he had progressed to a more fruitful line of enquiry. The aim of this next phase of enquiry was to determine the purpose of the survey, not (except as a subordinate aid) from its later use, but chiefly from the method and stages of its composition.

The first step in this new approach was taken in an article on the "Making of Domesday Book" published in the *EHR* in 1942, and the line of argument adopted in this article occupied him increasingly during the next thirty years. In form, the article was largely a polemic against J. H. Round's view of the stages of compilation and the purpose of Domesday Book. Round had believed that the prime purpose of the Domesday enquiry was to provide a basis for the reassessment of danegeld, the tax which the Norman rulers had inherited from their Anglo-Saxon predecessors. He also believed that he had discovered the way in which Domesday Book had come into existence. It had long been known that Domesday Book was the result of an enquiry conducted by royal commissioners who traveled round England in a number of different circuits. Round's achievement lay in giving the first detailed account of how they worked and how they arranged their material. In his view they traveled round each area, hundred by hundred, took evidence from local juries, and arranged their material on a strictly geographical plan. They then sent the results to Winchester, where royal clerks rearranged the material fief by fief within each county. On this Galbraith made the point, which had already been noticed but not fully appreciated by Round, that since danegeld was assessed by geographical units and not by fiefs, the reorganization of the material into fiefs would have nullified the value of Domesday Book as an instrument for the reassessment of danegeld. This difficulty could be overcome by arguing that the "feudal" reorganization of the material, and the compilation of Domesday Book as it now exists, had taken place several years after the survey, when the original purpose had either been accomplished or forgotten. This was the line that had been taken by several workers in the field after Round. But Galbraith produced evidence to show that this explanation would not work, because the feudal reorganization of the material had already taken place *before* the commissioners sent their material to Winchester. The proof of this, he believed, was to be found in a number of documents (notably the "Exon" Domesday, the *Inquisitio Eliensis*, and the "Little" Domesday) which had had no clear place in Round's reconstruction of the process of the enquiry. In Galbraith's view these documents could best be understood as intermediate stages in processing the raw material of the enquiry before it was sent to Winchester. From this it would follow that the feudal organization of Domesday Book was not an afterthought but an integral part of the original process of collecting and sorting the material; consequently, the reassessment of danegeld could not have been the main, or even a subsidiary, purpose of the operation.

The greater part of Galbraith's later work was an elaboration of the arguments put forward in the Ford Lectures of 1941 and the article of 1942. It is symptomatic of the great complexity of the problems which were thrown up in the course of this work that another article (in 1950) and three substantial volumes (in 1950, 1961, and 1974) barely sufficed for all that he had to say. The end of the discussion is not yet in sight, and a final judgment on his contribution to the solution of the problems of Domesday Book must be left to the future. What can be said is that he opened up a new view of the complexities of the Domesday problem, and developed new and promising lines of enquiry. Next to Round, no one has done so much to bring together the bewildering array of documents, to chart the gaps and ambiguities in the evidence, and to suggest new ways of looking at the first and most important of our Public Records. He has not left the subject tidier than he found it, but he has brought it to life.

V

The second enterprise which he started in Edinburgh, and which continued to absorb his energies for the rest of his life, was the series of texts, known first as Nelson's Medieval Classics, and now as the Oxford Medieval Texts. The series came into existence as a result of conversations between Galbraith and H. P. Morrison, the managing director of the famous Edinburgh publishing firm of Thomas Nelson & Sons, in 1941 and 1942. The two men first met in November 1941, and they took to each other at once. They both had a certain expansiveness, and an ability to encourage expansiveness in others, which each found immediately attractive in the other. Galbraith wrote on November 12, 1941: "I met a very interesting and delightful man called Morrison yesterday, and in conversation he told me he was anxious – very anxious – to extract a book... on the English Church to replace the now out of date... Wakeman." At the darkest moment of the war it took a very optimistic, or a very far-sighted, publisher to be "anxious – very anxious" about such a work. The war had put a stop to most publishing plans, but Morrison was already planning a great expansion in the religious and educational side of Nelson's business. The fruits of this vision began to appear in 1946 with the publication of the *Revised Standard English New Testament* and the continuation of Dom Schmitt's edition of the works of St. Anselm. It took another three years for the first volume of the Medieval Classics to appear, but work had been in hand since 1942. The series was an enterprise which Galbraith made peculiarly his own. It appealed to his belief in original texts as the foundation of all historical study even at the most elementary level, and it also expressed his conviction that even those who knew little of the original language would benefit from the opportunity to check a translation against the author's own words. He threw himself into the project with zest, and the search for texts and editors was never far from his mind during the next thirty years.

At the very beginning Galbraith had sought the editorial help of R. A. B. Mynors, and the names of these two editors appeared on all the volumes published in Galbraith's lifetime. The main responsibility for choosing the texts and editors lay with Galbraith; Mynors was responsible for examining (and in several volumes transforming) the account of the manuscript tradition, the Latin text, and the translation. The early volumes strongly reflected Galbraith's own interests, especially the three volumes edited by his old colleague at the PRO, Charles Johnson. In the course of time, and especially after 1959 when C. N. L. Brooke became one of the general editors, the series became very diversified, but to the end Galbraith's was the hand on the tiller. He fought for the series in every crisis: "after all," he wrote in 1963, when it seemed to be going on the rocks, "it was *not* Nelson's idea, nor Morrison's – but *mine* – the child of my old age, and I will not readily let it go."

Twenty volumes appeared between 1949 and 1963, when Nelson's was taken over by the Thomson organization. The new publisher had none of Morrison's starry-eyed view of the desirability and profitability of religious and educational volumes. For two years no new volumes were commissioned, though the three which were published included G. D. G. Hall's edition of Glanvill, one of the most important volumes in the whole series. Then in 1965, after a long negotiation, the series was taken over by the Oxford University Press, and its future was assured. Once more the flow of volumes began spreading over an ever-widening area of interest, and culminating (so far as Galbraith's editorship went) with the great edition of the *Historia Ecclesiastica* of Ordericus Vitalis by Dr. Marjorie Chibnall. Although this did not begin to appear until 1969, it had been commissioned in Nelson's day, and it is the finest monument to the collaboration between Galbraith and Morrison, his publisher. Taken as a whole the series can claim to be the most important publication of medieval historical texts undertaken in this country since the closing down of the Rolls Series in 1897.

While these two enterprises – the Domesday Book studies and the Medieval Texts – were in progress Galbraith made two moves, first to London, and then to Oxford. The change to London was made in 1944 when he became the Director of the Institute of Historical Research at a difficult moment in its history. The Institute was a unique creation of a single man, A. F. Pollard, who (in the words of Sir George Clark) had "hacked his way through the tangle of London academic politics virtually single-handed" to bring about its foundation in 1921. From 1921 to 1931, with Pollard as its director, the Institute had become the visible and institutional expression of his own powerfully expressed view of the way in which historical studies should be conducted. The Institute became a conspicuous landmark in the historical world, the only serious institutional rival to Manchester in historical research. But in 1931 Pollard had retired from his university chair, and from this date he was no more than the honorary director of the Institute, appearing about once a fortnight to conduct his seminar. This arrangement led to growing disagreements with the Committee, and finally to Pollard's resentful resignation in 1939. To add to its misfortunes, the Institute in 1938 had been moved from the rooms in Malet Street which it had occupied since its foundation, and it had begun a series of moves into temporary accommodation which did not come to an end until 1947. Deprived of its director and its permanent home, the war added the further misfortune of depriving the Institute of its students, and it remained in a state of suspended animation for the first four years of the war. By 1943, however, it was becoming clear that the war was nearing its end, though the end was slower in coming than many people expected. It was necessary to make provision for the future. Galbraith was invited, and with some hesitation he accepted this nebulous but potentially influential position. He resigned his Edinburgh chair on April 1, 1944, and moved with his family to Woburn Square within a few minutes' walk of the Institute. His early experience at the PRO, when he had lived at Hampstead, had taught him the value of living over the shop, and everyone benefited from his proximity. In October he began his first graduate seminar: "I am about (he wrote) to begin my first little seminar class here on Palaeography and Sources... As a matter of fact I am rather nervous at having to teach such advanced scholars as the three who are coming to me!"

With the end of the war life quickly returned to the Institute, and the "little Seminar Class" was soon filled to over-flowing. Galbraith provided just the stimulant needed by students returning from the war, and he saw this as his main task. It was work which appealed to him, and the memory of his own plight in 1919 must often have been in his mind. The magic of his presence was as potent as ever: "An hour with him (wrote one of his post-war students) was a kind of intoxication which kept up one's intellectual pulse for a week." After five years of war the restoration of intellectual pulses was a delicate operation, and probably no one could have succeeded in this task as he did: "When I was despondent it used to seem that if only I could get back for one hour with Galbraith all would be well," wrote a student of that time. And another: "His classes on palaeography and diplomatic were indeed exhilarating. He had the extraordinary gift of transforming an outwardly dull subject into a really exciting study. It was all so simple that we felt about diplomatic as Molière's Monsieur

Jourdain did about prose, that we had known and practised it all our lives without realizing it." These are the testimonies of hard-bitten men, who had been through the war, and were later to achieve distinction in academic life. But when it came to "hacking his way through the tangle of London academic politics" it was a different story. As he himself wrote to Sir Charles Clay in 1949: "My contribution (to the Institute) was a personal one, almost a social one, and no one knows better than you how I hated the great edifice of committees, estimates, fees, admissions – for which I am constitutionally unsuited. The professional administrators on our committees did not, after all, spare me, and my deficiencies as an administrator and a business man were – rather crudely – laid before me month by month...I loathe ADMINISTRATION with every fibre of my being, and London has been a painful revelation of academic men gratuitously inventing machinery to waste time that would have been better spent doing what we professors are – after all – paid to do, viz. teach and work."

By 1947 he felt that the work which he could best do in London – the reestablishment of the Institute as a place where young researchers would like to meet, and where those who had been battered by war for four or five years could find the enthusiasm necessary for picking up the threads of their intellectual life – had been done. So in June 1947, when the offer of the Regius Professorship at Oxford reached him, he accepted without much hesitation, and returned to Oxford in January 1948.

If the succession to Pollard in London was a difficult one, that to Powicke in Oxford was almost too easy. The key-note which he struck, not without overtones of ironic humor, in his Inaugural Lecture was, "Carry on Sergeant Galbraith." He and his predecessor were bound together by intimate ties of loyalty and common experience. They both shared the general view of the Manchester school about the way in which history should be taught. The special feature of the Manchester system was its combination of great generality in the treatment of the outlines of European history during the first two years of an undergraduate's career, with intensive and carefully supervised concentration on a special subject and thesis in the third year. Powicke had supposed (wrongly, as he found to his dismay) that he had been called to Oxford to introduce the Manchester system in Oxford, and he had tried hard to graft a year's specialization on to the Oxford course of study. Galbraith had been a tutor too long to believe that any such reformation was possible, and he left the curriculum severely alone. In so far as he brought the flavor of Manchester to his Oxford teaching, it was in his concentration on giving general lectures to undergraduates. His old fire was still alive, and he could still draw crowds of enthusiastic and admiring undergraduates. "I was surprised, and indeed embarrassed by finding myself with nearer 400 than

300 audience (he wrote at the end of his first year) and I still had two thirds of them at the last lecture." But if he had escaped the administrative responsibilities of London, he was weighed down with the load of other calls on his time – membership of the Halford Committee on listed buildings, of the Royal Commission on historical monuments, and many other academic committees of one kind or another, as well as a large general correspondence. Most of these activities continued for years after his retirement in 1957. During these years, both before and after retirement, he was less part of an institution than an institution in himself, written to, visited, and consulted by large numbers of pupils of all ages, who were anxious to hear his views on every kind of personal, professional, and scholarly subject. It was only in his late seventies that the pace became noticeably slower, and it was only in his eighty-fifth year that he sold his books to the new university of Ulster – back to his origins – and brought his life's work to an end. He died without pain or illness on November 25, 1976.

In general appearance Galbraith was small, wiry, and energetic. Despite his early stoop and white hairs, he gave an impression of perpetual alertness and vitality. His head was remarkably large, and his profile had a rugged distinction that was very memorable. He was careless in dress, and lacked any kind of pomp or sense of formal dignity. The colloquialisms and expletives of his lectures – relics of his days in the army – were abundant on all occasions when he was not chained to a written text, and his colorful expressions and uninhibited comments were the delight of his audiences.

As a scholar he will probably be longest remembered for his editions of chronicles and his contribution to Domesday studies. These are the weighty part of his work and they will long survive. But my own personal preference is for his smaller miscellaneous articles. These studies in which he unraveled the significance of documents of modest size, and threw light on the thoughts, circumstances, and difficulties in which they had their origin, seem to me the masterpieces of his critical art and his historical imagination. It was in these little studies that his sharp eye and keen sense of the historical occasion had their most satisfying fulfillment. I think especially of *Monastic Foundation Charters* (1934), which grew out of his discovery of the foundation charter of Quarr Abbey, and led to an elaborate account both of the diplomatic form of the document and of the way in which an extended baronial family made provision for its spiritual well-being; or of the *Literacy of the Medieval English Kings* (1935), which grew out of the study of the writs and charters of royal government, and developed into an account of the literary equipment of the kings under whose names these documents were issued; or of the article on the *Modus Tenendi Parliamentum* (1953), in which he was able to associate a historical fiction with the routine operations of royal clerks of the reign of Edward II. I think too of his many studies of the autographs and methods of composition of thirteenth- and fourteenth-century chroniclers – studies which spanned the whole sixty years of his working life. When he was engaged on any of these pieces of work he was wholly absorbed in his subject, and he would talk about it on every possible occasion. I often thought it strange that a man who had so little patience for administration should have had so much pleasure in the contemplation of the administrators of the past. He enjoyed the bustle of life; and in the bustle of their lives he was able to forget that they were probably quite as formal and boring as their modern counterparts. They came to life for him in their documents, and to the end the PRO, where he had learnt his trade, remained for him the happiest of hunting grounds. It was in his studies of documents that his writing was at its most lively. Yet, in the last resort, nothing that he wrote could be as vivid as the man himself, as he stood by the fire scattering his shafts of wit and wisdom, truth and error, in all directions, a fascinating study in himself, and a source of energy in others.

11

Richard William Hunt
(1908–1979)

Any account of Richard Hunt and his place in contemporary British scholarship has a peculiar shape imposed upon it by the surviving materials as
well as by the nature of the man and of the positions which he occupied
for most of his life.[1] He shunned publicity and the posts he held for over
forty years – a lectureship at Liverpool University followed by the Keeper-
ship of Western Manuscripts in the Bodleian Library – gave full scope to
his instincts for withdrawal from the limelight. Moreover, his publications
were relatively brief, by-blows (one might say) in a life of scholarship, the
results of chance encounters with Festschriften and meetings of societies.
His main influence was exercised in personal contacts with scholars from
all parts of the world. He was not an expansive writer, whether in public
or private. He looked on the written word as a vehicle for conveying
information as briefly as possible and he almost never allowed his private
feelings of grief or disappointment or frustration or, for that matter, of joy,
to rise to the surface of speech, much less of writing. To one who expressed sympathy with him in the bitterest of his personal griefs – the loss
of his first wife and expected baby after only one year of marriage – he
made a brief acknowledgment and passed without a pause to the description of manuscripts. It was not that he was heartless, far from it; but,
when there was nothing to say, he said nothing.

In these circumstances it might seem an impossible task to write a
memoir of these years without event. It must largely be a record of an
unremitting pursuit of learning, and even here there are obstacles to be
overcome. If we may crudely divide scholars into those who seek to know
in order to solve problems, and those for whom problems are just incidental occurrences in exploring as wide an area of learning as possible, Richard Hunt is almost as pure a specimen of the second category as it is
possible to find. He solved many problems in scholarship, but only in the
way in which he wrote articles or gave talks: they were by-products of
scholarship. It is not easy to arrange his work around any central issues.

His learning can only be understood in the broader picture of scholarly developments in his lifetime, especially, but not exclusively, in medieval studies. In this context, nearly everything he wrote is significant, whether he published it or not, and whether or not it was intended for any eyes but his own.

It is at this point that his biographer has an incomparable asset at his disposal. Although Richard Hunt published only a small proportion of what he wrote, and wrote only a small proportion of what he knew, he threw away very little. He was a most tenacious preserver of the written word. He may sometimes have destroyed papers, but not many. When he died he left a large mass of manuscripts, notes, descriptions of manuscripts, scholarly correspondence, lectures, and papers in chaotic abundance. These papers constitute a remarkable archive of scholarship. They contain the materials for several learned works, of which two or three are already in course of preparation. Hidden within the mass of paper there are hints and insights which may provide the starting points for many future enquiries. The devoted labor of Dr. Bruce Barker-Benfield has brought order into this chaos and in due course it is to be hoped that these papers will be available in the Bodleian Library for the use of other scholars. The essential task for a biographer, however, is not to catalogue the contents of these papers nor to forestall later enquirers, but to give some idea of the ways in which they illuminate Richard Hunt's scholarly interests and provide a guide to the development of medieval studies in this country in the last fifty years.

The events which I shall have to record are few and unremarkable; but the learned lines to be traced in these papers are of the highest interest, and they will sometimes require a lengthy explanation for their elucidation. By way of introduction it should be said that the half century after 1930 was a period of remarkable change in British medieval scholarship, and Richard Hunt was a central figure in this change. At the beginning of the period, medieval studies in Britain, apart from the study of vernacular literature, were still firmly contained within the secular and institutional limits broadly delineated by Stubbs and his successors since about 1850. Of course, there were and had always been some exceptional scholars who looked beyond these limits – such men as Edmund Bishop, Henry Bradshaw, M. R. James, to name only the most remarkable. But these men had had little influence on the main body of work in British universities. They had no patronage at their disposal and consequently they had little power to encourage young scholars in what were widely looked on as eccentric lines of enquiry. The result of this powerful canalization of effort was that British scholars had taken almost no part in some of the most important new areas of medieval study. The most striking example of this British isolation was in the study of medieval scholastic thought, which had undergone a huge expansion, largely as a result of the patronage of Pope Leo XIII, following his encyclical of 1878. The policy of this Pope had been one of many influences which extended the area of intensive enquiry into every corner of medieval philosophy, theology, and canon law, and to every other aspect of the disciplines of the medieval schools. The influence of this work had scarcely penetrated into British scholarship before 1930. The fate of the young C. R. S. Harris, who as a young Fellow of All Souls in the early 1920s had undertaken a study of Duns Scotus, may be mentioned as an indication of the total isolation of Oxford from medieval scholastic studies: in Oxford he could find neither supervisor nor guide in even the simplest matters of medieval disputations and their transmission. Despite his great ability, his two-volumed work on Scotus, which appeared in 1927, was fatally flawed by his ignorance of the basic disciplines of medieval scholastic thought.

The importance of the 1930s for British medievalists was that these rigid lines of demarcation which separated "serious" history from eccentricity began to dissolve. A very important influence in bringing this about was the Regius Professor of Modern History in Oxford, F. M. Powicke; but there were also more general influences working in the same direction which need not, at present, be elaborated. Suffice it to say that Powicke was concerned about Richard Hunt's future, partly because it was not easy for anyone with Hunt's interests to get a job at that time, and partly because he saw that in Hunt there was a young scholar capable of taking his place in an area of scholarship from which Britain had hitherto been isolated.

II

With these preliminaries I turn to the details of his career. He was born on April 11, 1908, in the Derbyshire village of Spondon, where his father was a general medical practitioner. His mother, Mabel Mary Whitely, came from a family of Nottinghamshire lace manufacturers. Their family consisted of three sons and a daughter, of whom Richard was the second son. As a family, they never left Spondon except for holidays in Suffolk and family visits to a grandmother in Felixstowe. They were not great travelers. In this steadfast immobility we may detect something which came naturally to Richard in later life. The family had the usual rather spartan comforts and interests of the professional class to which they belonged. They were brought up to have a love of Dickens and Scott and to engage, at a fairly low level of competence, in family games of golf and tennis, activities to which Richard long remained unexpectedly addicted. Financially they were only moderately well off, and scholarships were needed to send the sons to public schools. It seems to have been this need which determined the choice of Haileybury for Richard. In later years he never mentioned his school days, and he seems to have been mildly oppressed by the barbarities of boarding school life. Nevertheless, he made some lasting friendships, among them (Aelred) Sillem, later abbot of Quarr Abbey, and J. R. Liddell, who shared, and perhaps stimulated, his early interest in the Middle Ages.

If Haileybury was lacking in general intellectual stimulus, it provided him with a sound classical education. The Classics master was a former Balliol undergraduate and later Fellow of Merton College, R. G. C. Levens, and it may have been as a result of his encouragement that Richard tried for a Balliol scholarship. He failed to get a scholarship, but with some help from a family trust he was able to go to Balliol as a commoner in 1927. Here he came at once under the influence of his Balliol tutor, R. A. B. (later Sir Roger) Mynors, who will appear frequently in the following pages. In the arts of composition, which then dominated the Oxford study of Latin and Greek, Hunt was only moderately successful, but in his notes and essays which have survived from his undergraduate years we find some remarkable foreshadowings of his later interests and habits of thought. At that time, all undergraduates at Balliol during their first two terms were required to write a general essay each week on subjects chosen by the Master. All these early essays of Hunt's have survived, with careful notes of the tutors to whom they were read, and the remarks which they made about them. With hindsight, it is possible to see that these essays gave evidence of some unusual intellectual powers, and it is perhaps not very creditable to the search for brilliance which the tutorial system encouraged that they seem to have evoked no more than mild commendation. His essay on Lewis Carroll, written in his second term, already shows his extraordinary faculty for picking out bibliographical details which could be used to illustrate important themes. Moreover, at a time when the importance of logic in Lewis Carroll's writing was not as widely appreciated as it now is, Hunt saw that it was one of the mainsprings of Carroll's life and a permanent influence in his books.

> It also made him (he continued) very precise and meticulous. We are told that from January 1861 to the time of his death he kept a precis of every letter he wrote. There are 98,721, and all indexed with an ingenious system of cross-referencing devised by himself...His poetry was not the merely imaginative nonsense poetry of Edward Lear. It is mostly either parody or composed on scientific principles. Take the quatrain which appears in *Through the Looking Glass*, "'Twas brillig and the slithy toves...": this was made up in 1855 long before the rest of the book was thought of, and was originally meant as a parody of Anglo-Saxon poetry and fitted with a glossary...These books are thoroughly a part of our nursery tradition, itself perhaps the greatest in any language.

I do not know how competent he was at that time to pronounce on the nursery tradition in any language other than English, but the remark has the stamp of his mature years, and no one who knew him in later life can read these sentences without seeing the man who later wrote about the indexing symbols of Robert Grosseteste and the logical grammarians of the twelfth century.

More immediately important for the future, these years also saw the beginning of his lifelong habit of transcribing with meticulous accuracy the unpublished contents of medieval manuscripts. Among the earliest of these is a transcript of verses in a Trinity College manuscript (no. 34). Hunt noted its date (quite in his later style): "s.xii ex." and the record of his transcription: "copied in J. R. H. Weaver Esq.'s room in Coll. Trin. Nov. 1930."

Several notebooks survive which testify to the range of his undergraduate reading – not only Helen Waddell's *Wandering Scholars* and Haskins's *Twelfth Century Renaissance*, which many an undergraduate of that time read with a thrill of discovery, but also (which very few undergraduates can ever have looked at) the recently published edition (1930) of *Carmina Burana* by Alfons Hilka and Otto Schumann. His notes on this last publication show that Hunt had already thoroughly grasped the principles of the exhaustive German method of editing.

These are trifles, but they may be mentioned as the earliest symptoms of what was later to become his life's work. Practically, however, the main need for him in these years was to make sure of a First-Class degree if he was to have much hope of an academic career. This gave him a good deal of anxiety; but, after getting only a Second Class in classical Honor Moderations, he got a First in Greats, and this was followed by his election to a Senior Scholarship at Christ Church for two years from October 1931. In the circumstances of the time, and in view of Hunt's repugnance to presenting himself in a favorable light, it was an imaginative choice.

Without delay he set off for Munich, the fountain-head of the modern study of paleography, with the declared intention of working under the direction of Paul Lehmann. Lehmann in Munich and E. A. Lowe in Oxford were the most distinguished pupils of Ludwig Traube, who at the beginning of the century had shown how the scientific study of manuscripts could be used as an instrument of literary and intellectual history. Lehmann's contributions to medieval studies, like those of Traube himself, were far more than merely paleographical. He was an innovator in the study of medieval literary forms and in the study of medieval German libraries. It may be conjectured that it was this last interest which was the most powerful influence in taking Hunt to study under him. As long ago as 1907, Lehmann had started under Traube's inspiration to work on the library catalogues of Switzerland and Germany. In 1918 he had produced the first, and in 1928 the second, of the massive series of volumes containing the texts of these catalogues, and there were (and still are) more to come, in 1932, 1933, 1939, 1962, 1977, 1979.

The main inspiration in turning Hunt's attention in this direction came from Mynors, who was at this time urging Hunt to take on, or collaborate in, some kind of similar publication of English library catalogues. Hunt's first reactions were distinctly cool. The sight of Lehmann's icy persistence in a publication which, with all its scholarship, had many of the qualities of a telephone directory, was enough to chill the most enthusiastic admirer. Hunt spoke to Lehmann about it, and Lehmann was not encouraging: it was work, he rightly observed, which could not be undertaken as a spare-time occupation. Lehmann's scholarship made a deep impression on him. Looking back many years later, when he could see his development in perspective, he recorded: "I always feel grateful to Lehmann for putting me on to an analysis of a big fifteenth century florilegium which made me look around for sources." This work, dry though it was, taught him as nothing else could have done to understand the texture of medieval thought. He worked assiduously in Lehmann's seminar, visited the manuscript collections of Prague in his company, and generally learnt the trade of being a medievalist at its roots.

At the same time, stimulus of a different kind was coming to him from Powicke, who wanted him to write a DPhil thesis on Alexander Nequam. Here too Hunt's reactions were cool. If medieval library catalogues seemed too horrendous a task, Alexander Nequam somehow failed to satisfy the breadth of his interests. Yet Powicke was undoubtedly right. Alexander Nequam was a perfect subject for a DPhil thesis: he was an important scholar whose works covered a wide range of grammatical, scientific, and theological learning. His works are preserved in a large, but not overwhelmingly large, number of good manuscripts. They were (and still are) largely unprinted and unstudied; and they are a mirror of a large area of thought at a central moment in the Middle Ages. The arguments for "adopting" him as a subject were strong, but the impulse was weak.

This nagging choice overshadowed Hunt's last months in Munich in the summer of 1932, while around him a more horrific choice was reaching its fatal issue. Before long Lehmann would be starting his lectures with a Nazi salute. Meanwhile, Hunt certainly benefited from his technical expertise, and by the time he returned to England, he was probably better equipped than anyone in the country at that time with the skills necessary for using manuscripts for studying the literary and intellectual history of the Middle Ages.

His year in Munich had completed his technical education, but the problem of his future was becoming urgent. He had only one certain year of his Senior Scholarship left and he needed something to show for it.

Wisely (but perhaps with a slight sense of desperation) he chose Alexander Nequam, and registered as a DPhil student at Oxford under Powicke's supervision. In 1933, his Senior Scholarship was extended for a third year so that he could finish his thesis, and in 1934 he successfully applied for a Lectureship in Paleography at Liverpool in succession to J. A. Twemlow. In 1935 he reported that Alexander Nequam was still hanging heavy on his hands, and though he completed his thesis in 1936, it was by then clear that his heart was not in it.

As soon as the thesis was finished, for all practical purposes Hunt forgot about it. Then and later, his friends begged him to publish it, and common prudence urged the need for publication. As late as 1961, he was persuaded to bring it up to date for publication, and he took some half-hearted steps in this direction. Now, after nearly fifty years, it still remains and still deserves to be published, and it is being prepared for publication by Dr. Margaret Gibson.[2] It is a treasury of accurate information about many manuscripts and many points of learned detail over the wide range of subjects covered by Alexander's works. Even in its unpublished state, it has been used more extensively than most theses in the Oxford History Faculty. Why Hunt was indifferent to its publication remains something of a mystery. Of course, everyone is apt to lose interest in a subject after writing about it, and there are always more important things to do than refurbishing exhausted thoughts for publication. But Hunt's indifference to his longest piece of learned writing has deeper roots than this. Even while he was working on it, his mind was on other subjects, and among these subjects the history of medieval British libraries, which he had not been able to see his way through in 1932, was the most important. This was to be the biggest single interest of his scholarly life, combining, as it did, his early work as an undergraduate in Oxford, when he first discovered the fascination of medieval manuscripts, with his experiences in Munich, when he saw the subject in its full European setting. To understand the way in which the work developed, a certain amount of background explanation is needed.

III

An interest in the contents of medieval libraries was not new in England. It had a long and continuous history going back at least to the thirteenth century. But in modern scholarship, a new age of careful and scientific investigation began in France with the great Léopold Delisle's *Cabinet des Manuscrits de la Bibliothèque Impériale* (3 vols., 1868–81) followed in Germany by Becker's *Catalogi Bibliothecarum Antiqui* (1885), and then by Gottlieb's and Lehmann's long series of German and Austrian catalogues from 1895 onwards. In England the only scholarly work of comparable importance was that of M. R. James, notably in his publication of the catalogues of Canterbury and Dover (1903) and – most important for our present subject – his short analysis, published in 1922, of the catalogues associated with a fifteenth-century bibliographer, whom James identified with John Boston of Bury St. Edmunds.[3] It was from James at Eton that Mynors had learnt to study medieval manuscripts, and it was from Mynors that Hunt's interest in medieval manuscripts was given its first distinct impulse. Mynors saw Hunt as the scholar who could carry on James's work with the learning and method which had characterized the work of the Continental scholars. As we have seen, Hunt was at first reluctant; but no sooner was he fully committed to Alexander Nequam than the libraries of medieval England became a major feature of his thoughts and efforts. The evidence for this growing interest can be found in countless notes from the years from 1933 onwards. His earliest sketch of the subject goes back to an unpublished paper on *English Monastic Libraries* which he read to the undergraduate History Society of Keble College in the spring of 1934. Like his thesis, from which it was then an imprudent diversion, it deserves to be printed even after this long lapse of time, for it contains a sketch of the physical and mental conditions under which scribes and authors pursued their tasks in the face of wind and weather, neglect, imperfect information, and the disapprobation of their superiors, which can be found nowhere else so well portrayed. There is one passage which deserves to be quoted, for it contains the key to a great deal of Hunt's later career:

> In conclusion I should like to touch on the subject of how far books in one monastery were available to others. Little has been done on it so far. I think we may safely say that books were lent from one house to another for the purposes of transcription, though I cannot remember an instance of it later than the ninth century... Some scholars, as William of Malmesbury, journeyed round in search of materials. But if a book was not in the library of one's house, was there any means of discovering it without writing round until you struck a copy? It may be surprising to some people to discover that there was. The earliest example comes from France. There existed in the seventeenth century (two Benedictine scholars saw it) a catalogue of the library at Savigny, and bound up with it the catalogues of Mont St. Michel, Caen, Bec, Jumièges. The date is variously given as 1210 or 1240. Of it, Delisle says (*Cabinet des Manuscrits*, i, 527), "I do not know any document that shows so clearly how abbeys in the Middle Ages gave a real publicity to their catalogues, and how monk-scholars knew where to find books which were not in the library of their own house." A fragment (*ib*. ii, 42, 196, 513) has also been found of a general catalogue of the Paris monasteries for the use of students at the Sorbonne.

In England we have a much more ambitious scheme. There exists more than one copy of a work which contains the names and works of all the commoner writers (mainly theological) used in the Middle Ages. The number varies (in different versions) from seventy to ninety-two. Against each work, there is a number or a series of numbers. Each number represents a monastery. Thus if we turn up Alexander Nequam, the first work given is his commentary on the Song of Songs; and against it are the numbers 142, 108, 15, XII, 46. These numbers stand for the following monasteries: Rievaulx, St. Peter's Gloucester, St. Albans, Buildwas and St. Neots. The catalogue was almost certainly compiled by the Franciscans, for it arranges England into seven Custodies, and among the Custodies appears Salisbury, which ceased to exist before 1331. Further, there are very few libraries of friars mentioned, and those that do occur are almost certainly a later addition. Therefore, it looks as if it were drawn up before the friars had collected large libraries. It is closely connected with another composite work, a collection of references to the incidental comments of the fathers on the Scriptures, and both together are known as the *Tabula Septem Custodiarum*. Thus, on Prov. XXXI. 10 it gives references to Ambrose on Luke, Augustine Sermon 35, Bede on Luke, and St. Bernard's second homily on "*Missus est Angelus.*" It indicates whether these references are anagogical, allegorical or tropological and gives exact references to book and chapter, in each case using subdivisions "a" to "g" and the opening words of the passages. Together they were meant to be a help to the theologian and preacher.

In the fifteenth century it was much enlarged by, it seems, a monk of Bury called John Boston. His list includes 672 authors and gives some slight account of their lives, where there is an easily available source. For many works it does not note the existence (of any manuscripts). Of course it contains many mistakes. But so far as is known, there is no parallel in the rest of Europe.

The importance of this passage is that it was a first attempt to put in the larger setting of their purpose as aids to theological study the remarkable series of documents to which M. R. James had called attention in 1934. The passage also shows that, already in the spring of 1934, Hunt had done a great deal of detailed work on these lists. By the middle of 1935, with his thesis still unfinished, Hunt had prepared a transcript of the earliest of this series of texts, preserved in the Bodleian MS. Tanner 165. Hunt reported this achievement to Mynors on March 28, adding that he had also got some distance in understanding the method of compilation and the causes of confusions which were later to give much trouble to its editors. He had worked out that the composite catalogue was based on reports of manuscripts actually seen in the libraries enumerated. To this extent, therefore, it contained first-hand evidence of existing volumes; but reassuring though this was, there was the warning that "the compiler must have been absolutely at the mercy of the contributions sent in." Mynors's reaction to this news was immediate. On April 5 he wrote: "It is heroic of you to have transcribed already the vast mass of Tanner...It clearly ought to be the first volume of a Corpus Catalogorum under the auspices of the British Academy." On May 30, after studying the transcript, Mynors wrote again: "it marks an epoch in medieval studies." Almost certainly by this time Hunt had already completed some of the remarkable studies identifying the works and manuscripts mentioned in these lists, which are to be found among his notes. Two years later Mynors himself contributed to this venture by completing an elaborate annotated transcript of the later, larger, and even more baffling catalogue associated with John of Boston. By 1937, therefore, the study of this collection of catalogues and the identification of the works and manuscripts mentioned in them was well advanced. Why, then, did it not appear? Why is it still, even now, a project adopted by the British Academy for future publication?[4]

The main part of the answer to this question is that the project grew in complexity as it developed. The number of detailed enquiries necessary for turning bare lists of books and libraries into reliable accounts of real men, real libraries, and actual manuscripts became larger and larger. So far as Hunt was concerned, the range of these enquiries was soon extended to embrace a complete survey of all the existing British manuscripts of which the medieval provenance could be established. This soon became a distinct project on its own, and like the "Boston of Bury" project, it also had a tendency to grow as it progressed. The earliest evidence for the existence of such a project in the Hunt papers is a letter from Mynors of April 9, 1932, mentioning that he had started a "slip catalogue of manuscripts of known provenance, which has quickly reached over 800 slips." More collaborators, notably Hunt and Liddell, were quickly drawn in, and the accumulation continued from several different sources. Among Hunt's papers there is a list of manuscripts of monastic provenance in Cambridge University Library, with a note in his hand: "copied by Pink and given me by J. R. L(iddell), 1936." In this list the evidence for continuing activity is clearly apparent. The original list contained about 100 manuscripts, but there are many additions in Hunt's hand. So the process of collection was going ahead vigorously in the years from 1932 onwards, and it was given still further momentum under the impulse of C. R. Cheney. In November 1937 he suggested that a collaborative effort should be made to produce a list of all extant British manuscripts of known monastic provenance. From this time, work on this project (very soon extended to include secular as well as monastic libraries) went ahead with increasing vigor with a uniform system of descriptive cards, a single collecting center, and with N. R. Ker emerging as its editor and chief collector and executive, while Hunt was increasingly the member of the group to whom everyone turned for criticism, information, and an authoritative judgment on doubtful points.

The team was remarkable in bringing together in total harmony and mutual confidence four or five men of different talents but with a single object. Their work in the years before 1940 did more than anything else to lay the material foundations for the later study of intellectual life in England in the Middle Ages: in a unique way, it linked learning to the harsh realities of physical objects and available resources. It is hard to believe that this could have been accomplished in so short a time by any other combination of scholars. But there was a price to pay: quite abruptly the "Boston of Bury" project began to take second place to *British Libraries*. Hunt recognized that the later project was a necessary preliminary to the completion of "Boston." It will, he wrote, "save an endless labour" in locating manuscripts, and "be a means of making available the things we find by the way."[5] The consequence was that *British Libraries* took an increasing proportion of his time. His correspondence with Ker (it has survived on both sides in remarkable completeness) gives a picture of scholarly cooperation worthy of a better age. It will not be out of place to quote a small part of one long letter from Hunt to Ker as an example of the kind of cooperation which was quietly bringing about, at this most unfavorable moment, the publication of a remarkable piece of historical scholarship. The letter is dated from Liverpool September 25, 1940:

> I have been going through M(edieval) B(ritish) L(ibraries) with great enjoyment, slightly tempered by fears for the safety of the MS. The notes I have made speak for themselves, though some of them may give you some trouble, I am afraid, because I have not always been able to verify my queries: and some of them may turn out to be mare's nests.
>
> I have only checked thoroughly those houses, whose MSS. or catalogues I have gone into at one time or another. I would have done more, but have not had time. The library A.R.P. [Air Raid Precautions] regulation is that everyone "without exception or excuse" either leaves the building or descends to the lowest stack floor, which isn't furnished with books.
>
> Will you look up Berlin Phill. 1805 and 1904? We haven't the Berlin catalogues here and my notes are insufficient to show whether their provenance can be determined. According to my notes, C(orpus) C(hristi) C(ollege, Cambridge, MSS.) 28 and 182 both have erased inscriptions, but the MSS. were in CCC when Jock (Liddell) and I went through them, and we didn't try the ultraviolet.
>
> If there are things in my notes which are not intelligible, just send them back with fierce comments and I'll try to elucidate them.

This letter was almost the last which passed between Hunt and Ker on this subject before the volume, *Medieval Libraries of Great Britain*, was printed. On August 1, 1940, Cheney ("at three in the morning" after "pretty long hours in a government office") had written to Hunt: "Here is a sample page of our Med. Brit. Libraries for your comments and criticisms. If we can finish it off soon, we can get it printed and published by the R. Hist. Soc. at once – the printer has just enough paper and the Society is willing." The volume was in fact "finished off soon," and it was published by June 1941.

With this part of the "medieval libraries" enterprise successfully completed, the way was clear for a final push to finish the earlier "Boston of Bury" project. But the war was now pressing more closely than before. So far as Hunt personally was concerned, his second marriage in 1942, his growing family, and above all his increasing obligations towards Liverpool University (the Professor of Medieval History, Coopland, had retired in 1940; no successor was appointed till 1945, and in the interval a large part of his work was done by Hunt) all combined to make immediate progress on "Boston" impossible.

It was the fate of "Boston" to be continually thrust aside by other projects which appeared to be necessary to it either as a foundation or overflow. It was in this guise that, in the last months of 1937, yet another project began to present itself. This was a plan for a new periodical which would gather up the flow of new discoveries. On November 29, 1937, Hunt wrote: "I have been discussing lately with a friend (Dr. Raymond Klibansky) the possibility of starting a periodical to deal with medieval thought and learning. Such a periodical is badly wanted. There is no English periodical which will print material on medieval thought: it has to be sent abroad." The discussions thus started continued and broadened in scope during 1938. By the middle of the year the outline of the first number of the new periodical had been determined. It only remained to find a publisher, printer, subscribers, and to put out a prospectus. The indomitable energy of Dr. Klibansky was largely engaged in canvassing and solving these problems, and in the last days of 1938 a prospectus was issued for a periodical, familiarly and (in the circumstances of the time) sardonically known as *MARS*: it announced that *Mediaeval and Renaissance Studies* would appear twice a year, starting in October 1939 with an appetizing list of thirty contributions promised for the first numbers. The first number was ready in the summer and was sent to Belgium to be printed. It was lost in the turmoil of the following year, printed again in England, and finally appeared in 1941, with a further installment in 1943. Planned under the imminent threat of war, and brought into existence in the presence of war, it represented a concentration of the new spirit of medieval research which was stirring at that time. The periodical struggled on after the war with four further numbers from 1950 to 1968. The high standard of editing persisted and the need did not diminish, but the periodical languished amid manifold distractions. It deserves to be mentioned here as an expression of the hopes and efforts of the pre-war years.

IV

When the war ended, the "Boston of Bury" project was immediately revived. But two new obstacles now appeared. The first of these was a
minor international incident which, however slight its practical importance, elicited contrasting statements of rare interest from the groups of
Continental and British scholars interested in the project. To understand
the Continental point of view we have to go back to M. R. James's article
of 1922 which first brought to light the importance of the "Boston of
Bury" group of library catalogues. One of the earliest scholars to grasp
the significance of the discovery was the Belgian scholar Fr. Joseph de
Ghellinck, SJ. He wrote briefly about the discovery in a paper for a Congress of Librarians in 1923, and at greater length in a paper of extraordinary brilliance, "En marge des catalogues des bibliothèques médiévales," in
1924.[6] A brief quotation from this paper will give a clear idea of the point
of view and personality of this highly gifted scholar. The dry lists of books
in medieval library catalogues, he writes,

> *sont tout autre chose qu'une pétrifaction de la bibliographie rudimentaire
> antique... Elles recèlent la matière de tout un chapitre dans l'histoire de
> l'esprit humain;... ces notices anonymes jouent le rôle de témoins dans l'his-
> toire de la diffusion des écrits et de la transmission des idées;... elles nous
> donnent un tableau, souvent très net, de la transmission de la culture, de ses
> moyens de propagation et de leur rapidité, de la proportion des divers élém-
> ents qui y entrent; elles nous apprennent la mesure du succès des ouvrages, le
> rôle des pays et des époques, des écrivains et des groupements d'écrivains,
> dans la formation de la pensée médiévale.*
>
> ["are certainly not the mere petrifaction of an ancient and primitive bibli-
> ography. Hidden in them is the material for a whole chapter of the history of
> the human spirit. These anonymous notes play the role of witnesses in the
> history of the diffusion of texts and the transmission of ideas. They give us a
> picture, often very clear, of the transmission of culture, its means of propa-
> gation and its speed, the proportion of various elements within it; they tell
> us about the degree of success of the works, the part played by different
> countries and periods, of writers and groups of writers, in the formation of
> medieval thought."]

It would be difficult to make greater claims than these for any single body
of evidence. In Fr. Ghellinck's paper, they were supported by a scintillating
array of examples, including the "Boston of Bury" group of catalogues, of
which it is not unfair to say that, dazzling though they are in their variety,
they scarcely provide the illumination of *la transmission des idées* promised in the first paragraph. Fr. Ghellinck, however, was certainly the first

to appreciate the wider importance of the "Boston" catalogue which M. R. James had brought to his attention, and the English scholars always, though somewhat quixotically, accepted that he had a prior claim to any future publication. They were, therefore, reluctant to take any step towards publication without his agreement.

After the war, when contact with foreign scholars was reestablished, it soon became apparent that the kind of work which Hunt and Mynors had been doing before the war was not what Fr. Ghellinck wanted. He was not at all interested in the identification of the precise manuscripts referred to in these catalogues, nor in the detailed history of the libraries to which they belonged. He was interested only in the evidence which they provided for the use or disuse of the various works mentioned in the catalogues. That is to say, he was interested only in the light they could throw on the general history of Christian thought along the lines which he had laid down in 1924. A bare publication of the lists as they stood would (as he thought) satisfy his needs. With the raw material in front of them in print, it could be left to him and other widely ranging scholars to draw their own conclusions.

This view was entirely consistent with Fr. Ghellinck's earlier writings on the subject. But it struck at the foundations of the detailed work of Hunt and Mynors. With a view to getting a favorable hearing for their point of view they sought the help of W. A. Pantin, who wrote to Fr. Ghellinck giving the views of the English scholars. Ghellinck replied in a letter which is a masterpiece of wit and learned polemic. He first analyzed the contrasting points of view of the English and Continental scholars: he and his colleagues (he wrote) were interested only in this material as evidence for the diffusion and transmission of literary works, as a contribution to the history of thought and doctrine. Whatever went beyond this was superfluous: *non pas inutile, mais tout à fait secondaire* ["not without value but entirely secondary"]. The English scholars, by contrast, were interested in the history of libraries, or what he called *la documentation d'histoire bibliothéconomique* ["documenting the history of libraries as institutions"]. This latter constituted *la belle tradition anglaise dans l'histoire des bibliothèques, des Botfields, des Edwards, des Bradshaws, des James, etc.* ["the fine English tradition of the history of libraries, of the Botfields, etc."]. The English scholars were conducting an investigation into points of detail in which he and his friends had no interest. Nevertheless, despite his prior claim to these documents, he did not wish to deprive the English scholars of their chance of realizing their aim *essentiellement anglais par son objet et ses matières* ["essentially English in its object and its materials"]; but he pointed out that the researches of his English colleagues would take many years, and during this long time the learned world would be deprived of the use of documents which in their simple unadorned state would render *d'énormes services* ["enormous services"] to those who could use them for literary and intellectual history. What he and his committee therefore suggested was that the English scholars should prepare the documents for immediate publication with a minimum of introduction, and without any attempt to identify individual manuscripts or to describe the state of individual libraries. Once published, they could get on with their own researches at leisure without depriving the learned world of the documents which it needed. This manner of proceeding was, he claimed, a well-established practice. It would release the documents in a form that would provide *un remarquable ensemble de renseignements pour la tradition littéraire du moyen âge et pour les inspirateurs de sa pensée* ["a remarkable assemblage of information on the literary tradition of the Middle Ages and those who inspired its thought"] and it would give the English scholars ample time for their secondary investigations.

The contents of this letter must have given its recipients a *mauvais quart d'heure* ["bad moment"]. If Fr. Ghellinck was right they were relegated to the position of humble toilers at the coal-face, extracting ore to fuel the intellectual powerhouses of Europe, free in their long leisure to potter about among the old books, harmlessly engaged in finding out who had owned them, leaving the more serious work of tracing the intellectual history of Christian Europe to others. The strength of this view of the matter depended upon the correctness of Ghellinck's assumption that the material could be used for his grand purposes without further refinement. It was, therefore, essential, if the contrary view were to be maintained, to demonstrate that nothing could be made of these documents without the most careful assessment of the individual manuscripts, and the clarification of the many confusions embodied in the material available to medieval librarians. To neglect these facts could lead only to a superficial view of the European intellectual tradition.

It was left to Hunt to draft the reply to Fr. Ghellinck. His draft is a monument to his judgment. It also expresses an important principle in intellectual history – the principle that intellectual history cannot seriously be undertaken without the most exact attention to the material circumstances of intellectual work. The draft was later improved by his colleague, but this is the main part of what Hunt wrote:

Dear Fr. Ghellinck,
    We thank you very sincerely for your letter in which you state so clearly the grounds for producing a "provisional" edition of the *Catalogus librorum Angliae* and of Boston of Bury.[7] We very much welcome the frank and open exchange of views on the means of achieving the aim we all have in view, namely of making accessible to scholars the long awaited texts, so valuable, as you say, for the literary history of the Middle Ages.

From the point of view of the wider plan for a corpus of English mediaeval Library catalogues it would be a very great advantage to have printed texts of CLA and of Boston to work on; but we are not wholly convinced that a text with the minimum of introduction and a summary critical apparatus, but without any attempt to identify the works of the various authors, would be of great value to scholars. In view of the way the texts were compiled, some attempt at identification of the works mentioned seems necessary, and would surely be appropriate in a series like yours which is notable for the excellence of its apparatus. The examples of "provisional" texts to which you refer, the edition of the *Martyrologium Hieronomianum* by De Rossi and Duchesne and that of the *Corpus Juris Canonici* by Friedberg are on rather a different footing. There were many editions of both texts in existence already, and Friedberg does give the references to sources.

Here we should like to correct a false impression which our earlier letter created. You say that *l'œuvre que vous projetez se manifeste tout de suite comme une œuvre de documentation d'histoire bibliothéconomique* ["the work which you project can be immediately characterized as a work of documenting the history of libraries as institutions"], while the interest of the *Spicilegium* is in *la documentation... dont peut tirer parti l'histoire littéraire* ["documentation of which literary history can make use"]. We are no less anxious than you to make CLA and Boston really usable for scholars working on the literary history of the Middle Ages. The point we wished to emphasize was that they are texts *very dangerous to use for such enquiries* without a knowledge of the way their compilers worked and of the sources upon which they drew; and it would be impossible to bring this out by a few brief general observations in the introduction.

We think that the best way to make the point clear is to send you one or two specimens of the method of identification we should propose to adopt, (a) for patristic and (b) for mediaeval authors. For patristic authors we should give only a reference to a printed edition (normally Migne, *Pat. lat.* [*PL*]) without any discussion of the true authorship of individual works. For mediaeval authors we should go a little further and indicate summarily, as far as we can, the true author of any particular work. For there is a difference in the weight to be attached to the evidence of CLA and Boston for patristic and mediaeval authors. For patristic authors they merely reflect the manuscript tradition; for mediaeval authors, they may do something more. In both cases we refer to manuscripts only where a special point has to be made, e.g. where the attribution of particular works (or groups of works) to a particular author would be otherwise unintelligible, as in the enclosed specimen of Athanasius, or when the evidence derived from extant manuscripts makes certain the identification of works otherwise only to be guessed at, as in the enclosed specimen of Augustine.

To sum up, we should be prepared to attempt to construct a "provisional" edition of CLA and of Boston, but we should be very reluctant to see such an edition appear without the identification of the works included in them...

We should be glad if you would consider these observations, and send us the comments of the board of Directors of the *Spicilegium*.

So far as I know Fr. Ghellinck's answer has not survived, but in practice the views of the English editors prevailed.

I have described this controversy at some length for two reasons. The first is that, in the light of such criticisms as those of Fr. Ghellinck and, indeed, of thoughts which may arise in the minds of even sympathetic observers, Hunt's lifelong dedication to the task of describing the minutiae of a huge number of individual manuscripts requires justification, and here is its justification in his own words. I have said that Hunt did not easily or frequently think it necessary to explain himself. On this occasion he did so, and it is a striking tribute to the confidence which his colleagues had in his judgment that they left it to him to draft the reply to so formidable a critic as Fr. Ghellinck. His draft shows that their confidence was well justified. No one else could have demolished the thinly veiled dismissal of his and his colleagues' learned activity with more devastating brevity and force.

A second reason for dwelling at some length on this point is that a memoir of Hunt can only be of interest if it makes clear – what he himself never found it necessary to clarify in print – the general purpose served by the many detailed enquiries on which he was engaged throughout his learned life. This debate brings his work and that of his collaborators into the context of the general development of medieval scholarship during the period from 1930 to 1980. This half-century saw the culmination and decline of two great efforts in medieval scholarship: the English constitutional, and the Continental scholastic, interpretation of the Middle Ages. The first was defective in its parochialism; the second in its lack of parochialism. The first was strong in its grasp of times and places, but limited in its ideas; the second was strong in its grasp of doctrines, but weak in relating these doctrines to practical situations. The first was inspired by the belief that the institutions of government preserved all that was most important in the doctrines of the Middle Ages. The second was inspired by a conviction that the medieval tradition of scholastic thought was the continuing central theme of European civilization. Under the influence of this conviction, a mass of work was produced of great historical and intellectual importance. Its weakness was that it touched only lightly on the conditions which promoted scholastic thought and the pressures to which it responded. The conflict between Ghellinck and the group of scholars with whom Hunt associated was a confrontation between those, like Ghellinck, who wished to describe the stream of thought as an object in its own right, and those who insisted that material circumstances and limitations were an essential part of any realistic intellectual history. It is this contrast which gives the controversy a place of general interest and lasting importance in the history of medieval studies.

Whether or not Fr. Ghellinck was right in thinking that the bare lists of books and libraries would have rendered *d'énormes services* to medieval intellectual history, he was certainly right in predicting that the world would have to wait a long time to have the texts in the form which, as the English scholars insisted, alone made them capable of being used. One reason for this was that the end of the war brought new duties and distractions to all participants. Consequently, the project scarcely moved forward during the next fifteen years, until Richard and Mary Rouse took it up and brought new minds to the task. This is not the place to attempt to assess how much still remained to be done in editing the texts, identifying their contents, and investigating the circumstances in which they were planned and carried out. That is a story which will be told elsewhere.

V

In October 1945 Hunt left Liverpool and returned to Oxford as Keeper of Western Manuscripts at the Bodleian Library. Earlier, he had refused to be considered for important librarianships – notably at Liverpool – on the ground of his lack of administrative experience and skill. But he viewed the Bodleian offer with enthusiasm: "there is so much to be done in Bodley," he wrote on November 15, 1944, "and there surely ought to be possibilities for trying to be of some use to people who are working on manuscripts, though I am very vague about the actual duties of the Keeper." His enthusiasm grew as he learnt more: "It is a marvellous prospect," he wrote on January 14, 1945. "When telling me the duties of the Keeper, Craster (then Bodley's Librarian) put first helping and advising readers, for which I was very glad."

His immediate impressions on arrival confirmed these high expectations: "The work of the library is very exhilarating," he wrote in describing a sale of Harmsworth Trust manuscripts. "I fixed my attention on several manuscripts very inadequately described." This was his first venture to the sale-room to pick up manuscripts, which were not expensive, but which made significant additions to the Bodleian collections. The decade after the war was a golden age for acquiring unspectacular but interesting manuscripts. A number of important collections came on the market – not least the large residue of the Phillipps library – and the group of friends who before the war had collaborated in *British Medieval Libraries* and "Boston of Bury" were now largely instrumental in selecting manuscripts to add to the Bodleian collections. Until the mid-1950s prices were still low; yet the Bodleian expenditure on new acquisitions rose from an average of about £400 a year before the war to £3,450 in 1952–3 and to £13,362 in 1962–3. In 1975–6 (the year of Hunt's retirement) it reached the quite exceptional total of £58,472. This was not a symptom of lavish or indiscriminate buying, but of constant watchfulness. Hunt's eye for significant detail was equally active in finding sources of finance for new acquisitions and manuscripts which were worth buying.

In addition to purchases, his authority and persuasive power encouraged gifts and deposits. In 1958 Hunt wrote of the arrival of 185 boxes of personal papers of Sir Thomas Phillipps ("they will take some digesting"), followed by the remaining hoard of English topographical manuscripts: "They only arrived (Hunt wrote on Sunday, June 15), on Thursday afternoon, 15 tea chests. We still have these chests to unpack and haven't counted them, but there are over 500 vols., so we have our hands full" – this (he added) at a time when "the university has just decided that we shall keep the whole library open till 10 p.m. in term time and have given us no money for extra staff."

Another aspect of his new job, which he was quick to appreciate and act upon, was his responsibility for modern as well as medieval manuscripts, and for administrative as well as literary documents. Nothing was more conspicuous in his thirty-year tenure of the office than his concern for papers of every date and every type. Court rolls and modern diocesan records were among the earliest objects of his energy. On April 28, 1946, he wrote: "I am having a list of Court Rolls completed for the Register of Manorial Documents, and I am at work with a helper on the conspectus of shelf marks...It is exasperatingly fiddly work." Almost exactly a year later a new source of trouble made its appearance. On April 28, 1947, he wrote: "I've been a good deal concerned with Diocesan Records of late. We have taken in a large fresh batch of the Oxford ones...An old mill-stream rose up during the floods and entered the cellar of Church House where the records were kept...I got a team of volunteers and we removed all the wet papers and parchments, and tied each parish into a parcel and carted them all off to our New Building." These diocesan records kept on arriving for several years as they were released from ecclesiastical custody. Troublesome though they were, they proved to be an endless source of interest to him. He never looked at any documents, however mundane his immediate purpose, without going deeply into the reason for their existence and the forms of life of which they were the record. When the papers of Bishop Wilberforce were being sorted out, he wrote: "We have been able to learn from them how insufficient is our knowledge of the precise nature of ecclesiastical records." Characteristically, the chance which brought a growing bulk of diocesan records under his care caused him to revise several long-established judgments on the condition of the clergy in the eighteenth and nineteenth centuries, and also helped him to deal with practical problems when he was churchwarden of St. Barnabas in Oxford.

Everywhere in his work we see this same interplay between cataloguing, describing, understanding, and forming new judgments on men and their affairs. His judicious buying of manuscripts for the Bodleian was informed by a deep sense of the nature of the collections under his care and of their gaps. He had a special tenderness for the memory of those who were connected with the collections, as we can see in his researches into Archbishop Laud's books, and in his sympathy for Shelley whose letters form one of the main modern acquisitions among the Bodleian manuscripts. Some of Shelley's letters had been the subject of a forgery scare which he thought ill-judged, and he dealt with it firmly in the course of other business. On March 18, 1945, he wrote:

> I went up to London last Monday, partly to look at a MS. that was being sold at Sotheby's (a collection of fifteenth century theological treatises of some interest, which we got for the modest sum of £34), partly to see some of the B.M. [British Museum] people about the authenticity of a much disputed letter of Shelley to Mary. It belonged to the notorious T. J. Wise, but I am convinced it is genuine. To my joy it had an erased number on it which connects it with a series of letters Shelley wrote to Mary while he was eluding the sheriff's officers, and which were stolen from a desk they left at Marlow when they went to Italy (at least I think so). They were bought back by Mary from a disreputable man who pretended he was a natural son of Byron. He made forged copies of some of them which have caused the trouble. But most of it would have been avoided if only people would take the trouble to look at the originals.

This is a good example of the combination of sympathy and acumen which went with his daily work. This combination was nowhere more needed or more freely exercised than in his dealings with the growing number of researchers from all parts of the world who wanted advice, information, and help. It was the appearance of this growing army of workers which transformed the Bodleian from a quiet and scholarly institution with a small income and staff and an ingrained distrust of readers, into a big business with an annual budget of £1.6 million, a growing staff, and all the complications of a rapidly expanding number of readers. This was something which those who persuaded Hunt to return to Oxford in 1945 had not reckoned with. Another thing which they had not fully appreciated was his extraordinary devotion to readers and students of all kinds and ages. In 1945 he had welcomed the Librarian's assurance that the Keeper's first duty was to help and advise readers; but he carried out this duty with a zeal that was almost ferocious – he was a formidable and outspoken critic of shoddy work, and he had a genius for knowing what a reader needed. To all who came to him, whether casual readers, or members of his staff, or colleagues, he was a lavish source of help on a very wide range of subjects. Often he did not need to be asked: he simply noticed the need and met it. On one occasion it is recorded that he happened to notice that a reader had ordered two manuscripts, from which he deduced that a third, in a college library, would also contain relevant material. He promptly informed the reader, and added yet another to the long list of scholars who were indebted to him for timely information which they could have obtained from no other source. It was this part of his work which inspired the awe and devotion of scholars from all parts of the world: perhaps no one in this country except Henry Bradshaw at the Cambridge University Library a hundred years ago has made anything like the same impression on the workers in a library.

Some might think that his energies were dissipated by his availability to every caller and to every call on his time. This was the nature of the man. It was one aspect of his total absorption in the task of the moment. In his earlier years he had been a central point of reference on all points of scholarship for a few friends whenever they needed a steady judgment and a sharp eye backed by a retentive memory. In the second and longer phase of his career after 1945 he performed this function for all who came to study western manuscripts in the Bodleian. His scholarly work during the last thirty-five years of his life must largely be looked for in the books and articles published by others, and in his contributions – generally anonymous – to the cataloguing of manuscripts under his care. The acknowledgments of his help in prefaces and footnotes are beyond counting, and even if they could be counted they would give no idea of the extent to which his suggestions and knowledge of the sources, and above all his instinctive understanding of what other scholars were getting at, had transformed many of the works which he helped to bring into existence. He was content with this role. He felt no proprietorship in his learning. He knew that he was not a fluent writer, and he may have sensed that he lacked something – whether selfishness or ambition or a creative instinct – which makes for great productivity. He had none of the unease which lies at the root of a desire to create something new. His own imaginative life was in the writings of the past. He was in daily contact with one of the world's greatest collections of scholarly work, and he enjoyed this contact. He knew and had handled a large part of it. He gave his close personal attention to the work of cataloguing new accessions and revising the old catalogues of the main collections. His historical account of these collections, in the first volume of the Summary Catalogue, besides being lucid and accurate, is filled with little touches, which show that he understood the problems of his predecessors. In everything relating to books his judgment was both firm and clairvoyant. He had none of the instability of enthusiasm, but he was capable of explosive outbursts of joy in the presence of a sudden discovery, whether his own or another's. One colleague recalls "the day when he walked into my study just as I was about to return an Exeter College manuscript which had been deposited for photography. He opened it, and almost shouted, 'That's Petrarch's hand!'" It was this kind of incident which makes his memory live in the Bodleian. From 1945 onwards, his life was dedicated to an ideal. After he had been some years in the Bodleian, he wrote: "The more I reflect on librarianship in big 'research' libraries, the more I am sure that the librarian ought to be a scholar – not that he will have much time for scholarship, unless he has the energy of a Delisle. But without it, the place becomes devitalized, and the staff sink to be library clerks."

Although the pursuit of this ideal took up most of his time and left him "not much time for scholarship," it would be wrong to think of him only as a reference system for others. Although he got little pleasure from original writing, he got intense satisfaction from bringing to light and making intelligible the writings of scholars of all periods. He had early begun the practice of copying texts, and he continued this practice to the end. To copy texts which are difficult in subject-matter as well as script is not a mechanical process, but a process calling for deep knowledge and powers of interpretation. It was a process which gave him pleasure in exercising many kinds of skill. In his later years, his transcripts were largely of medieval grammatical texts. He was drawn to this subject partly no doubt because nearly all the writers whom he dealt with had had to learn Latin in the painstaking way in which he himself had learnt it, and their problems had been his problems. But later, the twelfth-century grammarians drew him into the higher reaches of the subject. Long before grammar had become a fashionable branch of modern philosophy, he had discovered that it was the foundation of all medieval thought and had deeply influenced their approach to philosophy and everything else. His first serious work on the subject was stimulated by the need to write something for the new periodical *MARS*. In July 1938 he visited Durham to study a twelfth-century manuscript in which he had found grammatical notes by a number of masters of the late eleventh and early twelfth centuries, and he went on to Paris to see two related manuscripts. This led to the first of his grammatical studies which appeared in *MARS* in 1943, followed by a continuation in 1950. The latest of his articles on this subject appeared in 1975.[8] Among his papers there are five boxes of grammatical texts and descriptions of grammatical manuscripts, of which some extracts will appear in the invaluable *cahiers* of the medieval Institute of the University of Copenhagen: an interesting illustration of the continuing truth of Hunt's remark in 1938 about the lack of a suitable periodical for such work in this country.

It would weary the reader, and make no essential addition to this sketch of his scholarly character and achievement, to record the many contributions which he made during the last thirty years of his life to cooperative works and learned committees. It must suffice to mention only one publication and two committees.

The publication is the revised edition of the *Oxford Dictionary of the Christian Church*, edited by Miss E. A. Livingstone and published in 1974. Hunt's contribution to this was second only to that of the editor herself. He read and revised nearly all the medieval articles, and he entirely rewrote several, notably those on Stephen Langton, Gottschalk, Florus of Lyons, Heiric of Auxerre, Gilbert de la Porrée, and Albertus Magnus. This was the kind of writing in which he excelled – correcting mistakes by stealth, adding new information anonymously, and bringing a wide range of up-to-date scholarship to bear on an article that might occupy half a page.

Of committees, the one which he enjoyed most was the Library Committee of Lambeth Palace, on which he served for many years. He liked it because it was a small and informal gathering of congenial colleagues, and it got things done – nothing less than the restoration and reorganization of a great historic library after its destruction in the war. The other committee which "got things done" was the manuscripts Sub-Committee of the Standing Conference of National and University Libraries, of which he was chairman from 1957 to 1975. It sounds like an administrative nightmare; but it was from this unglamorous height that he exercised an effective leadership in promoting scholarly publications which will form part of the permanent equipment of future medievalists. He succeeded in this, not by administrative skill or dominating personality, but simply by knowing the jobs that needed to be done and the people who could do them, and being obviously right. Two volumes of N. R. Ker's *Medieval Manuscripts in British Libraries* (with two more to come) and Andrew Watson's Catalogue of dated and datable Latin manuscripts in the British Library already testify to the efficacy of this unobtrusive form of leadership. It was work which he could promote and encourage without strain and without formality because he saw the whole field with the eye of a master and a friend.

A final extension of his genius for collaboration was occasioned by his election as a Fellow of this Academy [the British Academy] in 1961. This led to his becoming a member and then chairman of the Committees on the Medieval Latin Dictionary and British Medieval Texts. The editors of all the projects connected with these committees soon learnt like everyone else to draw abundantly from his overflowing well of knowledge.

VI

In the peculiar circumstances of Hunt's life and work – the brevity of his published work and the abundance of unpublished material, together with his wide and deep influence on contemporary scholars conveyed in short notes and verbal observations – it seemed proper to make this memoir a record of cooperative enterprises in which he played a major part even though his name was seldom publicly associated with them. I have tried to give a view of his work as it appeared from near at hand, and as it can still be found in his voluminous papers. To go further and attempt to portray the man, as he appeared to the many scholars who came to him in the Bodleian for work and in his home in Walton Street for refreshment, would go beyond the scope of what I have attempted. Everyone found him helpful to an astonishing degree – helpful both in the range of his original observations and in his willingness to communicate them freely. Everyone found his home life – largely shaped and colored by the immense good nature and exuberance of his second wife, Kit Rowland – a scene of warm and abundant hospitality. Everyone who knew him will remember his characteristic attitude at home, puffing his pipe under the eaves of his remarkably expressive eyebrows, often silent while others talked, breaking out at times into a deep chuckle or a body-shaking laugh. Not so many saw his rare outburst of indignation, or his stubborn persistence in defending some scholarly truth, or his outspoken enforcement of some simple rule like not smoking in a non-smoking compartment. With all his faculty for appreciating others, he could be very formidable, and even ruthless, as a critic.

The story would be seriously incomplete if these aspects of his personality were omitted. But one example of his absolute rigor on questions of scholarship or the plain rules of life must stand for all. I owe the example to Dr. Myres, formerly Bodley's Librarian, and I give it in his words:

> Did I ever tell you the tale about Richard's encounter with the old King of Sweden – another learned man – when he visited Bodley? Richard had set out for his inspection some MSS. to take his fancy in Selden End, including the one which figures Noah's Ark portrayed as a Viking Long Ship. The King was delighted with this, and ventured a date for it. "No, *No, NO!*" thundered Richard, thumping the table with indignation, and announced a different century. But the King stood his ground, pointing to details of construction and rigging, in justification of his date. Richard replied with equally decisive palaeographical considerations, and soon they were hard at it, like a couple of terriers, whom I and the royal equerries, with their eyes on the clock, had the greatest difficulty in separating. When they were eventually persuaded to let go of their respective ends of the bone of contention,

both seemed equally delighted with the learned rough and tumble, and equally oblivious of the tattered and irrelevant protocol.

There, in all his simplicity, is the scholar whom we knew.

After the death of his wife in December 1977, the vivacity went out of his domestic life, but he continued to work, and he was still at work when death came suddenly in the night of November 13, 1979.

12

Marjorie Reeves as a Historian

Marjorie Reeves's volume of 1969 on *The Influence of Prophecy in the Later Middle Ages* was a landmark in the opening up of a theme on European history which has been too much neglected. It is a theme which is sure to have a future, and since 1969 Dr. Reeves has played her part in shaping this future. But the purpose of this note is to trace the origins of the theme in the works which this volume commemorates. "It is pleasant," says Dr. Johnson, "to see great works in their seminal state, pregnant with latent possibilities of excellence; nor could there be any more delightful entertainment than to trace their gradual growth and expansion, and to observe how they sometimes suddenly advanced by accidental hints, and sometimes slowly improved by steady meditation." This is indeed too ambitious a program for a brief note, but it may be of interest to the readers of this volume to attempt to distinguish a few of the stages in the progress of the work. The story has a personal interest in recalling the struggles of a young historian to break out of the narrow channels in which the academic history of the 1920s was confined; and it has a broader interest in throwing light on the changing emphasis in historical writing during the last fifty years. One of the most important features of this changing emphasis has been the movement to give central place to thoughts and experiences in the past which had previously been banished to obscure corners by historians who looked on them as unsightly deviations from a great central tradition of Europe. No single figure was more firmly put in a corner than Joachim; no one has done more to reinstate him in historical respectability than Marjorie Reeves.

When Marjorie Reeves studied history at Oxford between 1923 and 1926 the prevailing mood was still adequately expressed by the then Regius Professor, H. W. C. Davis, when he said that "history is past politics." The merits of this tradition deserve recognition now when it has vanished beyond recall. Constricting though it was, and impossible as an ideal of historical scholarship, it gave a strength and unity to the undergraduate program of those days. It set clear bounds within which evidence could be sifted, judgment exercised, political values weighed, and common sense applied to common themes. It was history fit for the rulers of an Empire. The first sentences of the *Examination Regulations* which were then put into the hands of all undergraduates gave firm expression to this purpose: "The Examination in the School of Modern History shall always include the continuous History of England (including the History of British India and of British Colonies and Dependencies)" and "Every Candidate shall be required to have a knowledge of Constitutional Law, and of Political and Descriptive Geography." There was a beautiful simplicity in all this which showed itself also in the approach to the "Special Historical Subjects," which were to be "carefully studied with reference to original authorities." The weight of these Special Subjects was austerely political, and even the choice of original authorities for the Dante subject made it clear that the political background of the poet was to be studied rather than his poetry or world vision.

But all things, however clear-cut at first sight, have their ambiguities and blurred edges, not least history as viewed from Oxford in 1926. The Empire which informed so many of its presuppositions was visibly wobbling. That strangely Joachimite work, Spengler's *Decline of the West*, had recently been translated into English,[1] and though the book itself had no important influence, it expressed a new mood and it helped in a small way to open the cracks in the historical structure. Young Miss Reeves at St. Hugh's seems to have felt these tremors more than her teachers. I do not think that she was in any sense a rebel against the system, but she never confined herself within its limits. She duly got a First Class in 1926; but then she did what was not common in those days – she took the new Diploma in Education before teaching for two years in a grammar school. Then her mind turned back to her Dante Special Subject and she applied for a research fellowship at Westfield College with the idea of working on the Lombard communes under Eleanor Lodge. It was a subject which badly needed to be worked on, and I do not know that it has yet received the treatment that it deserves. But it failed to hold her interest, and within a few weeks her mind had turned to a more Dantesque subject – Joachim of Fiore. It was the turning-point in her historical development, the moment "pregnant with latent possibilities of excellence." By a curious but not irrelevant coincidence, it was also the turning-point in the history of post-war Europe, the moment of the Wall Street crash, and the emergence of the Nazis as the most powerful party in Germany. The crisis from which all that has since happened in the world had come about by a succession of easy transitions which might seem to have been foreordained. A fitting moment for the emergence of the apocalyptic man.

The immediate agent in this change of mind was a book which seems to have had a surprising popularity in College libraries at that time – Emile Gebhart's *L'Italie mystique*,[2] a work which contained a full and eloquent account of Joachim and his place in thirteenth-century spirituality and in Dante. By some strange intuitive process which defies analysis, Marjorie Reeves's subject and her life's work as a historian were settled once and for all. It was a leap in the dark, and from a prudential point of view it had almost everything against it. There was no one in England (with the possible exception of the learned recluse A. G. Little) who had more than a superficial knowledge of Joachim. A supervisor was found in Edmund Gardner, the Professor of Italian, a great and humane scholar in all things Italian, but no close student of strange doctrines. But supervision as then understood was generally considered to require no more than mild encouragement and sympathy, and this he could abundantly supply.

Here again we must recognize the merits of a system which has vanished. There are many scholars still alive who are glad to reflect that through the inadequate supervision of those days they escaped the pressure of more exacting and expert overseers, and enjoyed only the company, intermittent and unpredictable though it might be, of learned elders. Perhaps Marjorie Reeves is one of those who have reason to be grateful for this liberty. She had no alternative but to plunge without direction into the British Museum with its ragged collection of fat little volumes containing genuine and spurious works of Joachim in wild disarray in their earliest, the Venetian, editions of 1516–27. These strange intimidating works – the strangeness of their ideas emphasized by their contracted Gothic type and their bulging woodcuts illustrating the doom of nations – opened up a new view of history. And what a view! How different from the sane, rational, and comfortable picture of freedom slowly broadening down from precedent to precedent which the efforts of Oxford tutors had been designed to promote. It was a bold step for young Miss Reeves to commit herself, as one might say, to all this nonsense. Scarcely likely to commend her for an academic job! Nevertheless, she set to work, and three years later, in 1932, she presented her thesis: "Studies in the reputation and influence of the abbot Joachim of Fiore, chiefly in the fifteenth and sixteenth centuries."

The work was never published, but it still exists. When we look at it we naturally ask how far it contains the germs of later ideas, and in what ways it differs from the book which was published thirty-seven years later. How much can it tell us of the mood of that time, and of the changes that have taken place in historical writing since then? First we notice that in 1932 Miss Reeves thought that an apology, or at least an explanation, was needed to justify her choice of subject. The words in which she made this explanation are worth printing, for they contain the answer to some of our questions about the moment and the scholar:

To treat the fantastic as history may well require explanation. We are accustomed to throw the sensible and serious actions of political life against a background of contemporary thought which is equally sober. Most of the prophetic material upon which these studies are based wears an altogether different complexion: it is bizarre; it is fantastic; it seems, in itself, to be quite worthless. Yet such material forms an essential element in historical background, and one cannot truly appraise the texture of that background without it. Not only must one seek within the realm of fantasy for an understanding of those strange, abnormal creatures that occasionally move the world of politics – a Rienzi, a Savonarola, a Charles VIII – but further, one must recognize beneath the groundwork of normal political life, a far more general subsoil of prophetic belief, long since crumbled into superstition, than the rationalist is wont to admit. Thus the most calculated political action will sometimes display a root that goes far down below the conscious motive. Still more often, it will evoke a common interpretation which is manifestly the outcome of superstition.

A study of prophecy supplies that content to the title of Frederick III, and explains why Nicholas V could be so uneasy at the rumours of destruction which preceded the Hapsburg to Rome in 1453. Again, behind the Sack of Rome in 1527, there lies a wealth of prophetic forecast, and Charles V, we are told, did not neglect such matters. Indeed, his person proved so powerful a magnet for attracting all the most fortunate omens and oracles, that the opposition of one, at least, of his enemies, the Marquis Francis of Saluzzo, was overcome partly by prophetic persuasion. In such cases as these, a consideration of the fantastic enters into the field of practical politics. These examples are selected from the fifteenth and sixteenth centuries, and for a right appreciation of this period, the prophetic background must be accorded a value of its own. This background we believe to have been largely Joachimist.

There are a number of things which these words make clear. In the first place, much of the originality of Miss Reeves's treatment of the subject lay in her emphasis on the fifteenth and sixteenth centuries. Unlike her predecessors her thinking began, not from Joachim himself, but from his long-term influence on the political thought and action of the period immediately before and after the Reformation. From this point she worked backwards to Joachim himself. This approach was certainly right, that is to say it was the most fruitful and illuminating way of looking on the subject, and the one which could give full weight to the pervading influence of Joachim's ideas, not among heretics driven half crazy by persecution and pervasion, but among men of practical ability and impressive performance. In her Preface of 1932 Miss Reeves still regarded the ideas which these men entertained as fantastic and manifestly superstitious, but she brought them on to the center of the stage. Her political emphasis is very striking. Perhaps in this she reflected the political bias of the Oxford

School of History. At all events it was a valuable reminder of the realism which underlay the "fantasies" of the prophetic tradition.

Another important effect of this political orientation was that in directing attention to the political expectations and fears of the late Middle Ages, the distinctive pattern of history which Joachim evolved was given the importance which it deserves. All other questions such as those of Joachim's sources, of his heresies, or his influence on the Franciscans and the Fraticelli were relegated to a comparatively subordinate position. This emphasis on the importance of the prophetic pattern of history – a pattern which was still fully alive in Isaac Newton in 1700 – provides the key to Joachim's continuing importance.

Anyone who now reads the thesis of 1932 can see that the shape and emphasis of the later studies were in their main outline already fully formed. The work could have been printed as it stands, and I believe that the examiners, Professors Powicke and Claude Jenkins, recommended its publication. It was probably fortunate that they recommended in vain. The moment was not yet propitious. If it had been published, we should perhaps have heard no more about it. The delay meant not only that the work could be matured, but also that it would come out at a time which was more receptive to its message.

Twelve or thirteen years were to pass before Miss Reeves could return to the subject. Teaching in London and then in Oxford, with the stresses and obligations of the war, kept her fully occupied until 1945. Meanwhile, Joachimist studies had not stood still on the Continent. The most important event from the point of view of Miss Reeves was the publication in 1939 by Mgr. L. Tondelli of the *Liber Figurarum* which contains the authentic and diagrammatic summary of Joachim's universal plan of history. The book did not become available in England until 1945, and by then Miss Reeves had already gone beyond it. Following up some hints of Otto Pacht and Fritz Saxl, she had already examined the manuscript of the *Figurae* in Corpus Christi College, Oxford, and had at once seen that here, in a manuscript of the early thirteenth century, she had in a contemporary copy the book of the Abbot Joachim, which the Franciscan chronicler Salimbene had read with veneration in the 1240s, and to which he repeatedly looked for an explanation of current events. It must have been disappointing to find that Mgr. Tondelli had already gone a long way in the right direction. But Miss Reeves had gone further, and the combination of these two circumstances provided the stimulus that was needed.

Everyone who had lived through the war required an initial stimulus to restore their intellectual circulation. For Miss Reeves the Oxford manuscript and Mgr. Tondelli's book provided this stimulus which brought her back to Joachimite studies.

The fruit of this renewed study was the long article on the *Liber Figurarum* which appeared in 1950 in *Medieval and Renaissance Studies*. It at once established her as the leading authority on Joachim in the country, and it was the first of a series of articles which prepared the way for the two volumes which appeared in 1969 and 1972. By 1969 the world was ready for Joachim. When Tolkien comes, one might ask, can Joachim be far behind? These creators of visionary worlds had nothing in common except that they appealed to a generation to whom magic, astrology, visions, and apocalyptic expectations came more naturally than at any time since the seventeenth century. This broad basis of popular renunciation of conventional rationality laid the foundation of a new sympathy with Joachim's outlook on the world. Nor was this new receptivity confined to youthful enthusiasm. At a more scholarly level historians were more ready than ever before to consider forms of reasoning which had seemed merely superstitious forty years earlier. The political, constitutional, rational framework of history had almost everywhere broken down, and the scholarly world was ready to look at new ways of organizing the past.

Of course, these external changes had no influence on the development of Marjorie Reeves's thought, or the timing of her publications. The ideas she had had forty years earlier had simply needed more time to mature in the midst of many other duties. She had spent these years, not in adjusting to a changing climate of opinion, but in working out in detail many of the points which had been only briefly touched on in the earlier thesis. Nevertheless, the point of view of the 1969 volume is in some significant ways different from that of 1932. The Preface of 1969 no longer mentions fantasy or superstition as essential features of Joachim's interpretation of history. It speaks only of attitudes to the future, rules of predictability, and hopes and fears that are, at all times, the grounds for decision and action. It speaks of Joachim not as an aberration, but as an articulation of certain attitudes to the past, present, and future, which – while owing much to the fears and intellectual presuppositions of the late twelfth century – belong to a large and long-lived family of historical speculation. Joachim is no longer presented as an interesting but fantastic thinker; rather as a man whose presuppositions are no more absurd than any others, and whose imaginative and systematic power give him a permanent place in European historical thought. It no longer seemed necessary in 1969 to apologize; it could be taken for granted that attitudes and arguments, which have appealed to people of many generations and many levels of sophistication, require no further justification from the historian than the fact of their existence.

The volume of 1972 on the *Figurae of Joachim of Fiore* stands in the same relation to the article of 1950 as the volume of 1969 to the thesis of

1932.[3] It completes and develops the exposition of Joachim's scheme of history, and presents it as a view of universal history that has to be understood in all its complexity and not simply dismissed to the limbo of the unthinkable. Taken together, these two volumes form by far the most complete and penetrating account of Joachim's ideas on history in their earliest presentation and their later manifestations that we possess. No doubt much still needs to be done, but the foundations have been laid. There are many ways in which these studies may develop in the future. Perhaps the most immediate task is to fit Joachim into a wider tradition of prophetic writing.[4] He was, of course, not the original source of prophetic world visions: he was only the most powerful interpreter of these visions at an important stage of their transmission. Nor is prophecy always visionary: it comes in many different packages, and all of them deserve some examination. Like all historians who have enlarged our horizon, Marjorie Reeves has opened up many new fields of enquiry in the ramifications of history and prophecy. As she wrote in 1969, "Human beings in general can no more ignore their future than they can lose their past. Thus a theme common to all periods of history is that of attitudes towards the future. Such attitudes are determined by what one may term the contemporary rules of predictability." The "contemporary rules of predictability" from the thirteenth to the seventeenth centuries have been the center of her work during the last fifty years. It is a subject that is likely to occupy scholars for a long time to come, and many of those who follow this large and absorbing theme will look back to Marjorie Reeves as the initiator of their studies.

13

Beryl Smalley (1905–1984)

Beryl Smalley was born on June 3, 1905, the eldest of six children of Edgar Smalley and his wife Lilian, née Bowman.[1] Her father was a Manchester businessman who had inherited a firm of woolen and paper merchants, and in his younger days he had been a talented lacrosse player for Cheshire and for England. By the time of Beryl's birth he had prospered sufficiently to move with his family to a small country house at Cheadle in Derbyshire, and later to a larger house, Taddington Hall near Buxton. In these surroundings, he was able to indulge his taste for hunting with the High Peak Hunt, of which he rose to be joint Master in 1930–1. Beryl, who shared none of these tastes, grew up in an atmosphere of horse riding and other rural unbookish pursuits. As the eldest child she had a good deal to do in looking after the younger children. Later in life she remarked that she had done so much holding of the baby in her youth that she had never lost the knack. She also as a student attributed her disconcerting habit of absentmindedly muttering "Yes" or "No" while she was reading, to her automatic response to questions of the other children when she was studying. Despite these vexations, she retained a strong affection for her brothers and sisters and their children; but she was clearly the solitary member of the family, and some of the features of her early career reflect her reaction against the atmosphere of her childhood.

She was educated at Cheltenham Ladies' College and St. Hilda's College, Oxford, where she went as a Scholar to read history in 1924. Here the main influence on her was that of her tutor, Agnes Sandys (later Mrs. Leys). Some words which Beryl later wrote in the *Oxford Magazine* in memory of her may be quoted, not only as a description of her tutor, but also (*mutatis mutandis*) of herself:

> The intellectual movements at Oxford in her undergraduate days affected her very deeply. She became an ardent medievalist and was influenced by the Christian socialism which was a living force in Oxford at that time.

By the time that Beryl became an undergraduate, the link between Christianity and Socialism, which had been the inspiration of an earlier generation, had largely disappeared: the two components had been transmogrified into Catholicism and Communism, and stood in bitter opposition to each other. These two forces became successively the two intellectual principles of Beryl's life for the next twenty years; but neither of them displaced her enthusiasm for the Middle Ages, which proved in the end more lasting than either. As a student, she was distinctly wayward. Without taking too literally her own account that she would read nothing except Church history or, at a pinch, diplomatic affairs, she clearly had no inclination to read what the syllabus required. The result was that she finished her undergraduate years with an undistinguished Second Class. Perhaps the greatest service that Miss Sandys performed for her was to introduce her to Professor Powicke when he came to Oxford in her last undergraduate year to give the Ford Lectures in January 1927. These lectures were a landmark not only in Beryl's life but also in medieval studies in Oxford, so they deserve a brief excursion at this point.

Powicke had chosen as his subject the career of Archbishop Stephen Langton, with the intention of throwing some new light on the archbishop's influence on the struggle for Magna Carta and on the events of the minority of Henry III. But in the course of his preparation, he became increasingly aware of the large number of surviving manuscripts which preserved the substance of Langton's lectures at Paris during the last twenty years of the twelfth century. The existence of this material had long been known, but it had not been studied even by historians of scholasticism, still less of course by political and constitutional historians. Powicke was the first to realize that in this scholastic material there might lurk evidence of the highest importance for the formation of political attitudes. This was the inspiration which transformed his Lectures, and incidentally the whole of Beryl's later life. The story may be told in Powicke's own words:

> When I came to examine (Langton's) unpublished lectures, I found that the subject began to have a different and greater significance in my mind. What I had thought of as a restatement containing a few new suggestions was changed into a tentative introduction to a fresh, almost unworked, field of study. A happy result of the change has been that I have been able to gather together a little group of students... One of these is at work on Langton's *Questiones*, another on his commentaries (on the Bible), a third on his contemporary at Paris, Robert Curzon.

Beryl was the second of the students mentioned in this passage. The prospect of working on the Bible in the Middle Ages gave her just the stimulus she had been looking for: it was far removed from the kind of history that had bored her in the history syllabus; it brought her into the central intellectual tradition of the Middle Ages; and it struck a blow against the traditional Protestant view that the Bible was a discovery of the Reformation, with which she was disenchanted.

II

Inspired by these hopeful prospects, she at once registered herself as a research student at Manchester under Powicke, and spent the next three years engaged on a PhD thesis on the biblical commentaries of Langton and his contemporaries "viewed as historical material." This last phrase is worth quoting as evidence of an intention from which she was soon to break away.

After a year at home, making periodic visits to Manchester for consultations with Powicke, and working on the manuscripts in Cambridge and London, she went to Paris. Here she worked for the greater part of two years under the general direction of Georges Lacombe, who introduced her to the complexities of scholastic manuscripts. To sort out the huge bulk and many varieties of Langton's biblical commentaries was a task of great and – at least immediately – not very rewarding labor. But Lacombe's enthusiasm helped to give her the will to succeed, and the knowledge of authors and manuscripts which she gained in this work was the foundation of all that she did later. Immediately, however, large masses of repetitive commonplaces had to be waded through to reach rare moments of liveliness. To quote her own words:

> A very large proportion of Langton's work is composed of extracts from the Gloss, Biblical quotations, allegorical and moral excursions which recall the worst type of twelfth century sermon. It is often necessary to read through many folios of such material before arriving at an interesting *questio* or one of Langton's incomparably pithy *dicta*.

All her comments on the work of those early years give a sensation of back-breaking labor sustained by an eager sense of new discovery. The initial task of sorting out the various branches, types, and recensions of Langton's commentaries was completed with exemplary promptitude. She got her PhD in 1930, and the work was published in 1931. At this point Powicke advised her to turn to some more conventional and marketable form of historical research. He no doubt reminded her that the aim of her research had been to discover "historical material" in biblical commentaries. He tried to recall her to this task. But she was now thoroughly immersed in scholastic thought for its own sake, and she was not to be diverted.

One large problem was gradually taking possession of her mind. While working on Langton, she had become haunted by the presence of a great stream of earlier and almost unknown biblical exegesis on which he drew. In particular, the Gloss referred to in the passage I have quoted: What was it? Who made it? When was it made? How and when did it become a central textbook of the medieval schools? These were the questions she set about trying to answer.

Of the traditional answers to these questions the most deeply rooted was that the Gloss had been put together in the ninth century by a German monk, Walafrid Strabo, who had assembled a large body of patristic texts and attached them to appropriate passages of the Bible. Several scholars were beginning to express doubts about this legend – for legend in fact it was. In particular H. H. Glunz, in the course of a study of the text of the Vulgate, had put forward the view that the Gloss was a product of the early twelfth century. This was in fact broadly correct, but his argument was marred by a number of errors and wild conjectures which (somewhat unfairly) had brought his work into disrepute. As a result, the whole subject was in considerable confusion. The material for solving the problem was so abundant, so confused by anonymity and false ascriptions, that it was hard to know in which direction to turn for new light. The best clue was one which Beryl had found in a work of one of Langton's contemporaries. Writing at about the end of the twelfth century and looking back to a time a hundred years earlier, a Parisian master, Peter the Chanter, had written:

> It is regrettable that Master Anselm was prevented from completing his gloss on the whole Bible by the many demands made upon him by the canons whose dean he was.

This is one of those remarks which may be either a wild guess or a genuine tradition. It proved to be the latter. The more she worked on the manuscripts, the more the evidence accumulated which pointed to the school of Laon in the period from about 1080 to 1120, under the direction of its most famous master, Anselm, as the source of the gloss on the whole Bible, which was by the time of Langton beginning to be known as the *Glossa Ordinaria*.

Beryl followed this clue and the many others which gradually came to its support during the years from 1931 to 1935, and by the end of this time she had pieced together the main stages by which this essential tool of the schools had evolved from its earliest beginnings under Anselm and his brother Ralph, through its continuation and enlargement by a succes-

sion of pupils and masters, Gilbert the Universal, Gilbert of Poitiers, and
Peter Lombard, until it came into the hands of the Parisian masters of
Langton's generation. These researches were published in a number of
articles which are now known to all medievalists.

While completing these researches, Beryl had been lecturing at Royal
Holloway College from 1931 to 1935. In the latter year, through the
falling out of an already elected candidate, she became a research fellow
of Girton College, Cambridge. This new appointment made it a matter of
some urgency to write a book which would satisfy the requirements of the
College, and establish a claim to permanent employment thereafter.

The origin of the Gloss had come to dominate her work so much by this
time that her first thought was to write a volume on Anselm of Laon and
the *Glossa Ordinaria*. But fortunately two considerations deterred her.
The first was that a book on an unreadable compilation of patristic quotations by an unknown and barely knowable author would provide only a
meager claim to a livelihood. The second and happier reason was that in
the course of her most recent work, she had discovered a new character of
immense interest to her personally and of considerable potentiality for the
future: Andrew of St. Victor. A few words are needed to explain the large
role which this discovery played in her later development.

Andrew was a character for whom she felt the warmest sympathy. He
was an Englishman who had become a canon of St. Victor in Paris around
1125, returning to England in about 1145 to become head of a small and
remote community of Victorine canons at Shobdon and later at Wigmore
in Herefordshire. At St. Victor he had been the pupil of Hugh of St.
Victor, the most capacious thinker of the first half of the twelfth century.
Among many other achievements, he had stimulated two quite distinct
kinds of biblical exegesis – the symbolic and the literal. The first was
traditional and immensely popular, the second new and generally judged
to be uninteresting. Hugh's pupil Richard of St. Victor undertook the first,
and became one of the best-known writers of the Middle Ages. Andrew
undertook the second and was utterly forgotten until Beryl resurrected
him. She was later able to show that his work (its author forgotten) had a
considerable influence on later commentators; but his obscurity and his
stubborn, morose independence appealed to her – perhaps she saw in him
an image of herself: "Far be it from me (he wrote) to extend myself
beyond the limits of my powers; I prefer to rest solidly on my own foundations, rather than to be carried away into a void above myself." He
professed to confine himself to the literal meaning of Scripture because he
could not afford the many volumes in which the spiritual meanings had
been so abundantly explained. He doubted whether what he was doing
was worth much, but at least he might find out a little that was new. He
was not a man of towering intellect. He had no interest in natural science,

and none in dogmatic theology; and he had nothing to say about the fashionable political or ecclesiastical subjects of the day. "He is distinctly prosaic," wrote Beryl, "this is his virtue. Being merely a scholar, he is unknown to text-books, and almost unknown to modern works of reference." But she also saw behind the modesty of aim a grandeur of conception: "No Western commentator before him had set out to give a purely literal interpretation of the Old Testament." And humble though it seemed, this turning away from the allegory to the "undoctored incident that actually occurred" was itself a symptom of the great twelfth-century breakthrough into the world of physical reality which marked the beginning of modern science.

So in the end the obscure Andrew had a great future ahead of him. He was certainly not a man of superior genius. He lacked many of the historical and linguistic skills necessary for making a substantial contribution to the literal exegesis of the Bible, but at least he had made a start: "After all the first person in Western Europe who wanted to know what the authors of the Old Testament were trying to say to the Jews has a certain value." In order to understand what the Old Testament authors were trying to say to their contemporaries, Andrew turned to the Jews of his own day. He was not the first twelfth-century scholar to do this, but no one before him had made such systematic and constructive use of collaboration with contemporary Jewish scholarship.

In finding Andrew, Beryl had found in an obscure place the point of cohesion for which she had been looking. She had feared that her researches would drift into a quagmire of details about the growth of biblical glosses, and now she had found an unknown character to whom she responded with all her sympathy. At a time when anti-Jewish pogroms were one of the most loathsome symptoms of the breakdown of civilization she found relief for herself in turning to Jewish scholars for help in understanding a sympathetic predecessor. This form of collaboration played an important part in her later work. More immediately, she had also found a central theme for her book: the shift of emphasis from the allegorical to the literal interpretation of Scripture. So the newly discovered character both became the central figure in her projected book, and pointed to a future beyond the book.

Andrew of St. Victor had fully replaced the unexciting Anselm of Laon by the autumn of 1937, and from this date everything went with a swing: the introductory chapters on the Fathers and Carolingian scholars were rapidly written; the early articles on Anselm of Laon and the *Glossa Ordinaria* were shaped into a substantial section; Andrew was given the place of honor; Langton and his contemporaries were quickly disposed of; and a sketch of the later history of the literal interpretation of the Bible at the hands of the thirteenth-century friars – all the livelier for not having been too laboriously researched – was quickly put together. The book was finished in 1939 and sent to the press a few weeks before war broke out. It finally appeared in July 1941, under the title (arrived at with considerable misgivings), *The Study of the Bible in the Middle Ages*.

It was not a good moment for publicity, and there were not many reviews. Nor were they particularly favorable. It was complained that the contents did not fulfill the expectations aroused by the title, and the index was found remarkably defective. There was only one reviewer, A. G. Little, who spotted the essential quality of the work. "One does not," he wrote, "expect a book with this title to be exciting. But Miss Smalley's certainly is. One feels pervading it the thrill of fresh discovery, the adventurous and gay spirit of the pioneer." This is admirably put. The book was the record of an intellectual voyage of discovery undertaken under the influence of a new faith, and carried on in the midst of ill-health, of fears even of a total breakdown, and of distresses, both private and public, which brought much perplexity. The book itself reflects these circumstances both in its qualities and defects. Although the reviewers were quick to point out the latter, everyone can now see that the qualities are much more important. The book infused into a largely neglected subject a new spirit of discovery, all the more poignant for its troubled background.

III

At the time of the book's publication, Beryl had not yet succeeded in getting a permanent job. Her research fellowship at Girton had come to an end in 1940, and for the next three years she worked as a temporary assistant in the MSS. Department of the Bodleian Library. It was not until 1943, with the resignation of her old tutor, that she returned to St. Hilda's as fellow and tutor; and here she remained till her retirement in 1969.

This change in her circumstances affected the tempo and even perhaps the impulse which is so apparent in her earlier work. Most of her time was now devoted to the teaching of a busy College tutor. Then for the last twelve years before her retirement, from 1957 to 1969, she was also Vice-Principal of the College. She made light of the functions attached to the latter office, but they were time-consuming, and there were many College problems, which required attention. Besides, despite her cool and aloof manner of speaking to or about her pupils, she was devoted to their interests in many small ways which might have escaped the attention of more solemnly dedicated teachers. A few words will need to be said later about these matters. For the moment I am concerned only about their effect on her scholarly work, which – however central it remained in her life – could no longer be pursued with the passionate, almost desperate, energy of former days. These changes in her life after the war help to explain why her later studies consisted so largely of new probings in many different directions without any synthesis of the kind she had attempted in her first book. In comparison with the earlier period, the years after 1943 were a time of peaceful development along the lines already laid down. The exegesis of the Bible in the medieval schools continued to be the main area of her scholarly work; but two new areas (medieval political theory and medieval historical writing) were added in the course of time. In what follows I shall describe briefly the extensions of her biblical studies, and then mention the excursions outside this area.

The first notable landmark in her later biblical studies was the appearance, in 1951, of a second edition of *The Study of the Bible in the Middle Ages*. The main additions were of two kinds; first, the appearance of a new character who was to play a considerable role in Beryl's later work; and then secondly, an extension in time to include the work of the friars, the chief custodians of biblical studies from about 1230 onwards.

The new character was Herbert of Bosham. Everyone had known him as one of Archbishop Thomas Becket's stoutest supporters, and as the author of an extremely verbose, and on that account undervalued, *Life* of the archbishop. But of his scholarly work little was known. Glunz had written about his edition of Peter Lombard's glosses on the Psalms and Epistles; but it was left to Beryl to give substance and shape to our knowledge of his mind and aims. For this purpose the essential clue was provided by a manuscript of Bosham's own commentary on the Psalms in Jerome's version *iuxta Hebraicam veritatem*, which Neil Ker had found in the library of St. Paul's Cathedral and reported to Beryl. When she looked at this work, she found that Herbert was another man of the same stamp as Andrew of St. Victor. Like several of those who had been on the winning side in the Becket struggle, he passed the rest of his life in obscurity and unemployment. It was in the leisure of these later days that he reverted to the biblical studies with which he had been familiar in the schools. He had the independence of one who had seen greatness and was no longer interested in the world. He had always allowed himself the liberty of expressing dangerous thoughts, and this had earned him the reluctant admiration of his arch-enemy, King Henry II. He now brought all his boldness to the study of the Bible. In making a new commentary on the Psalms – the favorite hunting-ground of all allegorical interpreters of Scripture in the past – he broke away from this tradition and made a commentary solely on its *literal* sense.

Perhaps, like Andrew of St. Victor, he was partly influenced by the difficulty, in his penurious retirement, of getting the large number of books necessary for an allegorical study, but this cannot have been the main reason. He was inspired by a desire to get to the root of his text. In the first place, he chose to comment, not on the Vulgate, but on the version, the *Hebraica*, which was closest to the original Hebrew. He himself learnt some Hebrew (more, in the judgment of competent scholars, than any of his contemporaries); and he consulted – again more than anyone else – contemporary Jewish scholars, and he entered into their habits of thought more fully than was at all prudent. This led him into some curious speculations. "Supposing," he asked, "the Jews turn out to be right after all, and the Messiah has not yet come, will the faith of the Church still be meritorious? Will the sacrament of the Eucharist still be purer and more acceptable than the sacrifice of animals?" He also discovered that St. Paul had altered the text at one place (in Ps. 67: 19) to give it a more acceptably Christian interpretation, and he restored its original sense. Strange thoughts indeed for a twelfth-century theologian: they illustrate the existence of a range of doubts and hesitations generally, if they existed, left unspoken. I mention them here because they help to explain why Bosham, independent in action, restless in enquiry, solitary in his studies, appealed so strongly to Beryl.

The other, and more substantial, addition in the second edition was the extension to include the friars – Hugh of St. Cher, Guerric of St. Quentin, Bonaventure, Thomas Docking, Albert the Great, and Thomas Aquinas. In all of them she found an extension of interest in the literal meaning of the Bible spreading out in all directions. The list of names itself suffices to show that an emphasis on the letter of Holy Scripture no longer came, as it had in the previous century, from fiercely independent scholars on the edge of the scholastic world; it came from within the schools, especially from the friars, the chief custodians of biblical teaching. They brought to their interpretations a wide range of learning which incorporated Aristotle's newly translated scientific works; and they took an interest in ancient legends and classical antiquities, and used their biblical studies to promote the pastoral concerns of the new religious orders.

The mention of these diverse sources of inspiration will help to explain why no simple line of development can be found in Beryl's later work as it can in the work of her earlier years. The further she went, the vaster, the more unmanageable and unexplored, the subject became. Besides, she was never a great schematizer. She preferred to find a man or an aspect of the subject that elicited her sympathy, to work the subject up as far as she could, and leave it to others to carry on from there. That was how she always worked: the medium of her choice was an article, preferably for a Festschrift or some other special occasion; a book, if it came at all, arose from a combination of articles. She was always conscious in her post-war studies that the vastness of the materials and the many distractions of College duties would make it impossible for her to do more than illuminate a few points in a vast canvas. Nevertheless, they fall into a pattern, and it is possible to distinguish three main themes which offer a large prospect of further development. The themes are: the continuing growth of interest in the literal meaning of the Bible; the discovery of unusual characters whose solitude, dislike of public fame, and willingness to suffer for their independence made a special appeal to her; and finally – marking the last stage of her biblical studies – the increasing attention to the New Testament in the later Middle Ages. In much of her later work, these three themes become intermingled, but I shall try to give a brief account of each of them before turning to other things.

One consequence of growing interest in the literal meaning of the Bible was to turn the minds of commentators to the historical and mythological events of antiquity. It is rather strange that this antiquarian interest should have had its first flourishing in the midst of the violent controversies, famines, wars, and threats of war, of the early fourteenth century. Yet such was the case. Beryl was attracted to the investigation of this phenomenon partly because it lay in her path, but more forcibly because some of the pioneers in this early antiquarianism were men who appealed to her on other grounds – such men in particular as the Oxford Dominicans, Thomas Waleys and Robert Holcot. They were both men of marked individuality, and remarkably dissimilar.

The former was, like Beryl herself, a restless traveler. We get our first clear view of him at the papal court at Avignon in 1333, when he used the occasion of preaching in the Dominican convent to denounce the Pope's own much cherished opinion on the delay of the Beatific Vision till the Day of Judgment. This earned him a long period of imprisonment in the papal prison. I do not know that Beryl altogether approved of him, but she sympathized with his plight, and she admired his biblical work. Somehow in the midst of his tribulations he managed to write *Moralitates* on a large part of the Old Testament. The main contributions he made to scholarship in this work were his enquiries into ancient history and classical mythology. Waleys was evidently the kind of man who easily blunders into trouble, but there was a natural and carefree quality in him which she liked: "The type of lectures that he favoured (she wrote) resulted in a quaint mixture of sacred and profane; ... it stimulated browsing and book-hunting... the lecturer on Scripture from now onwards could indulge his secular interests and perform his statutory duties at one and the same time." Not the highest form of academic commendation, but close to the real life of an Oxford tutor. His existence helped to dissolve the idea of a monolithic and dehumanized Middle Ages, and this she always welcomed.

Like Waleys, Robert Holcot was a Dominican friar, but in all other ways he was a complete contrast. While Waleys spent much of his life abroad, involved in high-level controversies, Holcot is not known to have traveled further from Oxford than Cambridge, or perhaps Durham. He spent all his adult life as a lecturer in various Dominican priories within one or two days' journey from each other. But, stationary though he was, he was something of a gadfly intellectually, gathering picturesque material from every kind of classical and medieval source. Beryl described him as preferring decoration to decorum. The mixture was not uncongenial, and the extension of biblical studies into the field of ancient antiquities, to which he also was addicted, became the subject of much of Beryl's later work. In 1960 she gathered her various studies into a volume on *The Friars and Antiquity in the Early Fourteenth Century*, in which both Waleys and Holcot have a prominent place.

It will be seen that none of her favorite characters fits easily into any preconceived pattern of medieval piety or intellect. They all have strongly marked idiosyncrasies which might have made them more at home in an Oxford Common Room than a medieval lecture-room or cloister. This remark applies equally to my next example of her later work, and the one which may be expected to have the greatest future: her discovery of the lost biblical lectures of Wycliffe.

It had long been known that Wycliffe had lectured on the Bible. Indeed, as a Bachelor and then Doctor of Divinity, working in Oxford with only one period of absence between 1370 and 1382, he could scarcely have failed to give some biblical lectures. But it came as a complete surprise to find, not only that he had lectured on the whole of the Bible during these years, but that an almost complete record of his lectures had survived, chiefly in Oxford manuscripts. This is what Beryl discovered, and almost everything about the discovery was surprising. The range of Wycliffe's lectures was unique for their time. Nicholas of Lyre, who had finished his lectures nearly fifty years earlier, had been the last lecturer, so far as we know, to cover the whole Bible. Moreover, nearly all the important biblical lectures of the century were the work of friars, and Wycliffe was nothing if not secular. By a strange coincidence, Stephen Langton, nearly two hundred years earlier, had been the last secular doctor with a comparable range of biblical lectures to his credit. So the wheel of history, like that of her own studies, had come full circle.

It was a thrilling discovery. It allows us to see, for the first time, the most controversial figure in Oxford before Newman going about his daily task steadily, patiently, voluminously, year after year over a period of some ten years in a time of growing intellectual crisis. Much still remains to be done to extract from these lectures all that they can tell us about Wycliffe and the University of his day. They were not intended to be controversial; they were only the bread and butter of the theology course; but anyone who opens them at random will be unlucky not to find some traces of a remarkable man with something new to say.

Yet it must be recorded that Wycliffe was the only man about whom she made an important discovery for whom Beryl had no sympathy.

Broadly speaking, there were two medieval characters to whom she felt a
strong aversion. Joachim of Fiore was the first. In his perceptive review of
her book in 1941, A. G. Little had noticed this: "Her charity seems to fail
her when she is dealing with Joachim," he wrote, "yet Joachim made one
of the great guesses at the riddle of human history." He put his finger on
both the fact and its explanation. Beryl had no patience with guesses; she
wanted certainty, even if the certainty was only about points of grammar
or the literal meaning of words. She had no use for the lofty structures of
eccentric genius. So Wycliffe fell under the same condemnation as
Joachim. She liked the qualities which he had in common with such
favored characters as Waleys and Herbert of Bosham: his courage and
independence, his persistence in his daily task, and his historical insights.
But she could not tolerate his stridency and his putting the Bible above the
Church. That was too reminiscent of the position she had broken away
from when she first struck out on her own. She could not tolerate his
claim that flashes of insight, which (she wrote) "come to many a scholar,"
might actually come from God. Consequently she thought him – and it
is a very harsh judgment against the background of all that she had
waded through over the years – "the most arbitrary interpreter of Biblical
texts of the Middle Ages." Even his forsaken death moved her to no
compassion, and she was content to repeat McFarlane's judgment, which
tells perhaps more about the temper of our generation than about
Wycliffe: "He ended his life as a mere bore, inventing fresh insults in
default of new ideas."

There is much more that might be said about Beryl's later work, but it
must suffice simply to mention its scope. In her Ford Lectures of 1969 on
The Becket Conflict and the Schools she returned to the subject of the
political consequences of scholastic thought which Powicke had wanted
her to work on from the beginning. This change of direction reflected a
change in her own outlook on life, and it showed itself in several of her
later essays. Similarly, her volume *Historians of the Middle Ages*, published in 1974, reflects her growing interest, which all historians must feel
as they approach the end of their work, in the processes, aims, and incen-
tives of earlier historians. It is a delightful book, not least for the remarkable evidence it provides of her original and extensive knowledge of
illuminated manuscripts. It also gave her an opportunity to exhibit to her
wider public her talent for picking unusual characters out of the huge
mass of featureless authors: "I hope," she wrote, "to convey some idea of
the bewildering richness and variety of medieval historiography. Specialists
may think that I pay too much attention to the freaks; but the student can
correct me by browsing in run-of-the-mill chronicles and annals."

Finally, no account of her work would be even tolerably complete without mentioning her final persistence in producing a last group of studies

drawing attention to one of the great developments in the literal interpretation of the Bible in the later Middle Ages: the increasing concentration
on the New Testament. This was a development of immense significance
for the popularization and practical application of the Bible in the later
Middle Ages. It raised questions of great consequence about the inerrancy
of the Bible, which was the fundamental basis of all medieval – not to say
much modern – thought and practice. As always in her later work, Beryl
could do no more than open up new lines of enquiry. But, in the long run,
this may prove to be as important a contribution to our understanding of
the Middle Ages as any that she made in the course of her long and
dedicated researches.

IV

It remains only to add a few words about her personality, her work as a
tutor, and the impression she made on her colleagues and friends. In
speaking of these matters, I must first mention a constraint under which
this brief memoir has been written. She was an extremely private person,
very reluctant to allow even her friends and colleagues to see much of her
hopes and fears, her spiritual perplexities and emotional distresses. She
kept these things to herself, partly because these were battles she preferred
to fight alone; partly also perhaps because she kept the various sides of
her activity, and even of her personality, in watertight compartments. Nor
did she wish much to be known after her death. Before she died she
ordered the destruction of all her papers, all her unfinished pieces of
work. Nevertheless, despite this final expression of her lifelong reserve,
the warmth and simplicity of her character become increasingly evident in
retrospect. The mystery of her personality remains, but the sense of exclusion disappears. The pooling of recollections brings out an unexpected
range of sympathies and charities, which should not go unrecorded. Also,
a sense of harmony and unity takes the place of the fragmentation that
had seemed so conspicuous in life. For reasons which I shall touch on, she
seemed quite glad that I should write about her work, and she must have
known that this could not be done without some reference to the events
which moved her. But she did not wish her privacy to be unduly violated.

She and I had known each other for over fifty years. We had some
important things in common: we both had experienced the brief sunshine
of the late 1920s before the abominations of the '30s; we both had similar
academic beginnings in the undemanding and variously stimulating
Oxford History School of those days; we both had come under the influence of Powicke, and had both followed – with only intermittent contact –
parallel courses in our historical interests. For long periods we lost sight of

one another completely; but in the last years of her life, what we had had in common became more evident. I think some recognition of this must have lain behind her willingness that I should write some words about her after her death. She wanted to be remembered as one of a group. Her attempts to find a place in one or other of the universal groups of our time had ultimately failed. There only remained the group within which she had found her scholarly home. The inner circle of this was defined in the only photograph of herself which she preserved. It was a snapshot in which she was a diminutive figure in the company of Billy Pantin, A. B. Emden, Fr. Callus, and Richard Hunt. They – and especially the last – were the people with whom she most wished to be associated in retrospect; and, since they were all dead and had also been my friends, it was left to me to say whatever needed to be said.

I have said what I can about the growth of her scholarly work; but, for the latter half of her life, we must turn to her pupils and College colleagues, who were the chief observers and admirers of her personal qualities. To her pupils she presented a fascinating, daunting, and fastidious personality, both visually and mentally. One of her abiding interests throughout her life was in the changing modes and (I suppose) principles of feminine fashion. As far back as I can remember, she was a conspicuous object in the striking elegance and clear-cut severity of her appearance. At a time when dyed hair, painted fingernails, and cosmetics were held in the greatest abhorrence among "right-minded" women, she quietly, but not inconspicuously, and when necessary with steely words in shocked ears, registered her dissent. To the uninstructed observer, she had something of the appearance of an exceptionally clearly defined wraith – very thin, austere, remote, but distinctly visible. As a visual object, especially in the days of post-war austerity, she was adored by the junior members of her College.

Her voice was exceptionally clear, rather slow, but precise; her words few and unambiguous; her judgments decisive, and more often favorable than seemed at all likely. To her undergraduate pupils she was formidable and mild at the same time. As one put it: "She inspired in me equal parts of love and terror." The moment after finishing the reading of an essay was apt to be more than usually alarming in the long pause which followed; but then apprehension would be followed by relief as she took up the points one by one, and went round the room picking up books to illustrate them. She kept to the point and rarely obtruded her special interests, though her pupils eagerly examined her remarks for traces of Marxism, or Catholicism – or could it be Buddhism? They found it hard to know. It certainly wasn't Protestantism or Liberalism: that, they would say, was "for sure."

Gradually, and mainly after they had gone down, they got to know better another side of her: the wide extent of her kindness and hospitality.

Hospitality was one of her duties as a tutor, and it was one for which she had a peculiar genius. She was not in the least convivial, but she cared greatly about people in an austere way and would take endless trouble over their minor needs – major ones were their own affair. She liked to keep in touch with them in later life: "she delighted," wrote one of them, "in hearing of personal events – marriages, births, etc., and kept up an enormous correspondence, especially at Christmas." To another, who was visiting Oxford with her family, she wrote, "Four school girls constantly come to tea in my room, so I'm quite used to providing for large numbers and appetites."

Several years before she retired – in 1964 to be precise – she acquired a flat in Oxford to retire to. At once it became a place of hospitality for old, and for some future, pupils. She was always ready to put it at their disposal for family holidays: "My flat," she wrote, "can sleep only five unless two children can share a single bed or you can bring a mattress; but Tessa could stay in College with me perhaps. College will be almost empty at the time, so she won't be frightened."

Many pupils have recollections of this kind, and they are worth reporting because they show a quite different side of her from that which she displayed in public: the private warmth of a singularly independent character in a world which she found, not so much hostile, as extremely testing and ultimately unfathomable.

Her death was in keeping with her life. Her surgeon had told her that she had only a few months to live, and she accepted this warning with gratitude and equanimity. "The honesty of my surgeon," she wrote, "has given me the chance to finish everything... my last book is about to appear... There will be no *Nachlass*." She planned to finish as much of her work as possible, and to destroy everything that could not be left in a fit state for publication. The collection of essays, *The Gospels in the Schools, c.1100–c.1280*, which appeared posthumously, was the main result of the work of her last months. By the time she died all had been punctually accomplished. Meanwhile she would accept only the bare minimum of nursing. "Dying," she said to Menna Prestwich, her closest colleague, "is an experience like any other." What might have been bravado in others, in her was no more than a statement of a bleak fact, which she had once hoped to find untrue. In 1929 she had been received into the Roman Catholic Church, and about ten or twelve years later had become a member of the Communist Party. The connection between these two loyalties remained a mystery to all but herself. But by the time of her death she had quietly dissociated herself from both of them. These were her only attempts to find a home in a universal community. When these failed her, she sought no others, and accepted her solitary fate with unflinching courage and steadfastness. She bequeathed her books to her old College, and directed that there should be "of course, no memorial service."

Notes

Introduction

1 *PBA* 120: *Biographical Memoirs of Fellows* 2 (2003), pp. 413–42.

1 Aspects of the European Tradition of Historical Writing 1: The Classical Tradition from Einhard to Geoffrey of Monmouth

1 In Germany these studies have been much more frequent, as may be seen from the following selection of recent works which throw light on the pattern of historical writing in the period discussed below: H. Beumann, *Widukind von Korvei* (*Abhandlungen über Corveyer Geschichtschreibung* 3, Weimar, 1950), and *Ideengeschichtliche Studien zu Einhard und anderen Geschichtsschreibern des früheren Mittelalters* (Darmstadt, 1962); H. F. Haefele, *Fortuna Heinrici IV Imperatoris* (Graz and Cologne, 1954); L. Bornscheuer, *Miseriae Regum* (*Arbeiten zur Frühmittelalterforschung* 4, Berlin, 1968); A. Schneider, "Thietmar von Merseburg über kirchliche, politische und ständische Fragen seiner Zeit," *Archiv für Kulturgeschichte* 44 (1962), pp. 34–71; G. Simon, "Untersuchungen zur Topik der Widmungsbriefe mittelalterlicher Geschichtsschreiber bis zum Ende des xii Jahrhunderts," *Archiv für Diplomatik* 4 (1958), pp. 52–119; 5–6 (1959–60), pp. 73–153.

2 Aristotle, *Poetics* 1459a.

3 Ibid., 1451b.

4 For the connection between history and rhetoric in the ancient world, see H. Peter, *Die Geschichtsliteratur über die römische Kaiserzeit* (2 vols., Leipzig, 1897), 1, pp. 3–107; 2, pp. 179–210; and especially Quintilian, *Instituta oratoria*, I, viii, 18–21; X, i, 31–4; XII, iv; Pliny, *Epistolae*, v, 8; vii, 33; Cicero, *De Oratore*, II, ix, 36–8; xii, 51–xvi, 68; *Rhetorica ad Herennium*, i, 8–9.

5 There is a penetrating analysis of Sallust's view of historical causation in Gordon Williams, *Tradition and Originality in Roman Poetry* (Oxford, 1968), pp. 619–33.

6 John of Salisbury, *Policraticus*, ed. C. C. J. Webb (2 vols., Oxford, 1909), 1, p. 211, calls him *historicorum inter latinos potissimus* ["most powerful of the Latin historians"], and his popularity as a school-book (to take a random sample) is attested by the existence of no less than eight copies of his works in the library of Christ Church, Canterbury, about 1170 (M. R. James, *The Ancient Libraries of Canterbury and Dover* (Cambridge, 1903), p. 9).

7 G. Simon, in the studies cited above, has collected a number of samples of typical apologies for literary shortcomings, but the list could easily be extended.

8 His edition appeared in the series of *Classiques de l'histoire de France au moyen âge* in 1923 (2nd ed., 1938) [there are English translations in *Two Lives of Charlemagne*, trans. Lewis Thorpe (Penguin Classics, 1969), and *Charlemagne's Courtier: The Complete Einhard*, trans. P. E. Dutton (Peterborough, Ontario, 1998)].

9 Chapter 9 (Halphen, pp. 28–9).

10 Ed. H. Bresslau, *MGH, SRG* (1915) [there is an English translation in *Imperial Lives and Letters of the Eleventh Century*, trans. Theodor E. Mommsen and Karl F. Morrison (New York, 1962)].

11 They have been carefully uncovered with much penetrating comment by Alistair Campbell in his edition in the Royal Historical Society, Camden Third Series, 72 (1949) [repr. with a supplementary introduction by Simon Keynes (Cambridge, 1998)].

12 Ed. F. Barlow (Nelson's Medieval Texts, 1962); an indispensable edition [2nd ed., OMT, 1992].

13 For the origins of the Frankish legend see E. Lüthgen, *Die Quellen und der historische Werth der fränkischen Trojasaga* (Bonn, 1875). The sources are in *MGH, Scriptores rerum Merovingicarum*, 2, ed. B. Krusch (1888), pp. 45–6, 194–200, 241–6: J. M. Wallace-Hadrill has some useful comments on them in *The Fourth Book of the Chronicle of Fredegar* (Nelson's Medieval Texts, 1960), pp. xii–xiii.

14 Fredegar, iii, 4–8, ed. Krusch, pp. 45–6.

15 *Rerum gestarum Saxonicarum libri tres*, ed. P. Hirsch, *MGH, SRG* (1935), pp. 4, 20–1. It is clear that he knew the legend only (as he tells us) from oral tradition for he thought that these Macedonian fugitives were Greeks, not Trojans as the literary version made clear.

16 Ibid., pp. 46–8.

17 The best edition is still that by J. Lair in *Mémoires de la Société des Antiquaires de Normandie* 23 (1865) [there is now an English translation, *History of the Normans*, trans. Eric Christiansen (Woodbridge, 1998)].

18 *MGH, SS* 6 [*Frutolfi et Ekkehardi Chronica*, ed. Franz-Josef Schmale and Irene Schmale-Ott (Darmstadt, 1972)]. Ekkehard describes his aims in the Preface (p. 9): *Cum tota intentio huius libri tam Romani imperii quam Teutonici regni deserviat honori, quorum coniunctio cepit a Karolo Francigena,*

necessarium duximus tam nobilissimae gentis... altius originem repetere, et sic per antiquissimae nobilitatis generationes usque ad eundem Karolum narratione deducta, qualiter ipse capesseret rem publicam labefactam et qualiter deinde Romanum imperium per successiones regum istius gentis excellentissime gubernaretur... digerere ["Since the whole intention of this book is to serve the honor of both the Roman Empire and the German kingdom, whose conjunction began with Charles the Frank, we have considered it necessary to trace the more distant origin of such a noble people and thus, taking the tale through the generations of most ancient nobility down to that Charles, to expound how he took hold of the state, as it was tottering, and how thereafter the Roman Empire was governed most excellently by a succession of kings of that people"]. In those words we see the signs of a sharper political propaganda than in earlier works.

19 The process of transferring the whole Frankish legend to the Capetian monarchy can be followed in the historical collections of St. Denis in MS. Bibl. Mazarine 2013 and Bibl. Nat. lat. 12710. On the second of these manuscripts, see J. Lair in *Bibliothèque de l'Ecole des Chartres* 35 (1874), pp. 542–80 (esp. pp. 551–7 where the notes of the compiler of the chronicle show how, and from which sources, he intended to patch together his story linking the Capetian kingdom with Troy).

20 Geoffrey of Monmouth is too large a subject for annotation in this brief sketch, but I should like to record my thanks to Professor Idris Foster for his help, though I cannot claim his authority for anything I have said here.

21 A comparison of Richer's *History* with the *Annals* of Flodoard on which it is largely, and sometimes wholly, based will provide an illuminating example of the various types of expansion, invention, transposition, and *suggestio falsi* which a serious and ambitious historian could permit himself in turning his raw material into a finished history.

2 Aspects of the European Tradition of Historical Writing 2: Hugh of St. Victor and the Idea of Historical Development

1 See *De Civitate Dei*, xxii, 30. For an account of the early history of the division into seven Ages, see R. Schmidt, "Aetates Mundi: die Weltalter als Gliederungsprinzip der Geschichte," *Zeitschrift für Kirchengeschichte* 67 (1955–6), pp. 288–317.

2 For Bede's speculations on universal history see *Bedae Opera de Temporibus*, ed. C. W. Jones (Medieval Academy of America, 1943), pp. 201–2, 303, 307–15 (=*De Temporum Ratione* 10; *De Temporibus* 16; *Epistola ad Pleguinam*). In his Introduction, pp. 130–9, Professor Jones gives an illuminating account of Bede's use of his sources.

3 For a different view, with many penetrating observations on the authors discussed below, see M.-D. Chenu, "Conscience de l'histoire et théologie au XIIe

siècle," *Archives d'histoire doctrinale et littéraire du Moyen Age* 21 (1954), pp. 107–33 [available in English in M.-D. Chenu, *Nature, Man and Society in the Twelfth Century* (English translation, Chicago, 1968), pp. 162–201].

4 For a study of the evidence, see R. Baron, *Etudes sur Hugues de St-Victor* (Paris, 1963), pp. 9–30.

5 There is a convincing description of his school by Lawrence of Durham, later abbot of Westminster, in B. Bischoff, *Mittelalterliche Studien* 2 (Stuttgart, 1967), pp. 182–7.

6 Hugh of St. Victor, *Didascalicon*, VI, iii, *De historia*, ed. C. H. Buttimer (Washington, DC, 1939); translated with valuable notes by Jerome Taylor (Columbia University Press, 1961).

7 *De Sacramentis*, II, 14, i (*PL* 176, 551–2). On this subject more than any other we can catch a glimpse of the confusion and controversies which went far beyond the walls of the schools. As Hugh wrote: *Quando dicimus hominibus...ut confiteantur mala quae fecerunt, dicunt nobis, "Date auctoritatem"* ["When we say to people that they should confess the wrongs they have committed, they say to us, 'Give an authority'"]. Many of the works of the period testify to the difficulty of meeting this demand.

8 *De Meditatione*, c. 3 (*Hugues de St. Victor: Six Opuscules Spirituels*, ed. R. Baron (Paris, 1969), p. 48).

9 The sources for this sketch of Hugh's historical ideas are his *De Sacramentis*, I, 1, iii; I, 3, iii; I, 8, iii, xi; I, 10, iv, vi–vii; I, 11, i–vii; I, 12, i, iii, vi (*PL* 176, 187–364); *De Sacramentis legis naturalis et scriptae Dialogus* (ibid., 17–42); *De varietate mundi*, ii–iii (ibid., 716–30). See also *Summa Sententiarum*, IV, i–ii; V, i (ibid., 117–20, 127–8). Several of the same ideas are found also in Lawrence of Durham's report on Hugh's lectures in Bodleian Library, MS. Laud misc. 277.

10 For the background of Newman's idea of development, see O. Chadwick, *From Bossuet to Newman: The Idea of Doctrinal Development* (Cambridge, 1957).

11 Abelard's main attack on Hugh (he does not mention him by name, but the source of the doctrines attributed to a master in France, *qui se quasi singularem divinae paginae magistrum omnibus praefert* ["who presents himself to everyone as if he were the only master of theology"] is unmistakable) is in *Theologia Christiana* (*PL* 188, 1285) [ed. E. M. Buytaert, *Opera theologica*, 2 (CCCM 12, 1969)]. In his *Problemata Heloissae* (ibid., 698), Abelard's position with regard to salvation in a state of natural law is in practice very similar to Hugh's, except that he still insists on a special revelation of Christian doctrines as a requirement for salvation. Hugh's appeal to St. Bernard is known only from St. Bernard's reply, *Tractatus de Baptismo aliisque quaestionibus*, 3 (*PL* 182, 1038–46).

12 The substance of Hugh's argument is reported by St. Bernard with the remark that he had almost nothing to add (*PL* 182, 1038–9).

13 *Expositio in Hierarchiam coelestem*, II, I (*PL* 175, 948).

14 Eusebius-Hieronymus, *Chronica*, ed. R. Helm (Berlin, 1956) (see esp. annals for 1684, 1637, 1569, 1471, 693 BC); Isidorus, *Etymologiae sive Origines*,

ed. W. M. Lindsay (Oxford, 1911) (see esp. I, 3, iv; II, 2, i; II, 24, iv–v, vii; III, 2, i; 10, i; 16, i; 25, i; IV, 3, i); Remigius, *Commentum in Martianum Capellam*, ed. C. E. Lutz (2 vols., Leiden, 1962–5) (see esp. 1, pp. 145, 175; 2, pp. 3, 12–13, 15–16, 26, 179–80).

15 Hugh's waverings on this point are analyzed by D. van den Eynde, *Essai sur la succession et la date des écrits de Hugues de St-Victor* (Rome, 1960), pp. 41–2.

16 *Didascalicon*, I, i: *Naturae nostrae dignitas...reparatur per doctrinam, ut nostram agnoscimus naturam, et ut discamus extra non quaerere quod in nobis possumus invenire* ["The dignity of our nature...is restored through learning, so that we may recognize our nature and learn not to seek outside ourselves what we can find within"]. For some further discussion of this view of man's nature, see R. W. Southern, *Medieval Humanism and Other Studies* (Oxford, 1970), pp. 29–60.

17 *Epitome Dindimi in Philosophiam*, in *Opera propaedeutica Hugonis de S. Victore*, ed. R. Baron (Paris, 1966), p. 193.

18 *Didascalicon*, I, xli.

19 Ibid., II, xi. For the origin of the legend of Parmenides, see R. Klibansky, "The Rock of Parmenides," *MARS* 1 (1943), pp. 178–86.

20 *Didascalicon*, I, xii, where he appears to reject the view of Remigius of Auxerre (*Commentum in Martianum Capellam*, ed. C. E. Lutz (2 vols., Leiden, 1962–5), 2, p. 3) that Grammar was the earliest of the arts.

21 The mechanical, no less than the liberal, arts were *opera artificis imitantis naturam* ["works of a craftsman imitating nature"]: hence they served to develop the powers of human reason (see *Didascalicon*, I, x). Hugh would find the seeds of this idea in Remigius, op. cit., 1, p. 208; 2, pp. 299, 302–3.

22 The Chronicle has never been printed in its entirety; hence it is difficult to study it in detail. Professor A. Vernet, who has kindly communicated to me his views, has made the closest study of the manuscripts, and he has doubts about the authenticity of the work. It is clear that some of the manuscripts preserve additions which could not have been written by Hugh himself. Nevertheless I accept it as in the main a genuine work of Hugh of St. Victor. The Preface is printed by W. M. Green in *Speculum* 18 (1943), pp. 484–93, and some of the lists of rulers in *MGH, SS* 14, pp. 88–97. There are convenient descriptions of the contents of the work in Green, op. cit., pp. 492–3, D. van den Eynde, op. cit., pp. 90–2, and in R. Baron, "La chronique de Hugues de S.-Victor," *Studia Gratiana* 12 (1967), pp. 167–80.

23 *Didascalicon*, VI, iii.

24 *Sunt quaedam fundamenta scientiae, quae si memoriae firmiter impressa fuerint, facile cetera omnia patescunt. Haec tibi in subiecta pagina eo ordine disposita praescribemus quo ipsa volumus animo tuo per memoriam inseri, ut quicquid postea superedificaverimus solidum esse possit* ["there are certain foundations of a science, which, if they are firmly imprinted on the memory, easily make everything else clear. We will write them down for you in the following pages in the order in which we want you to implant them in your memory, so that whatever we shall build on them afterwards can be secure"],

Praef., ed. Green, op. cit., pp. 490–1. An interesting parallel to Hugh's method in his Chronicle is to be found in contemporary penitential literature: the *circumstantiae peccatorum* ["circumstances of sinners"] begin at this time to play a part in moral theology similar to the part of the *circumstantiae gestorum* ["circumstances of history"] in Hugh's Chronicle. See J. Grundel, *Die Lehre von den Umständen der menschlichen Handlung in Mittelalter (Beiträge zur Geschichte der Philosophie des Mittelalter 39, 1963).*

25 Green, op. cit., lists sixteen manuscripts, nearly all in Northern France.

26 Richard of St. Victor, *Liber Exceptionum*, ed. J. Chatillon (Paris, 1958). The editor lists about 170 surviving manuscripts, and discusses their influence and usefulness (pp. 81–6). For other works of Richard of St. Victor in which the influence of Hugh's historical ideas can be found, see his *Opuscules Théologiques*, ed. J. Ribaillier (Paris, 1967), pp. 237–41, 256–80 (*PL* 196, 995–1010).

27 Anselm of Havelberg, *Dialogi*, I, ed. G. Salet (*Sources Chrétiennes* 118, 1966), p. 34 (*PL* 188, 1141).

28 I have not found any verbal dependence on Hugh of St. Victor, but the *Dialogi*, I, i–iv, op. cit., pp. 48–50 (*PL* 188, 1145–6) adopt the main lines of Hugh's view of religious development.

29 Op. cit., p. 116 (*PL* 188, 1160).

30 *Dialogi*, I, i–iv, pp. 64–6 (*PL* 188, 1148–9).

31 Otto, bishop of Freising, *Chronica sive Historia de duabus Civitatibus*, ed. A. Hofmeister, *MGH, SRG* (1912), pp. 7, 67–8, 285 [there is an English translation, *The Two Cities*, trans. C. C. Mierow (New York, 1928)].

32 Ibid., p. 309.

33 *Gesta Frederici*, ed. G. Waitz, *MGH, SRG* (1912), p. 65 [there is an English translation, *The Deeds of Frederick Barbarossa*, trans. C. C. Mierow (New York, 1953)]. For the contrast with his earlier view, cf. *Chronica*, p. 7.

34 *Chronica*, p. 8.

35 Ibid., p. 227.

36 Alexander Nequam, *De Naturis Rerum*, ed. T. Wright (RS, 1863), p. 398.

37 Bishop Berkeley, *Verses on the Prospect of Planting Arts and Learning in America.*

38 *An Universal History from the earliest Time to the Present, compiled from Original Authors, and illustrated with Maps, Cuts, Notes, Chronological and other Tables* (8 vols., London; J. Batley and others, 1736–50). The work was started by the Arabic scholar George Sale and continued by "many learned men" chiefly from Oxford and Cambridge. It was never finished. A parallel French work, but much more timid in its scholarship, is Dom Augustin Calmet, *Histoire Universelle, sacrée et profane, depuis le commencement du monde jusqu'à nos jours* (8 vols., Strasbourg, 1735–47).

39 It is interesting to observe how the eighteenth-century scholars dealt with the materials used by Hugh of St. Victor six centuries earlier: they had more materials and more assurance, and criticized their predecessors with greater freedom. But their point of view had scarcely changed: see for instance 1, pp. 81 (on Seth), 117 (on Shem), 122–3 (on Nimrod), 218 (on Egypt), 2, p. 222 (on the astrology of the Chaldaeans). These scholars were more learned and

in a sense more rational than Voltaire, whose *Essai sur les mœurs et l'esprit des Nations* (1756) was the first really damaging attack on the whole system of history which had dominated European historical thought since the time of Eusebius. But Voltaire's suspicions about this whole edifice of learning happened to be right.

3 Aspects of the European Tradition of Historical Writing 3: History as Prophecy

1 *Summa Theologica*, IIa IIae, 171, art. 1 and 3.
2 Ibid., IIa IIae, 171, art. 3: *Ultimus autem gradus est eorum quae sunt procul ab omnium hominum cognitione, quia in seipsis non sunt cognoscibilia, ut contingentia futura, quorum veritas non est determinata* ["the ultimate level is (knowledge) of things beyond all human cognition, which are intrinsically unknowable, such as future contingents, whose truth is not determined"].
3 Ibid., IIa IIae, 172, art. 4 and 6.
4 Ibid., IIa IIae, 171, art. 6, ad 2.
5 For instance Gebeno (see below) defended Hildegard's prophecies against those who refused to read her writings because of their obscurity by retorting that they did not understand, *quod hoc est argumentum verae prophetiae* ["for this is a proof of true prophecy"] (J. B. Pitra, *Analecta Sacra* 8 (1891), p. 483).
6 R. H. Charles, *Commentary on the Book of Daniel* (Oxford, 1929), p. 170.
7 Daniel 7: 24–5.
8 *PL* 25, 1352–3.
9 The main text is Paulus Albarus, *Indiculus luminosus* (*PL* 121), on which see E. P. Colbert, *The Martyrs of Cordoba (850–859): A Study of the Sources* (Catholic University of America, Studies in Medieval History, New Series, 17, Washington, DC, 1962).
10 Revelation 6: 1–17; 8: 1.
11 Bede, *Commentum in Apocalypsim* (*PL* 93, 129).
12 Anselm of Havelberg, *Dialogi*, ed. G. Salet (*Sources Chrétiennes* 118, 1966), pp. 68–106.
13 See B. Smalley, "Ralph of Flaix on Leviticus," *Recherches de théologie ancienne et médiévale* 35 (1968), pp. 35–82, for a contemporary protest (pp. 39–42) against the general indifference to the coming of Antichrist. I have to thank Miss Smalley for calling my attention to this passage.
14 The fundamental work on the sibylline literature in the Middle Ages remains E. Sackur, *Sibyllinische Texte und Forschungen* (Halle, 1898). For some interesting examples of translations from the Greek between the seventh and ninth centuries, see B. Bischoff, "Die lateinische Übersetzungen und Bearbeitungen aus den Oracula Sibyllina," *Mittelalterliche Studien* 1 (Stuttgart, 1966), pp. 150–71; and for a valuable account of the Byzantine tradition, see P. J. Alexander, *The Oracle of Baalbek: The Tiburtine Sibyl in Greek Dress* (Washington, DC, 1967), and "Historiens byzantins et croyances eschatologiques," *Actes du XIIe Congrès Internationale des Etudes Byzantines, 1961* 2 (Bel-

grade, 1964), pp. 1–8 [repr. in *Religious and Political History and Thought in the Byzantine Empire* (London, 1978), no. XV].

15 Abelard gives a striking testimony to the role of the sibyls in broadening the stream of Revelation: *Cum itaque Dominus, et per prophetas Iudaeis et per praestantes philosophos seu vates gentibus, catholicae fidei tenorem annuntiaverit, inexcusabiles redduntur tam Iudaei quam gentes si ... ipsos non audiant. Et quidem multi ex gentibus, nonnulli ex Iudaeis, in hoc quoque a doctoribus populi sui instructi fidem sanctae Trinitatis recognoverunt, in uno corpore ecclesiae quasi duo parietes coniuncti* ["Therefore, since the Lord announced the tenor of the catholic faith through the prophets to the Jews and through outstanding philosophers or seers to the gentiles, neither the Jews nor the gentiles have any excuse if they did not listen to them. Indeed many gentiles and some of the Jews, instructed in this by the teachers of their own people, acknowledged belief in the Holy Trinity, joining in one body of the Church like two walls"], *Theologia Christiana*, 1, 136 (*PL* 177, 1166).

16 For this incident see H. Grundmann in *Deutsches Archiv für Erforschung des Mittelalters* 16 (1960), p. 491.

17 The text was the *Sibylla Samica* (ed. O. Holder-Egger in *Neues Archiv* 15 (1890), p. 177).

18 The text of Merlin's prophecies forms chapters 112–17 of Geoffrey of Monmouth's *Historia Regum Britanniae*, in E. Faral, *La Légende Arthurienne* (3 vols., Paris, 1929), 3, pp. 191–202 [ed. Neil Wright (Cambridge, 1984), pp. 74–84; English translation, *The History of the Kings of Britain*, trans. Lewis Thorpe (Penguin Classics, 1966), pp. 171–85]. There is a lively account of the huge literary success of the prophetic genre founded by Geoffrey of Monmouth in P. Zumthor, *Merlin le Prophète* (Lausanne, 1943) (with full bibliography), where the emphasis is too exclusively on literary invention rather than historical thought.

19 *Ep. 176* (*PL* 199, 171) [John of Salisbury, *Letters*, ed. W. J. Millor, H. E. Butler, and C. N. L. Brooke (2 vols., OMT, 1979–86), 2, pp. 134–7 (ep. 173)].

20 The *Prophetia Merlini cum expositione Johannis Cornubiensis* was printed rather inaccurately from Vatican MS. Ottobonianus 1474 by C. Greith in his *Spicilegium Vaticanum* (Frauenfeld, 1838), pp. 98–106, with an address to *R. Oxoniensi*; but Delisle (*Bibliothèque de l'Ecole des Chartres* 37 (1876), p. 518) reported that the correct reading is *R. presuli Exoniensi* [ed. M. J. Curley, *Speculum* 57 (1982), pp. 217–49, reading *R. presul Exoniensis*]. This could be either Robert Warelwast 1137–55, or Robert of Salisbury (or Chichester) 1155–60. But since the prophecy seems to refer to the death of Count Conan in 1171, and since John of Cornwall was probably still studying in France in 1160, it seems likely that "R" is a mistake for B(artholomew), bishop of Exeter 1161–84. For John of Cornwall's career, see E. Rathbone, "John of Cornwall; a brief biography," *Recherches de théologie ancienne et médiévale* 17 (1950), pp. 46–60.

21 This is what Gerald calls his *Expugnatio Hibernica* (*Opera Omnia*, ed. J. S. Brewer, J. F. Dimock, and G. F. Warner (RS, 1861–91), 1, p. 414; 3, p. 333; 8,

p. 159, etc.), in which he made full use of the prophecies of Merlin and the Celtic bards; but the concluding book in which, as Gerald announced, he would collect and translate further, orally transmitted prophecies, was never written [*Expugnatio Hibernica: The Conquest of Ireland*, ed. A. B. Scott and F. X. Martin (Dublin, 1978)].

22 William of Newburgh's main objection to Merlin's prophecies was that he received his knowledge of the future from his demon father. Since demons, being shut out from the light of God, have no knowledge of the future, but can only make plausible conjectures about it, Merlin's testimony (quite apart from Geoffrey of Monmouth's fraudulent additions) was not to be relied on (*Historia rerum Anglicarum*, ed. Richard Howlett, in *Chronicles of the Reigns of Stephen, Henry II and Richard I*, 1–2 (RS, 1884–9), 1, p. 12. This objection may be compared with the explanation given to Dante by Farinata in *Inferno*, x, 100–5, that the damned have an imperfect vision of distant events and no knowledge of present events on earth. These were both highly personal views. Thomas Aquinas expressed a more general view when he granted the validity, within limits, of demonically inspired prophecy (*Summa Theologica*, IIa IIae, 172, art. 5 and 6).

23 For her letters and consultations, see J. B. Pitra, *Nova S. Hildegardis Opera*, *Analecta Sacra*, 8 (1891), and *PL* 197, 145–382. There is a useful account of her main book of visions with reproductions of contemporary illustrations and a German translation by M. Böckeler, *Hildegard von Bingen, Wisse die Wege (Scivias)* (Salzburg, 1954). In the Preface to this work Hildegard tells us that she began to understand her visionary experiences in 1141, when she was forty-two years old. After this date her fame as a consultant steadily grew [*Epistolarium*, ed. L. Van Acker (CCCM 91, 1991–), *Letters*, trans. Joseph L. Baird and Radd K. Ehrman (New York, 1994–8); *Scivias*, ed. A. Führkötter (CCCM 43, 43a, 1978), trans. Colombia Hart and Jane Bishop (New York, 1990)].

24 *Ep*. 199 (*PL* 199, 220) [John of Salisbury, *Letters*, ed. Millor, Butler, and Brooke, 2, pp. 222–5 (ep. 185)].

25 In 1222 Gebeno, prior of Cîteaux, made a selection and arrangement of Hildegard's visions to elucidate *ea quae de futuris temporibus et de Antichristo prophetavit* ["those things she prophesied about future times and about the Antichrist"]. His purpose was to confute "the frivolous and vain prophets of the present day" who said that Antichrist had already been born.

26 The earliest book of practical astrology which circulated in the West from the eleventh century onwards was Julius Firmicus, *Mathesis*. This was a literary and philosophical work which provided no basis for measurement or scientific observation. Nevertheless it was already attracting attention by the beginning of the twelfth century, as we know from the comments made when Gerard, archbishop of York, who died suddenly in 1108, was found dead with a copy under his head (William of Malmesbury, *Gesta pontificum*, ed. N. E. S. A. Hamilton (RS, 1870), pp. 259–60) [there is an English translation, *Deeds of the Bishops of England*, trans. David Preest (2002)]. For the introduction of the astrolabe which made measurement possible, and for the

Arabic tables which made measurements generally accessible, see C. H. Haskins, *Studies in the History of Medieval Science* (Cambridge, Mass., 1924), pp. 82–128. I have traced the progress of the subject at Worcester in the early twelfth century in *Medieval Humanism and Other Studies* (Oxford, 1970), pp. 168–71.

27 Roger of Howden has preserved the predictions which *universi fere orbis conjectores tam Graeci quam Latini* ["the interpreters, both Greek and Latin, of almost the whole world"] wrote for 1186 (Benedict of Peterborough, *Gesta regis Henrici secundi*, ed. William Stubbs (2 vols., RS, 1867), 1, pp. 324–8; *Chronica Rogeri de Hoveden*, ed. William Stubbs (4 vols., RS, 1868–71), 2, pp. 290–8).

28 For the links between astrology and prophecy in the later Middle Ages see D. Kurze, *Johannes Lichtenberger (1503): Eine Studie zur Geschichte der Prophetie und Astrologie* (Lübeck, 1960) (summarized in the author's "Prophecy and History," *Journal of the Warburg and Courtauld Institutes* 21 (1958), pp. 63–85); also T. O. Wedel, *The Medieval Attitude towards Astrology* (Yale Studies in English 60, 1920), where the sources are discussed. There is a very interesting scholastic treatment of the whole subject by the early fourteenth-century English theologian Henry de Harkeley in his *Quaestio Utrum Astrologi vel quicumque calculatores possint probare secundum Adventum Christi* ["Whether astrologers or interpreters of any kind can demonstrate the Second Coming of Christ"] (ed. F. Pelster, *Archivio italiano per la storia della pietà* 1 (1951), pp. 328–76).

29 This passage occurs in an introductory summary of the *Opus Maius*, which Bacon wrote in 1266–7 (ed. A. Gasquet, *EHR* 12 (1897), pp. 514–15 [ed. E. Bettoni (Milan, 1964)]). There is a similar passage in the *Opus Maius*, ed. J. H. Bridges (3 vols., Oxford, 1897–1900), 1, pp. 268–9, where instead of "other pagan prophets" he mentions "Aquila, Sesto, Joachim and other prophets."

30 M. E. Reeves, *The Influence of Prophecy in the Later Middle Ages: A Study in Joachimism* (Oxford, 1969).

31 For the development of Joachim's thought see Reeves, op. cit., pp. 3–30. Among older works H. Grundmann, *Neue Forschungen über Joachim von Fiore* (Marburg, 1950), and "Joachim von Fiore und Rainer von Ponza," *Deutsches Archiv* 16 (1960), pp. 437–546, are especially valuable. In addition to the contemporary records edited by Grundmann, the account of Joachim's early writing by Lucas of Casamari (*Acta Sanctorum*, Maius, 7, 91–2), the record of his interview with Richard I in 1190 (Benedict of Peterborough, op. cit., 2, pp. 151–5, and Roger of Hoveden, op. cit., 3, pp. 75–9), and his interview with Adam of Perseigne (Ralph of Coggeshall, *Chronicon Anglicanum*, ed. Joseph Stevenson (RS, 1875), pp. 67–71) are of fundamental importance.

32 The essential text on this point is 2 Thess. 2: 7, which was always taken to mean that Antichrist would not appear so long as the Roman Empire, or alternatively the temporal power of the papacy, lasted. For the later medieval developments of the theme see M. E. Reeves, op. cit., pp. 293–392, "Antichrist and the Last World Emperor."

33 *Registrum*, xvi, 28 (*PL* 216, 817–22).
34 For this aspect of Joachim's thought, see Reeves, op. cit., pp. 303–5.
35 For these successive postponements, see Reeves, op. cit., pp. 48–51, 54, 58–9, 83, 228, 246, 308, 313–14, 316, 322, 368.
36 *Opera*, ed. S. Horsley (5 vols., London, 1779–85), 5, pp. 297–491. The first edition appeared in 1733. William Whiston's *New Theory of the Earth from its Original to the Consummation of all Things* (London, 1696), and *Astronomical Principles of Religion Natural and Revealed* (London, 1717), which were dedicated to Newton, make an interesting attempt to combine biblical prophecy with Newtonian astronomy. Newton may originally have welcomed the attempt, but he later rejected the author.
37 Ibid., p. 449.
38 Ibid., p. 305.
39 Ibid., p. 364.
40 Ibid., p. 450.

4 Aspects of the European Tradition of Historical Writing 4: The Sense of the Past

1 William of Malmesbury, *Gesta regum*, ed. William Stubbs (2 vols., RS, 1887–9), 1, p. 278 [ed. and trans. R. A. B. Mynors, R. M. Thomson, and M. Winterbottom (2 vols., OMT, 1998–9), 1, pp. 414–16].
2 William of Malmesbury, *Gesta pontificum*, ed. N. E. S. A. Hamilton (RS, 1870), p. 202.
3 The monastic reaction in Germany has been intensively studied in recent years, especially in the persons of Rupert of Deutz and Gerhoh of Reichersberg. For the former, see especially the remarkable article of H. Grundmann: "Der Brand von Deutz 1128 in der Darstellung Abt Ruperts von Deutz," *Deutsches Archiv* 22 (1966), pp. 385–471; also R. Haacke, "Die Überlieferung der Schriften Ruperts v. Deutz," ibid., 16 (1960), pp. 397–436, and H. Silvestre, "A propos de la lettre d'Anselme de Laon à Heribrand de St-Laurent," *Recherches de théologie ancienne et médiévale* 28 (1961), pp. 5–26 [see also Southern's *Scholastic Humanism and the Unification of Europe*, 2 (Oxford, 2001), pp. 7–24].
4 *Gesta regum*, 2, p. 304 [OMT ed., 1, p. 456].
5 *Hemingi Chartularium Ecclesiae Wigorniensis*, ed. T. Hearne (2 vols., Oxford, 1723), 2, p. 391. For the composition of the cartulary see N. R. Ker, "Hemming's Cartulary," in *Studies in Medieval History presented to F. M. Powicke* (Oxford, 1948), pp. 49–75.
6 The main part of the manuscript was probably written between 1120 and 1122, with corrections and additions to 1130. The chronicle of Marianus Scotus on which it was based was brought to England by Robert, bishop of Hereford 1079–95, and no doubt introduced to Worcester by Wulfstan. Unfortunately no manuscript takes us back to the early stages of compilation at Worcester before the death of Florence, the original compiler, in 1118; but the corrections and additions vividly illustrate the continuing tradition of histor-

ical work after Florence's death [John of Worcester, *Chronicle*, ed. R. R. Darlington and P. McGurk (2 vols. to date, OMT, 1995–), esp. 2, pp. xxi–xxxv].

7 For the objects associated with the journey of St. Cuthbert's body see *Symeonis Monachi Opera Omnia*, ed. T. Arnold (2 vols., RS, 1882–5), 1, pp. 39, 57, 64, 66, 67, 74–5, 79–80 [Symeon of Durham, *Libellus de Exordio atque Procursu istius hoc est Dunhelmensis Ecclesie*, ed. David Rollason (OMT, 2000), pp. 60, 102, 114, 116, 120, 134–6, 146–8]; and for Athelstan's gifts, 1, pp. 75, 211 [ibid., pp. 134–6; *Historia de Sancto Cuthberto*, ed. Ted Johnson South (Cambridge, 2002), p. 64]. For the Durham manuscripts mentioned above, see R. A. B. Mynors, *Durham Cathedral Manuscripts* (Oxford, 1939), nos. 5, 13, 15, 16.

8 Eadmer, *Historia Novorum*, ed. M. Rule (RS, 1884), p. 1. For historical studies and their background at Canterbury, see R. W. Southern, *St. Anselm and his Biographer* (Cambridge, 1963), pp. 229–336.

9 See below.

10 The essential text is BL, Cotton MS. Claudius C ix, ff. 105–203, badly edited by J. Stevenson, *Chronicon Monasterii de Abingdon* (2 vols., RS, 1858), and first given its due importance by F. M. Stenton, *The Early History of the Abbey of Abingdon* (Reading, 1913) [*Historia Ecclesie Abbendonensis: The History of the Church of Abingdon*, 2, ed. John Hudson (OMT, 2002)].

11 The most important writer at Evesham was Prior Dominic, on whom see J. C. Jennings, "The Writings of Prior Dominic of Evesham," *EHR* 77 (1962), pp. 298–304, and "The Origins of the 'Elements Series' of the Miracles of the Virgin," *MARS* 6 (1968), pp. 84–93; also the texts in *Chronicon Abbatiae de Evesham*, ed. W. D. Macray (RS, 1863), pp. 1–100.

12 The main manuscripts are St. John's College, Oxford, MS. 17 with BL, Cotton MS. Nero C vii from Thorney, written (with additions) in the period from 1085 to 1125 (see N. R. Ker, *British Museum Quarterly* 12 (1938), p. 131); and BL, Cotton MS. Tiberius C i, ff. 2–42 with Harleian 3667 from Peterborough, written in 1121–2. For the Easter Tables in the Thorney MS. with their uniquely long series of annals from 528 to 1536, see C. Hart, "The Ramsey Computus," *EHR* 85 (1970), pp. 29–44.

13 The works of this most expert of all post-Conquest students of Anglo-Saxon can now be studied in a facsimile edition with a full analysis and introduction by Peter Sawyer, *Early English Manuscripts in Facsimile*, 7 (1957) (*Textus Roffensis*, Pt. i), and 11 (1962) (*Textus Roffensis*, Pt. ii).

14 For a recent survey of his life and works, see H. Farmer in *JEH* 13 (1962), pp. 39–54 [Rodney Thomson, *William of Malmesbury* (Woodbridge, 1987)].

15 The contaminated text is printed in T. Hearne, *Adami de Domerham Historia de rebus Glastoniensibus* (Oxford, 1727), pp. 1–122. For the original text see J. Armitage Robinson, *Somerset Historical Essays* (Oxford, for the British Academy, 1921), pp. 1–25, and his later study, *Two Glastonbury Legends: King Arthur and Joseph of Arimathea* (Cambridge, 1926) [John Scott, *The Early History of Glastonbury: An Edition, Translation and Study of William of Malmesbury's "De antiquitate Glastonie Ecclesie"* (Woodbridge, 1981)].

16   *Gesta pontificum*, p. 2.
17   Most of William's descriptions of places throughout England occur in his *Gesta pontificum*, and it seems likely that he did most of his traveling in preparation for this work between the completion of the *Gesta regum* in about 1120–1 and the *Gesta pontificum* in 1125.
18   *Memorials of St. Dunstan*, ed. William Stubbs (RS, 1874), pp. 287–8, 317.
19   The best accounts of his career are Conyers Read, *William Lambarde and Local Government* (Ithaca, NY, 1962), and Wilbur Dunkel, *William Lambarde, Elizabethan Jurist, 1536–1601* (New Brunswick, 1956). Robin Flower, "Laurence Nowell and the Discovery of England in Tudor Times," *PBA* 21 (1935), pp. 47–73, has a valuable account of the relations between Lambarde and Nowell, based on the Nowell transcripts (which belonged to Lambarde) in BL, Additional MSS. 43703–10, but he exaggerates the importance of Nowell in Lambarde's development. Lambarde is scarcely noticed in F. S. Fussner, *The Historical Revolution: English Historical Writing and Thought, 1580–1640* (London, 1962), where his contemporaries are discussed at length.
20   For Lambarde's career in Parliament as member for Aldborough (Yorks) in 1563 and 1566, see J. E. Neale, *Elizabeth I and her Parliaments, 1559–1581* (London, 1953). The main evidence for the identification of William Lambarde with the Mr. Lambert who made a speech in Parliament on the succession in 1566 is a small treatise on Parliament (in *Harleian Miscellany* 5 (1810), pp. 258–67), which gives an account of the speech of 1566 made by "this writer, W. L." The treatise and (more especially) the collection of documents of which it forms part clearly reflect William Lambarde's manner of composition. The title, "Some certaine notes of the Order, Proceedings, Punishments, and Priviledges of the Lower house of Parliament Gathered by W. Lambert," generally given to the treatise, really refers to the whole collection in BL, Additional MS. 5123, in which the treatise is only one item.
21   The dates are provided by the family diary which Lambarde started, printed in *Miscellanea Genealogica et Heraldica* 2 (1876), pp. 99–101.
22   The work was not printed until 1576, when Thomas Wotton (the father of Sir Henry) published it with a dedication to the "Gentlemen of Kent." Lambarde had sent it to Wotton on January 31, 1571 with a letter, which is printed in the second edition of 1596. A draft of the letter to Wotton with Lambarde's numerous corrections for the second edition is in the Bodleian copy of the Perambulation (4° Rawl. 263). Another copy with an autograph letter from Lambarde to Sir Henry Sydney, dated June 1, 1576, explaining the circumstances of the composition and publication of the work, is also in the Bodleian (4° Rawl. 587). It is from this letter that I have taken (with slight abbreviation and modernization of spelling) the extract quoted above. Lambarde, of course, had an estate in Kent before his marriage, but there is no evidence that he ever lived on it. After 1570 he divided his time between the Kentish family-estates of his wives and Lincoln's Inn.
23   The original draft of 1579 is BL, Additional MS. 41137. The title page has Lambarde's signature (in Anglo-Saxon characters) with the date August 1579 followed by notes of the revisions to 1594. For a full description of the

manuscript see B. H. Putnam, "The Earliest Form of Lambard's *Eirenarcha* and a Kent Wage Assessment of 1563," *EHR* 41 (1926), pp. 260–73. For Lambarde's work as a JP, see J. H. Gleason, *The Justices of Peace in England 1558–1604* (Oxford, 1969).

24 As with most of his works, Lambarde continued to revise and to produce enlarged editions (1587, 1594, 1599) until the end of his life.

25 For his conclusions on the development of these courts, see *Archeion* (1635), pp. 21, 27.

26 The manuscript of the work which Lambarde sent to Sir Robert Cecil in 1591, with the dedicatory letter in his own hand, is in the Bodleian, MS. Carte 174. The work was not printed until 1635. There is a modern edition by C. H. McIlwain and P. L. Ward (Cambridge, Mass., 1957).

27 See above.

28 *Reports of Causes in Chancery Collected by Sir George Cary one of the Masters of the Chancery in Anno 1601 out of the labours of Master William Lambert* (printed 1650). There is an important study of the collection of material from which these "Reports" were drawn, by P. L. Ward, "William Lambarde's Collections on Chancery," *Harvard Library Bulletin* 7 (1953), pp. 271–98. For Lambarde's work as a Master in Chancery, see W. J. Jones, *The Elizabethan Court of Chancery* (Oxford, 1967), pp. 103–17.

29 Bodleian Library, MS. Rawlinson B 471, ff. 1–13. This MS. also contains a text and translation of Walter of Henley, an analysis of the members and officials of the Court of Chancery, and extracts from Bracton, etc., on the "writing and making of Deeds or Muniments in Law."

30 Bodleian Library, MS. Rawlinson B 198. The other MSS. mentioned in this paragraph are BL, Cotton MSS. Vespasian A v and Julius C ix, and Additional MS. 43705. The Easter Table is in Bodleian MS. Hatton 41.

31 The notes for this work were printed by Fletcher Gyles in 1730. The last addition which can be dated was made in 1577 (p. 410).

32 See the memoirs of William Lambarde Esq. in *Bibliotheca Topographica Britannica*, 1 (London, 1790), p. 512.

33 *Perambulation of Kent* (1596), pp. 526–7. The drafts for this passage, which show Lambarde's anxiety to give Camden his full due, are in the Bodleian copy (4° Rawl. 587), p. 378.

5 The Shape and Substance of Academic History

1 These figures are taken from an article on "The Distribution of Undergraduate Population," *Oxford* (1959), pp. 9–11, and from the *Oxford University Gazette*, October 5, 1961, p. 123. For other universities they have been supplemented by the annual reports of the University Grants Committee.

2 *Report of the Royal Commission on Oxford University* (1852), p. 58.

3 E. Abbott and L. Campbell, *Life and Letters of Benjamin Jowett* (2 vols., London, 1897), 1, pp. 176–7.

4 *The Fourth School* (1850) (an anonymous broadsheet raising objections to the establishment of the School of Law and Modern History).

5 "Suggestions on the Best Means of Teaching English History," in *Oxford Essays* (1855).

6 Sidney Lee, *King Edward VII* (2 vols., London, 1925–7), 1, p. 77.

7 For the testimony of Acton and Mark Pattison to the extraordinary impact in England of this not very powerful work of Newman, see O. Chadwick, *From Bossuet to Newman: The Idea of Doctrinal Development* (Cambridge, 1957); "Newman's Essay did more than any other book of the time to make the English think historically, to watch the process as well as the result" (Acton); "Is it not remarkable that you should have first started the idea – and the word – Development, as the key to the history of church doctrine, and since then it has gradually become the dominant idea of all history, biology, physics and in short has metamorphosed our views of every science and of all knowledge" (Mark Pattison, writing to Newman in 1878).

8 Stubbs gave four lectures on the development of historical studies in Oxford. The first was his Inaugural in 1867, the second pair was a survey of his first ten years delivered in 1876, the last was a valedictory address in 1884. They are printed in his *Seventeen Lectures on the Study of Medieval and Modern History* (3rd ed., Oxford, 1900), pp. 1–80, 427–43.

9 Paul Frédéricq, *De l'enseignement supérieur de l'histoire en Ecosse et en Angleterre: notes et impressions de voyage* (Paris, 1885). His report on French and German universities, which he visited in 1881 and 1882, has also been published (English translation, Johns Hopkins University Press, 1890).

10 Paul Vinogradoff, *Collected Papers* (2 vols., Oxford, 1928), 1, p. 33.

11 J. H. Newman, *The Idea of a University* (Everyman Library), p. 141.

6 The Historical Experience

1 The *Journal and Notebooks on Transmutation of Species* have been edited by Sir Gavin de Beer, *Bulletin of British Museum (Natural History), Historical Series* 2 (1959–63), pp. 3–21, 27–200. The *Autobiography* has been edited by N. Barlow (London, 1958), and in *Autobiographies* (of Darwin and Huxley) by Gavin de Beer (Oxford, 1974). The *Voyage of the Beagle* first appeared in 1839 as vol. 3 of the *Narrative of the Surveying Voyages of HMS Adventure and Beagle*, and more fully – and in some respects in a more primitive form – in a second edition in 1845. There are a number of recent works which supplement this material in various ways: see especially N. Barlow, *Charles Darwin and the Voyage of the Beagle* (London, 1945); G. de Beer, *Evolution by Natural Selection* (with an edition of Darwin's early sketches of 1842 and 1844 of the *Origin of Species*) (Cambridge, 1958); Gertrude Himmelfarb, *Darwin and the Darwinian Revolution* (London, 1959); H. E. Gruber, *Darwin on Man* (with an edition of his early notebooks by P. H. Barrett) (London, 1974); and, for some valuable remarks on the influence of Lyell on

Darwin, M. J. S. Rudwick, "The Strategy of Lyell's *Principles of Geology*," *Isis* 61 (1969), pp. 5–33.

2 *Voyage*, October 8, 1835 (ed. of 1845).

3 *Journal*, p. 7. The passage runs as follows: "In July opened first notebook on 'Transmutation of Species' – Had been greatly struck from about Month of previous March on character of S. American fossils – and species on Galapagos Archipelago. These facts origin (especially latter) of all my views."

4 Ibid., p. 8.

5 *Notebooks*, p. 160. The page which contains most of the entry for October 3 was torn out by Darwin in 1856 when he was working on the *Origin of Species*: it was his practice at this time to remove pages which he thought might be useful for his work, but he left a few sentences at the end of the entry for October 3, presumably because they were no longer of interest to him.

6 Letter of April 20, 1861 to F. W. Hutton (*More Letters of Charles Darwin*, ed. F. Darwin (2 vols., London, 1903), 1, p. 184).

7 T. Mozley, *Reminiscences, chiefly of Oriel College and the Oxford Movement* (2 vols., London, 1882), 1, p. 389.

8 *Apologia pro Vita sua* (London, 1864), p. 205.

9 Ibid., pp. 208–10.

10 Sermon, "On the Theory of Developments in Religious Doctrine," in *Sermons, Chiefly on the Theory of Religious Belief, Preached before the University of Oxford* (London, 1843), pp. 315–17.

11 For the letters quoted here, see Marx–Engels, *Collected Works* (London, 1975–), 2, pp. 385–546.

12 For Engels in Manchester, see S. Marcus, *Engels, Manchester, and the Working Class* (London, 1974). There are some interesting details in M. Jenkins, *Frederick Engels in Manchester* (pamphlet published by the Lancashire and Cheshire Communist Party, 1951). Engels's *Condition of the Working Class in England*, the main product of his experience in Manchester, was published in German in 1845, but not until 1887 in English: the English text with some useful annotation is in Marx–Engels, *Collected Works*, 3, pp. 295–596; there is a critical edition by W. D. Henderson and W. H. Chaloner (Oxford, 1958; 2nd ed., 1971), which in my view gives a much too unfavorable account of its historical quality.

13 *On the History of the Communist League* (1885), quoted in *Frederick Engels: A Biography*, ed. Institute for Marxism-Leninism of Germany (1972), from the Moscow edition of *Selected Works of Marx–Engels* (1970), 3, p. 178. For a more readily available edition see K. Marx and F. Engels, *The Cologne Communist Trial*, ed. R. Livingstone (London, 1971), p. 44.

14 *Souvenirs d'enfance et de jeunesse*, in *Œuvres complètes*, ed. E. Psichari (Paris, 10 vols., 1947–61), 2, pp. 807–8.

15 Ibid., p. 813. Renan's development during these years and his growing commitment to historicism can be followed, though imperfectly, in his notebooks, ed. J. Pommier, *Renan, Travaux de jeunesse* (Paris, 1931), pp. 183–4.

16 *L'Avenir de la science* (*Œuvres complètes*, 3, p. 867), written in 1848–9, but not published until 1890.

17   Ibid., 3, p. 1121.
18   Ibid., 3, p. 723 (Preface of 1890 to *L'Avenir de la science*).
19   *Souvenirs d'enfance et de jeunesse*, in *Œuvres complètes*, 2, p. 852. This passage was written in 1881.

7   *The Truth about the Past*

1   "A Carolingian Renaissance Prince: The Emperor Charles the Bald," *PBA* 64 (1978), pp. 155–84.

9   *Sir Maurice Powicke (1879–1963)*

1   Throughout his life Powicke carried on a very active correspondence with friends, colleagues, and pupils, and many of his letters survive. They contain a great deal of information about academic affairs as well as many highly personal touches. I am indebted for the loan of letters in their possession and for details, corrections, and advice of all kinds to the following: Lady Powicke, the Misses Powicke, Professor H. H. Bellot, Sir George Clark, Professor C. R. Cheney, Professor V. H. Galbraith, Dr. R. W. Hunt, Professor E. Hughes, Mr. R. V. Lennard, Dr. Margaret Sharp, Professor E. L. G. Stones, Dr. M. Tyson, and Mr. J. M. Wallace-Hadrill. The autobiographical sketch in the possession of Dr. Alys Gregory has been very valuable, especially for Powicke's early years. I have also made use of some unpublished papers and addresses.
2   The recollections of the Free Library are printed in the *Library Association Record*, September 1950; the other recollections of childhood and youth come from an autobiographical fragment in the possession of Dr. Alys Gregory.
3   There are some personal recollections of this period in "The University of Manchester, 1851–1951," *History Today*, May 1951, pp. 48–55, at p. 55.
4   [Greek and Roman classical literature, philosophy, and ancient history.]
5   F. M. P. made some corrections to this account in a review in the *Oxford Magazine*, March 2, 1944.
6   Letter to T. F. Tout, July 8, 1905.
7   A small biography of Bismarck published in 1914 in a forgotten series (The People's Books: Jack) may be mentioned as a curiosity. Powicke once told me that he had been greatly interested in Bismarck's mother and in his religious upbringing. This characteristic remark aroused my curiosity, but the book has long been missing from the Bodleian and I have never seen a copy.
8   This unpublished paper is dated in Powicke's handwriting "?1930."
9   August 14, 1928 to Edward Hughes.
10   April 13, 1948 to C. R. Cheney.
11   Public and academic honors came then in abundance: honorary fellowships at Balliol, Merton, and Oriel; doctorates at Cambridge, Durham, St. Andrews, Glasgow, Manchester, Liverpool, Belfast, London, Oxford, Harvard, and

Caen; the associateship of the Académie des Inscriptions, fellowship of the Medieval Academy of America, and of course of this Academy [the British Academy]; and in 1946 a knighthood.

12 *Councils and Synods with Other Documents relating to the English Church 2 (1205–1313)*, ed. F. M. Powicke and C. R. Cheney (2 vols., Oxford, 1964).

13 April 9, 1944 to C. R. Cheney.

14 *EHR* 52 (1937), p. 153.

15 It should perhaps be explained that the Regius Professorship of Modern History at Oxford carries with it a Fellowship at Oriel College.

16 From an unpublished paper "read to Owen's College Literary Society sometime in the period 1896–9."

17 From an Address to the Friends of the Bodleian Library, June 20, 1944.

18 January 10, 1928.

19 April 27, 1902 to his mother.

20 *Three Lectures* (Oxford, 1947), pp. 85–6.

10   Vivian Hunter Galbraith (1889–1976)

1 Among the many who have helped me by supplying material or correcting mistakes, I am especially grateful to Professor J. S. Roskell, who copied for me the relevant parts of Galbraith's letters, and other letters about him, in the papers of James Tait and T. F. Tout, now deposited in Manchester University Library; also to Professors Lionel Stones, George Cuttino, C. N. L. Brooke, and Gerald Graham, who sent me letters, which they had received over many years, and gave much advice. For information about Galbraith's experiences in the First World War, I am indebted to the remarkable memories of (to give them the titles appropriate to those days) Captain P. C. Duncan, MC, Lieutenant Reginald Jennings, and Sergeant S. W. Vinter. For his years in the Public Record Office, I have benefited greatly from the help of Mrs. H. C. Johnson, who directed my attention to Galbraith's official journal, and Dame Mary Smieton, who has given me a vivid account of the impression he made on his colleagues at that time. Professor H. A. Cronne has allowed me to quote extensively from a privately circulated account of his years at Balliol from 1925 to 1927. Professor M. D. Legge has given me some memories of Galbraith at Edinburgh, and Mr. A. T. Milne has provided valuable information of his years at the Institute of Historical Research. Mrs. Galbraith has been unendingly patient and helpful in providing information about the family and in correcting my mistakes. For the rest, I have relied on Galbraith's publications, of which there is a list down to 1957 in *Facsimiles of English Royal Writs to A.D. 1100*, ed. T. A. M. Bishop and P. Chaplais (Oxford, 1957), and on my own memory.

2 [In *Domesday Commemoration*, 1 (*Domesday Studies*), ed. P. E. Dove (London, 1888).]

11 Richard William Hunt (1908–1979)

1 The compilation of this record has been made possible by the help of many friends of Richard Hunt. I am especially indebted to Dr. N. R. Ker, Sir Roger Mynors, and Mrs. Joan Varley who have allowed me to use a large collection of letters in their possession, which illuminate different phases of the works described above. They, together with Dr. Beryl Smalley, Professor and Mrs. Richard Rouse, Mrs. G. D. G. Hall, Dr. J. N. L. Myres, Dr. Bruce Barker-Benfield, Dr. A. C. de la Mare, and other members of the Bodleian staff, have enabled me to fill many gaps and correct many errors in my memory of events and in my knowledge of the complicated business of the Bodleian.

2 [R. W. Hunt, *The Schools and the Cloister: The Life and Writings of Alexander Nequam* (Oxford, 1984).]

3 Dr. R. H. Rouse has shown ("Bostonus Buriensis and the Author of the *Catalogus Scriptorum Ecclesiae*," *Speculum* 41 (1966), pp. 471–99) that the compiler of the catalogue was not "John Boston" but a Henry of Kirkstede (probably Kirstead in Norfolk), a monk and librarian of Bury who died in about 1380. But since Hunt and his colleagues referred to the author as "Boston of Bury" in all their discussions, I have retained this label.

4 The work is now well advanced, and the long-awaited edition of these catalogues, edited by Richard and Mary Rouse, will appear before long [*Registrum Anglie de libris doctorum et auctorum veterum* (London, 1991)].

5 The question of priority between the two projects was probably never explicitly faced, partly because M. R. James's judgment that the publication of the "Boston" catalogue was an essential preliminary to "any really thorough investigation of ancient English libraries" was accepted without dispute. Hunt's contrary judgment was the result of several years' work, which had shown that "Boston" presented a mass of problems, which could only be resolved by a detailed study of the surviving books from the constituent libraries. For M. R. James's initial judgment, see his study of the library at Bury St. Edmunds in *Cambridge Antiquarian Society Octavo Publications* 28 (1895), p. 34; and R. W. Pfaff, *M. R. James* (London, 1980), p. 201, for a general account of these developments.

6 *Miscellanea Francesco Ehrle*, vol. 5, *Studi e Testi*, 41 (1924), pp. 331–63.

7 The first of these texts (generally abbreviated to "CLA") was the thirteenth-century catalogue made by the Franciscans preserved in the Bodleian manuscript which Hunt had transcribed in 1935; "Boston of Bury" was the catalogue derived from this and preserved in the Cambridge University Library manuscript which Mynors had transcribed in 1937.

8 These articles have now been collected and republished, not altogether satisfactorily, in a single volume [*The History of Grammar in the Middle Ages*, ed. G. L. Bursill-Hall (Amsterdam, 1980)].

12   Marjorie Reeves as a Historian

1 [Oswald Spengler, *The Decline of the West 1: Form and Actuality*, authorized translation with notes by Charles Francis Atkinson (London, 1926).]
2 [(1890). English translation by Edward Maslin Hume, *Mystics and Heretics in Italy at the End of the Middle Ages* (London, 1922).]
3 It is appropriate here to mention Miss Reeves's collaborator in the 1972 volume, Dr. Beatrice Hirsch-Reich, an independent scholar and student of medieval symbolism, whose help in interpretation Miss Reeves enlisted after she had identified the contents of the Oxford manuscript. Their collaboration continued until Dr. Hirsch-Reich's death in 1967, and in her Preface to the 1972 volume Miss Reeves paid a generous tribute to her help and identified the parts of the volume for which she was responsible.
4 Miss Reeves has already made a substantial contribution to this development in her recently published *Joachim of Fiore and the Prophetic Future* (London, 1976).

13   Beryl Smalley (1905–1984)

1 I am grateful for help in preparing this memoir to Marion Gibbs, Alys Gregory, Susan Hall, Menna Prestwich, and John Roskell; also to the following pupils, who sent me their recollections: Stephen Ferruolo, Daphne Simon, Anne Summers, Jennifer Sweet, and Lucy Torode. I have also to thank Katherine Walsh and Diana Wood and Messrs Basil Blackwell, the editors and publisher of *The Bible in the Medieval World: Essays in Memory of Beryl Smalley* (Studies in Church History, Subsidia 4, 1985), for allowing me to use parts of my contribution to that volume.

Bibliography of the Publications of R. W. Southern

* Included in the present volume

1933

"Ranulf Flambard and Early Anglo-Norman Administration" (Alexander Prize Essay), *TRHS*, 4th ser., 16, pp. 95–128 (rev. and repr. in *Medieval Humanism and Other Studies*, 1970, pp. 234–52).

1937

Review: *St. Bernard of Clairvaux* by Watkin Williams, *History* 21, p. 367.

1938

"Some New Letters of Peter of Blois," *EHR* 53, pp. 412–24.

1939

"An Alphabetical List of Dukes, Marquesses and Earls, 1066–1603," in *Handbook of British Chronology*, ed. F. M. Powicke et al. (Royal Historical Society).

1941

"St. Anselm and his English Pupils," *MARS* 1, pp. 3–34.

1943

"The First Life of Edward the Confessor," *EHR* 57, pp. 385–400.

1948

"Lanfranc of Bec and Berengar of Tours," in *Studies in Medieval History Presented to F. M. Powicke*, ed. R. W. Hunt, W. A. Pantin, and R. W. Southern (Oxford), pp. 27–48.

1949

Review: *The Religious Orders in England* by David Knowles, *Journal of Theological Studies* 50, pp. 98–100.

1950

"A Note on the Text of 'Glanville,' *De Legibus et Consuetudinibus Regni Angliae*," *EHR* 65, pp. 81–9.
"View from the Osler Pavilion," *Cross-Section: The Magazine of the Oxford United Hospitals*, Summer, pp. 26–8.
Review: *Ways of Medieval Life and Thought* by F. M. Powicke, *Oxford Magazine*, June 15, pp. 558–60.

1951

Reviews: Odo of Deuil, *De Profectione Ludovici VII in Orientem*, ed. and trans. V. G. Berry; and Oliver of Paderborn, *The Capture of Damietta*, trans. J. J. Gavigan, *Medium Ævum* 20, pp. 84–6.
The Episcopal Colleagues of Archbishop Thomas Becket by David Knowles, *EHR* 67, pp. 87–90.

1953

The Making of the Middle Ages (London).
Reviews: *Tithes and Parishes in Medieval Italy and the Historical Roots of a Modern Problem* by Catherine E. Boyd, *Medium Ævum* 22, pp. 109–10.

Richard of St. Victor, *Sermons et Opuscules Spirituels*, ed. J. Chatillon and
W. J. Tulloch, *EHR* 68, pp. 632–3.

1954

"St. Anselm and Gilbert Crispin, Abbot of Westminster," *MARS* 3, pp. 78–115.
"Exeter College," in *Victoria History of the County of Oxford*, 3, *The University
of Oxford*, ed. H. E. Salter and M. D. Lobel (London and Oxford), pp. 107–18.

1955

"The Tenth Century," *Encyclopedia Americana*.
Review: Otto of Freising, *The Deeds of Frederick*, trans. C. C. Mierow and
R. Emery, *EHR* 70, pp. 315–16.

1956

Reviews: *The Growth of Papal Government in the Middle Ages* by Walter Ull-
mann, *EHR* 71, pp. 635–8.
Richard III by P. M. Kendall, *The Economist*, January 21, pp. 199–200.
An Introduction to Anglo-Saxon England by P. Hunter Blair, *The Economist*,
March 24, p. 645.
A History of the English Speaking Peoples, 1. The Birth of Britain by Winston
S. Churchill, *The Economist*, April 28, p. 3.
History of the Byzantine State by G. Ostrogorsky, trans. Joan Hussey, *The Econo-
mist*, September 29, p. 1040.
Angevin Kingship by J. E. A. Jolliffe, *Oxford Magazine*, March 1, pp. 322–3.
Christianity and the State in the Light of History by T. M. Parker, *Oxford Maga-
zine*, November 1, pp. 76–8.
From Becket to Langton: English Church Government, 1170–1213 by C. R. Che-
ney, *Times Literary Supplement*, August 17, p. 482.

1957

Reviews: *The Eastern Schism* by Steven Runciman, *EHR* 72, pp. 101–3.
The Letters of John of Salisbury, 1. The Early Letters (1153–1161), ed. W. J. Miller
and H. E. Butler, revised by C. N. L. Brooke, *EHR* 72, pp. 493–7.
Theobald Archbishop of Canterbury by Avrom Saltman, *History* 42, pp. 218–20.
Ordericus Vitalis: ein Beitrag zur Kluniazensischen Geschichtsschreibung by Hans
Wolter, *JEH* 8, pp. 232–3.

The Religious Orders in England, 2, by David Knowles, *Journal of Theological Studies*, N.S. 8, pp. 190–4.
Analecta Monastica 2 (Studia Anselmiana 31) by J. Leclercq, *Journal of Theological Studies*, N.S. 8, pp. 194–6.
A History of Technology, 2. *The Mediterranean Civilizations and the Middle Ages, c.700 B.C. to c.A.D. 1500*, ed. Charles Singer, E. J. Holmyard, A. R. Hall, and Trevor I. Williams, *The Economist*, January 5, pp. 26–7.
Feudal Britain by G. W. S. Barrow, *The Economist*, January 12, pp. 109–10.
A History of Medieval Europe from Constantine to St. Louis by R. H. C. Davis, *The Economist*, December 14, p. 957.
Frederick II of Hohenstaufen by Georgina Masson, *The Economist*, December 28, pp. 1112–16.

1958

"The Canterbury Forgeries," *EHR* 73, pp. 193–226.
"The English Origins of the 'Miracles of the Virgin,'" *MARS* 4, pp. 176–216.
Reviews: *Fritz Saxl 1890–1948: A Volume of Memorial Essays*, *EHR* 73, pp. 752–3.
Warwick the Kingmaker by P. Kendall, *The Economist*, January 4, p. 30.
The Sicilian Vespers by Steven Runciman, *The Economist*, March 29, Spring Books, p. 6.
Political Thought in Medieval Times by J. B. Morrall, *The Economist*, August 30, pp. 664–7.
The Northern Seas: Shipping and Commerce in Northern Europe, 300–1100 by A. R. Lewis, *The Economist*, October 18, p. 226.
The Life of Edward II by the so-called Monk of Malmesbury, ed. and trans. N. Denholm Young, *Oxford Magazine*, February 27, p. 333.
Medieval Thought from St. Augustine to Ockham by Gordon Leff, *Time and Tide*, June 28, p. 802.

1959

"Pope Adrian IV," *The Times*, September 1 (rev. and repr. in *Medieval Humanism and Other Studies*, 1970, pp. 234–52).
Reviews: *The Intellectual Heritage of the Early Middle Ages* by M. L. W. Laistner, *EHR* 74, pp. 713–14.
The King's Two Bodies: A Study in Medieval Political Theology by Ernst H. Kantorowicz, *JEH* 10, pp. 105–8.
Medieval England, 2 vols., ed. A. L. Poole, *The Economist*, January 10, p. 121.
Rural England, 1086–1135 by Reginald Lennard, *The Economist*, September 5, p. 726.
The Origins of Russia by George Vernadsky, *Listener*, March 26, pp. 563–4.

1960

"The Place of England in the Twelfth Century Renaissance," *History* 45, pp. 201–6 (rev. and repr. in *Medieval Humanism and Other Studies*, 1970, pp. 158–80).

Review: *Untersuchungen über Inhalt und Datierung der Briefe Gerberts von Aurillac* by Mathilde Uhlirz, *EHR* 75, pp. 293–5.

1961

*The Shape and Substance of Academic History (Inaugural Lecture as Chichele Professor of Modern History, Oxford), repr. in *The Varieties of History from Voltaire to the Present*, ed. Fritz Stern, 2nd ed. (London, 1970), pp. 403–22.

1962

Western Views of Islam in the Middle Ages (Cambridge, Mass.).

The Life of St. Anselm by Eadmer (Nelson's Medieval Texts, repr. OMT, 1972).

"The Place of Henry I in English History," Raleigh Lecture on History, *PBA* 48, pp. 127–69 (rev. and repr. in *Medieval Humanism and Other Studies*, 1970, pp. 206–33).

Review: *The Religious Orders in England*, 3, by David Knowles, *Journal of Theological Studies*, N.S. 13, pp. 469–75.

1963

St. Anselm and his Biographer: A Study of Monastic Life and Thought, c.1059–c.1130, Birkbeck Lectures, Trinity College, Cambridge, 1959 (Cambridge).

"Commentary," in *Scientific Change: A Symposium in the History of Science, 9–15 July 1961*, ed. A. C. Crombie, pp. 301–6.

"The Church of the Dark Ages, 600–1000," in *The Layman in Christian History*, ed. S. C. Neill and H. R. Weber, pp. 87–110.

"A Wonder of the Victorian Age: Balliol Celebrates its 700th Anniversary," *Oxford Mail*, June 28, p. 8.

Review: *Medieval Technology and Social Change* by Lynn White Jr., *History of Science* 2, pp. 130–5.

1964

Foreword to *Oxford Studies Presented to Daniel Callus* (Oxford Historical Society, N.S. 16), pp. v–viii.

*"Sir Maurice Powicke (1879–1963)," *PBA* 50, pp. 275–304.

"Expanding Christendom, i. Bede, ii. Anselm, iii. Meister Eckhart," *Listener*, February 13, February 20, March 20, pp. 267–9, 308–10, 425–7 (rev. and repr. in *Medieval Humanism and Other Studies*, 1970, pp. 1–26).

1965

"Medieval Humanism, i. Religious Humanism, ii. Scientific Humanism, iii. Practical Humanism," *Listener*, August 20, September 9, pp. 303–5, 377–80, 412–15 (rev. and repr. in *Medieval Humanism and Other Studies*, 1970, pp. 29–60).

Reviews: *The Historian and Character* by David Knowles, *EHR* 80, pp. 570–1.

The Life of Edward the Confessor, ed. and trans. F. Barlow, *History* 50, pp. 197–9.

The Martyrs of Cordoba (850–859): A Study of the Sources by E. P. Colbert, *JEH* 16, pp. 228–9.

The York Psalter in the Library of the Hunterian Museum, Glasgow by T. S. R. Boase, *Medium Ævum* 34, pp. 139–40.

1966

"1066," *New York Review of Books*, November 17, pp. 33–6.

1967

Reviews: *Magna Carta* by J. C. Holt, *EHR* 82, pp. 342–6.

The Letters of Frederic William Maitland, ed. C. H. S. Fifoot, *History and Theory* 6, pp. 105–11.

Augustine of Hippo by Peter Brown, *New Statesman*, September 22, pp. 360–1.

1968

"Thomas Aquinas," *International Encyclopaedia of the Social Sciences*, 1, pp. 375–7.

Reviews: *The Letters and Charters of Gilbert Foliot* and *Gilbert Foliot and his Letters* by Adrian Morey and C. N. L. Brooke, *EHR* 83, pp. 784–9.

Letters of Peter the Venerable, ed. Giles Constable, *Times Literary Supplement*, March 7, p. 234.

1969

Memorials of St. Anselm, ed. with F. S. Schmidt (*Auctores Britannici Medii Ævi* 1).

1970

Western Society and the Church in the Middle Ages (Pelican History of the Church 2).
Medieval Humanism and Other Studies (Oxford).
*"Aspects of the European Tradition of Historical Writing 1: The Classical Tradition from Einhard to Geoffrey of Monmouth," *TRHS*, 5th ser., 20, pp. 173–96.
"A Meeting of the Ways in Oxford," *The Tablet*, October 31, pp. 1062–3.

1971

*"Aspects of the European Tradition of Historical Writing 2: Hugh of St. Victor and the Idea of Historical Development," *TRHS*, 5th ser., 21, pp. 159–79.
Reviews: *The Letters of Innocent III (1198–1216) Concerning England and Wales: A Calendar with an Appendix of Texts* by C. R. and M. G. Cheney, *EHR* 86, pp. 796–9.
Hubert Walter by C. R. Cheney, *EHR* 86, pp. 829–30.

1972

*"Aspects of the European Tradition of Historical Writing 3: History as Prophecy," *TRHS*, 5th ser., 22, pp. 159–80.

1973

*"Aspects of the European Tradition of Historical Writing 4: The Sense of the Past," *TRHS*, 5th ser., 23, pp. 246–63.
"Dante and Islam," in *Relations between East and West in the Middle Ages*, ed. Derek Baker (Edinburgh), pp. 133–45.

1974

Review: *Fontes Harleiani: A Study of the Harleian Collection of Manuscripts in the British Museum* by C. E. Wright, *EHR* 89, pp. 113–16.

1976

"Master Vacarius and the Beginning of an English Academic Tradition," in *Medieval Learning and Literature: Essays Presented to R. W. Hunt*, ed. J. J. G. Alexander and M. T. Gibson (Oxford), pp. 257–86.

"A Benedictine Monastery in a Disordered World," an address given on the opening of a new monastic library at Mount Angel, Oregon, in May 1970, *Downside Review*, 94, pp. 163–77.

"A Commemoration Sermon on William Laud," in *The Beauty of Holiness*, ed. Benedicta Ward (Fairacres Publication 57), pp. 1–8.

1977

*"The Historical Experience," *Times Literary Supplement*, June 24, pp. 771–4 (the Rede Lecture, delivered in the University of Cambridge, May 3, 1977).

1978

*"Vivian Hunter Galbraith (1889–1976)," *PBA* 64, pp. 397–425.

1979

Platonism, Scholastic Method and the School of Chartres, Stenton Lecture, 1978 (Reading).

1980

*"Marjorie Reeves as a Historian," in *Prophecy and Millenarianism: Essays in Honour of Marjorie Reeves*, ed. Ann Williams (Harlow), pp. 1–9.

1981

*"Richard William Hunt (1908–1979)," *PBA* 67, pp. 371–97.

1982

"The Schools of Paris and the School of Chartres," in *Renaissance and Renewal in the Twelfth Century*, ed. R. L. Benson and G. Constable (Cambridge, Mass.), pp. 113–37.

Review: *La Naissance du Purgatoire* by Jacques Le Goff, *Times Literary Supplement*, June 18, pp. 651–2.

1983

"Anselm at Canterbury," *Anselm Studies* 1 (New York and London), pp. 7–22.
"Outlines of a National Church in the Thirteenth Century," in *Annual Report of the Friends of Lambeth Palace Library* (London), pp. 11–21.

1984

"From Schools to University," in *The History of the University of Oxford, 1: The Early Oxford Schools*, ed. J. I. Catto (Oxford), pp. 1–36.

1985

"Beryl Smalley and the Place of the Bible in Medieval Studies, 1927–84," in *The Bible in the Medieval World: Essays in Memory of Beryl Smalley*, ed. Katherine Walsh and Diana Wood (Studies in Church History, Subsidia 4, Oxford), pp. 1–16.
"Peter of Blois and the Third Crusade," in *Studies in Medieval History Presented to R. H. C. Davis*, ed. H. Mayr-Harting and R. I. Moore (London and Rio Grande), pp. 107–18.
The Monks of Canterbury and the Murder of Archbishop Becket, lecture to the Friends of Canterbury Cathedral (The William Urry Memorial Trust) (Canterbury).

1986

Robert Grosseteste: The Growth of an English Mind in Medieval Europe (Oxford).
*"Beryl Smalley (1905–1984)," *PBA* 72, pp. 455–71.

1987

"The Changing Role of Universities in Medieval Europe," *Historical Research* 60, pp. 133–46.

1988

"Sally Vaugh's Anselm: An Examination of the Foundations," *Albion* 20, pp. 181–204.

1989

"Michael Wallace-Hadrill," *Addresses of All Souls College Oxford* (Oxford), pp. 199–205.

1990

Saint Anselm: A Portrait in a Landscape (Cambridge).

1991

"Intellectual Development and Local Environment: The Case of Robert Grosse-teste," in *Essays in Honor of E. B. King*, ed. R. G. Benson and E. W. Naylor (Sewanee, Tennessee), pp. 1–22.

1992

"The Necessity for Two Peters of Blois," in *Intellectual Life in the Middle Ages: Essays Presented to Margaret Gibson*, ed. L. Smith and B. Ward (London and Rio Grande), pp. 103–18.

"Anselm and the English Religious Tradition," in *The English Religious Tradition and the Genius of Anglicanism*, ed. G. Russell (Wantage), pp. 33–46.

Second edition of *Robert Grosseteste* (1986) with "A Last Review," pp. xvii–lxvi.

1993

"Lorenzio Minio (1907–1986)," in *Luoghi cruciali in Dante. Ultimi saggi. Con un inedito su Boezio e la bibliografia delle opere*, ed. F. Santi, *Quaderni di Cultura Mediolatina* 6 (Spoleto), pp. 3–8.

"Richard Dales and the Editing of Robert Grosseteste," in *Aspectus et Affectus: Essays and Editions in Grosseteste and Medieval Intellectual Life in Honor of Richard C. Dales*, ed. G. Freibergs (New York), pp. 3–14.

1994

St. Anselm at Canterbury. His Mission of Reconciliation, a lecture delivered in Canterbury Cathedral on September 25, 1993, on the 900th Anniversary of the Enthronement of St. Anselm (Canterbury).

1995

Scholastic Humanism and the Unification of Europe, 1: The Foundations (Oxford).
"Towards an Edition of Peter of Blois' Letter-Collection," *EHR* 110, pp. 925–37.

2001

Scholastic Humanism and the Unification of Europe, 2: The Heroic Age, with notes and additions by L. Smith and B. Ward (Oxford).

Forthcoming

Biographical articles on "Anselm of Canterbury," "Peter of Blois," and "Robert Grosseteste," in the *Dictionary of National Biography* (Oxford).

Index

Where dates come after office, they refer to tenure of that office; otherwise dates are for lifespan, or only death-date is given.